W9-BNA-672

GODS OF DEATH

Around the World, Behind Closed Doors,
Operates an Ultra-Secret Business of Sex and
Death. One Man Hunts the Truth
About Snuff Films.

YARON SVORAY

with Thomas Hughes

SIMON & SCHUSTER

SIMON & SCHUSTER
Rockefeller Center
1230 Avenue of the Americas
New York, NY 10020

Copyright © 1997 by Hermannes Bosman
All rights reserved, including the right of reproduction
in whole or in part in any form.

SIMON & SCHUSTER and colophon are registered trademarks
of Simon & Schuster Inc.

Designed by Leslie Phillips
Manufactured in the United States of America

10 9 8 7 6 5 4 3 2 1

Library of Congress Cataloging-in-Publication Data
Svoray, Yaron.
Gods of death: around the world, behind closed doors,
operates an ultra-secret business of sex and death: one man
hunts the truth about snuff films / Yaron Svoray with Thomas Hughes.
    p. cm.
  1. Children in pornography.   2. Death in motion pictures.
3. Child sexual abuse.   4. Erotic films.   5. Sex crimes.
6. Hate crimes.   7. Racism.   I. Hughes, Thomas.   II. Title.
HQ471.S895   1997
791.43'092—dc21
[B]   97-11784   CIP
ISBN 0-684-81445-5

ACKNOWLEDGMENTS

My thanks to

my wife, my love, my life, and my sanity: Mikhal

my children, who are my guiding lights: Enosh, Elie, and Ohad

my voice, my devil's advocate, my personal censor, and, most important, my writing partner: Tom Hughes

Robert, who made it all come together

my advisor and mentor in all things American: Jody Hotchkiss

Yehoda, Rachel, and Ori Svoray, my dad, mom, and only brother

and many others who have advised me, helped me, and generally pointed me in the right direction

To you all, thank you. This story has to be told. Without your help this book would never have seen the light of day.

This book is the result also of the bravery, tenacity, intelligence, and sacrifice of Ako, Andreas, and Tara, who knew the risks and yet decided to stick by me.

This book is dedicated to Dorit.
She would have been so proud.
Her memory will always live
within my heart.

CONTENTS

CONTENTS

The story you are about to read is essentially a true one. I say "essentially" because, due to the nature of the story, the way I work, and the people with whom I had to deal during the course of my investigation, various changes and omissions have been made to protect myself, to protect others, and, less dramatic, to transform the two years I spent conducting my investigation into a cohesive narrative.

Almost all of the names in this book have been changed. The sequence of events has, in certain instances, been compressed, while other events have been omitted altogether. This was done for two reasons. First, although in some cases longer periods of time passed between events in the narrative than is indicated, what happened in between had no bearing on the investigation and would only have detracted from the urgency of the story that I set out to tell. Second, when events were omitted altogether, that was because certain aspects of investigatory work become repetitive. For example, I spent more time in Europe than is indicated in the book. However, the meetings that I recount in the narrative were the ones that turned out to be the most important. Others were more or less the same kind of encounter with the same kind of people, the only difference being that they did not produce any real results and therefore did not move the investigation forward.

Also, the conversations recounted in this narrative have mostly had to be reconstructed from memory and from notes made after the fact. The people I was dealing with and the fact that I was presenting myself as one of them (that is, a criminal) made it impossible to take notes at the time the conversations took place. I did, however, make extensive notes as soon as I had the chance. Furthermore, much of what was said to me had to be taken at face value. Due to the circumstances of my investigation I could not, in many instances, ask for independent verification of facts. I saw enough with my own eyes, however, to know that while the details of some stories might or might not have been true, the overall picture that emerged in many cases was as true as it was tragic.

Furthermore, I would like to say that my main goal in producing this book was to make accessible a world that most people know very little about. It was never my intention to write a scholarly tome on the evils of pornography. I am not a scholar. I am an investigator and I am a man with my own feelings and opinions regarding the subject of pornography and its consequences. Very early on I realized that I wanted to write a book about the very real people who trade in the lives of others. It was my aim to make them as human as possible and, in so doing, make it impossible to ignore the fact that these are not men and women from some faraway place where things like this happen and people are naturally evil. They are very much like everyone else. It is really only their indifference that allows them to do what they do, and that is the most horrifying part.

I could not remain indifferent.

YARON SVORAY

The feeling is so good, it makes everything
else seem so trivial, so stupid. Can you understand this moment of sheer joy? I am God.
I decide if she lives or dies.

—RAYMOND A., porn filmmaker

1 BEGINNINGS

A small room with a screen at one end. Men wearing patch-work semblances of Nazi uniforms. A box of tissues being passed around.

The film starts. Five men, faces covered, raping, torturing, and murdering a girl—maybe eight, maybe ten years old—on the screen.

The girl's eyes are terrified beyond words, and dilated. She is lifted off the ground by her hair, her short legs dangling in the air. Another man plunges a knife into her chest, killing her instantly. Blood bubbles out of her mouth.

My name is Yaron Svoray. A year ago I emerged from the neo-Nazi underground in Germany after investigating the hatred and the burgeoning power of Germany's fanatical far right for over nine months. I uncovered information on the reemergence of fascism in Germany and presented proof of it to the government of the recently reunited Republic of Germany. I uncovered undeniable links between this reemergence and the

19

growing power of various far-right groups in the United States and elswhere. I was shot at and had to fight for my life on more than one occasion. As a Jew, the son of Holocaust survivors, I had been sickened by what I witnessed. I had been appalled and I had been frightened—very frightened.

■ ■ ■ ■

My two youngest children, Elie, age seven, and Ohad, age four, run around in their pajamas trying not to go to bed, while my oldest, Enosh, looks on from his superior perch. He is the wise old man of ten, stifling a yawn. He's tired too, but he's intent on not taking a step toward the stairs leading to his bedroom until the younger kids are rounded up.

Watching my wife, Mikhal, trying to round up the kids irritates me unaccountably. I find that since my return from Germany I have been more and more irritable and hard to live with.

And then there are the nightmares.

I was born in the kibbutz of Guolot, in Israel. From the window of the house I was born in I could see the Gaza Strip and hear the muezzin calling the faithful to prayer from the top of the minaret overshadowing the mosque in Gaza. Guolot means "borderline" in Hebrew.

The inhabitants of Guolot were almost entirely Holocaust survivors. My father was a German Jew. My mother was a Romanian Jew. My grandfather fought for Germany in World War I and was awarded a medal by the kaiser himself for bravery.

The ironies of history.

The first I knew of the Holocaust was when my father asked me what I wanted for my fifth birthday and I told him that I wanted numbers tattooed on my arm like everyone else at the kibbutz.

My childhood was as uneventful as any childhood can be in a country surrounded by enemies. I attended primary school and high school and then became a soldier, assigned to an elite paratrooper unit. Less than six months after I survived basic training, Israel found itself involved in open hostilities with Syria, Lebanon, Egypt, and forces from Iraq. The year was 1973, and that war has become known as the Yom Kippur War. I fought first in the Sinai and then in the Golan Heights. A lot of people died in that war—a lot of people whom I knew, and many more whom I did not know. In the army, I learned how to lead. After close to three weeks, an eternity in the lifetime of a country about the same size as Rhode Island, the war was over. I finished out my hitch as an active member of the Israeli armed forces, fighting terrorism both overtly and covertly. I was wounded several times; I had learned both to lead and to follow; and looking back on it now, I consider my time in the army as my first step on the long road to my present career.

Of course, I would never have thought of it like that back then. It takes time to get perspective on things, and I have learned over the years that patterns are rarely discernible from ground level. It is one of the most important lessons I have brought with me to my work as an investigative journalist. Only when I have finished an investigation am I able to see how one thing led to another. Under fire, literally or figuratively, there is often very little to see at all besides smoke.

At the end of 1977 I left the army and traveled the world. I herded cattle in Australia and drove limousines in New York City, eventually coming back to Israel and going to school at the Hebrew University of Jerusalem. After earning a degree in political science and international affairs, I became a detective. I enjoyed the work and enjoyed my life as a detective—that is, until I met a lovely woman who presented me eventually with a very simple proposition. She told me that it was either her or the police; and since she was much prettier than the police, she became my wife. I have never regretted my decision.

We went to the States. I studied communications at Queens College in New York and supported my wife and myself by working with various international investigatory agencies, running down leads from Bermuda to Paraguay, making many connections and further preparing myself for the strange turn of events that would lead me to a life as a journalist.

Also, due to my background as well as my scholarly expertise, I lectured before Jewish organizations on the topic of international terrorism.

And it was after one of these lectures, in Bangor, Maine, that everything I had been doing came together in one of those accidental explosions which happen very rarely in life and make all the difference in the world.

An elderly Jewish gentleman approached me after my talk. "I would like to tell you an interesting story," he told me.

I probably winced unconsciously. I am proud to be a Jew and I love my people, but every elderly Jewish gentleman has a long story to tell, and I remember quite clearly that I was not in the mood to hear one.

"I'm sorry, but I'm very tired. Please forgive me," I told him.

He smiled at me. "Well, if you don't want to hear a story about diamonds worth $200 million buried on the French-German border, it's OK. Sorry to bother you," he told me, turning away.

I stayed and listened to him for nine hours. He told me an incredible story of World War II intrigue and buried loot in Alsace near the Saar River. Five months later I went to find the diamonds.

I never found them. Instead, quite by accident, after being introduced to a local historian who confided to me quite easily that he had once been a Nazi officer, I found the organized remnants of the Third Reich, still terrifyingly alive and well in the heart of the Republic of Germany.

And I came back with the story. The problem for me was that

nobody seemed to care. I testified before government panels both in the United States and in the Republic of Germany. I presented proof of the illegal rallies in Germany where swastikas were openly worn and saluted and the Jewish people were openly vilified as enemies of humanity. Nothing happened. I was thanked for my good work, assured that it would all be looked into in due course, and dismissed.

In the end I returned to Israel satisfied with a job well done, only to find the taste of satisfaction souring in my mouth as I realized I had made no difference at all.

Not long afterward, the dreams began. As part of my initiation into the neo-Nazi underground, I had been made to watch a film. The film was made up of newsreel footage of Hitler haranguing his troops, intercut with images that were seared into my eyes and that I have never forgotten. They were the images of an eight- or nine-year-old girl being brutally raped and then murdered.

Of all the horrible things that I witnessed during my investigation in Germany, that girl's face was the one that appeared to me again and again, waking and sleeping. Slowly but surely my visions of her became more frequent. Unaccountably, ridiculously even, I found myself feeling somehow personally involved. I found myself feeling responsible. I became more and more angry with myself that I had watched the film and done nothing, said nothing, because it would have endangered my investigation.

I gave lectures regarding what I had found out in Germany, and I spoke often about the film and the girl; it made me feel better.

Then I was visited by a woman named Catharine MacKinnon and a friend of hers. Catharine is a professor of law at the University of Michigan, a lawyer, and the author of *Toward a Feminist Theory of the State*, among other books. She had accepted a speaking engagement in Israel in order to track me down. According to her, in eight years of investigating snuff pornography she had not found anyone before me who had ever said in print that he had seen a snuff film.

We talked, the end result of our conversation being that I was now more determined than ever to do something about the eight- or nine-year-old girl and any others out there.

We talked about my experience of seeing a snuff film. It was amazing to me that there were people in the world who doubted that such things existed. I had seen them. I knew what was out there, and I realized that if I were ever to be able to stop dreaming about the girl in the film, I would have to do something about it. I would investigate the world of snuff pornography and come back with a story and, I hoped, a film that would prove, once and for all, that this horrible thing exists among us.

I just had to talk it over with Mikhal first.

■ ■ ■ ■

I walked slowly upstairs, looked in on the children one by one, and entered the room that Mikhal and I have shared since we were married, fourteen years ago.

Mikhal was already in bed. She lay with her dark hair spread out on a pillow and a book propped up on her flat stomach. The light on her side of the bed was on. She looked up from her book and smiled at me.

"Mikhali," I said quietly.

She smiled again. "Mikhali" is a pet name.

"Are your guests gone?" she asked, pulling herself up in the bed to a sitting position.

I nodded and wandered around the room. I fingered the pictures of us and the kids on the dresser. I went and looked out the window, sniffing the salt air.

"So?" she asked.

So? I made a flying leap onto the bed, captured my wife around her waist, and held her to me, burying my face in her stomach.

"Have I ever told you that you are the most beautiful woman I have ever met?"

"Yes."

"Can I tell you again?"

"If you want."

"If I want!?" I demanded in mock anger. I slid upward until my face was even with hers and I could look into her bright— brilliantly bright—eyes. "Look, if you get tired of hearing it, just let me know—there're plenty of other things I could tell you."

"Yeah, like what?" I could feel her breath on my face. Her eyes are black.

"Like, I love you more than anything else in the world. Like, thank you for our beautiful children. Like, how the hell after three kids do you stay so sexy to me that every time I see you all I want to do is—"

She put her hand on my mouth and held it there while she laughed. Not that she didn't believe me. But she knew there was something else on my mind.

She knew because I discuss everything with her. Mikhal is the center of my life. She is my best friend and my partner and my lover and . . .

I looked at her, wishing I could explain myself. It is not that I am inarticulate, and it is not that I don't like to talk about my motives for doing what I do. It's just that more often than not I don't understand them until after the fact. There was no reason for me to walk the edge. There was no reason for me to face vicious skinheads on their own territory and stare them down —except that I could.

After a silence of about two minutes, Mikhal patted me on my bald head.

"There might be a hell of a story in this, Mikhal," I told her eagerly.

"There probably is."

"And, Mikhali—" I paused.

She looked at me, waiting for me to continue. She already knew, somehow, what I was going to say.

"Mikhali, I dreamed about her again, the girl, last night."

She looked at me and smiled gently. "I know. I heard you," she told me.

I kissed her face. I kissed her eyes and her mouth. "Maybe I can finally do something for that little girl," I whispered.

"I hope you can."

"I love you, Mikhali."

"I love you too," she told me. Then she grabbed my face with both hands. "And don't forget that!" she said sternly. "Go and do this and come back—and don't get hurt or I'll kill you!"

It was done. I laughed and Mikhal laughed with me.

"No—no, it won't take long." I ran downstairs. The hunt was on! I was excited as I dug through the file cabinet in my office and came up with my book of contacts. It is a little black book. It is totally inconspicuous from the outside, but its contents are invaluable. In it are the names, addresses, and telephone numbers of almost everyone I have ever known. In that book are the names of criminals who owe me favors and friends from my childhood. The man whose number I was looking for at that moment was both.

I came back upstairs, leafing through the book.

"So where are you going to start?" Mikhal asked. She would never admit it, but in her own way, she was as excited as I was at the beginning of each investigation.

I found the name and number I was looking for and smiled at her.

It was the number of a man I will call Dany.

"You remember Dany?" I asked her.

2 BANGKOK

Dany had told me, no deals over the phone. If I wanted to talk to him I would have to go to Bangkok.

The flight from Israel to Thailand is a long one. I sat in the plane looking out the window and going over in my head what I had done in the last week and what I was planning to do once my plane landed.

Dany and I had grown up together. He had become a criminal, and I had become a cop. I had done him a favor once, helping him out with a minor marijuana-possession charge for old times' sake.

My plane landed at 1 A.M. at Bangkok's international airport. I picked up my bags, went through customs, and stepped outside into the long humid night of Thailand.

It took me four hours to get downtown. The traffic was a vision of chaos, and my dark-haired, fine-featured cabdriver swore in Thai as we crept along the eight-lane road leading into the city. Cars and motorcycles seemed to fly at us from every direction, horns blaring, lights arcing through the grimy windshield as my shirt crept closer to me, sticking to my body as it soaked up the perspiration running down from under my arms and the crooks of my elbows.

This was Bangkok, the internationally recognized sex capital of the world. I thought to myself that if I was going to find out about snuff films anywhere, it was going to be here. Here in this city where the largest percentage of employed Thai women are employed in the sex industry, and where, as far as I knew, just about anything could be had, any fantasy indulged—however perverse—if the price was right.

I found a hotel, got a room, and went to sleep.

The next morning, at about 11:30 A.M., I got a cab and gave the driver the address Dany had given me. The Hotel New Orleans.

What struck me most as we wound our way through the teeming streets of Bangkok was the shrines. They were everywhere, small ones and large ones—spirit shrines with stone Buddhas tucked into them—and they were respected. Once, as I stood at the intersection of two of the massively wide main thoroughfares that crisscross the city, a man on a motorcycle stopped for a red light, put his hands to his forehead, and bowed his head to the shrine. With all the press that Bangkok gets as a sex capital, I thought this was an interesting and little-talked-about dichotomy: the devotion and piety of a people known for catering to the basest needs of most of the developed world.

The Hotel New Orleans was not hard to find. And it was not, as far as I could tell, a hotel. It was more discreet than a lot of the other places I had passed; the carports were covered, hidden by curtains, so that the customers could not be identified by their automobiles. I learned later that the "hotels," especially the ones named after American cities, were mostly for locals—Thai gentlemen who wanted their visits to be kept secret.

It was early afternoon when I entered the Hotel New Orleans. The interior was dark and cool and filled with the insistent hum of an overworked air conditioner. There were tables and chairs scattered around the large room, all facing what looked like a huge fish tank. It was a large transparent wall of glass or plastic—and inside were the fish. Teenage Thai girls with the knowing eyes of forty-year-olds sat behind the wall combing their hair and doing their nails while they chatted, inaudibly, amongst themselves. They had on sheer baby-doll-type nighties with red numbers pinned to them and seemed to be completely underwhelmed by my sudden appearance in the otherwise empty hotel. I realized only later that, due to the glare created on their side of the barrier by fluorescent lights, and the darkness in the rest of the room, they couldn't see me at all.

At the other end of the room was a bar, mirrored and brassed in a perfectly good semblance of the late twentieth century's ideal of luxury. Behind the counter, a large, well-groomed Thai man was busy wiping glasses.

I walked purposefully over to the bar and laid my hands on its cool metal top.

"We closed now—come back one hour," the barman told me before I had opened my mouth.

I smiled my most winning smile, explained who I was, and asked for Dany.

I was cut off by a familiar voice.

"Shalom, Yaron."

And there was Dany. He walked over to us, said something in Thai that sent the barman back to his glasses, and slapped me on the back. "What the hell are you doing here, Yaron?" he asked me.

"I came to see you, Dany."

"To see me, or *that*?" he asked, indicating the girls behind the plastic.

"To see you and to find something—something I thought you might be able to help me with."

Dany smiled. "Whatever you want in Bangkok, I can help you find it," he assured me.

"That's what I was hoping," I told him.

■ ■ ■ ■

You're really bothered by all that shit, aren't you?" Dany asked me.

We were sitting in the coffee shop at the Dusit Thani Hotel, a real hotel not far from the Pat Pong.

"Yeah, it does bother me, and you know what? It's not the death that bothers me—I've seen plenty of that. What bothers me is that it's about power. It's about the power to kidnap young girls and then torture them and cut them open like animals *because you can.* It's about being a Nazi. So that's why, when this woman came to me, I knew that the whole stinking German story was not over—because that girl is still there, and hundreds or maybe thousands of girls like her. She—that one I saw—she's in my head. And all the other ones are just waiting. Waiting to meet the wrong sicko and—and get killed. Not for any reason—just because killing an innocent makes them feel like God and—"

The more I talked, the more excited I got, so I shut up. Dany looked at me from across the table, his face blank and unreadable. Then I remembered whom I was talking to and I almost laughed. I was a cop. I hadn't been one for years, but that didn't matter—because Dany was still a criminal. He was a criminal who some of the detectives back in Israel said had killed more than his share of guys—drug dealers mostly. He had killed them in cold blood, for drugs. And he had worked women. He had worked them on the streets and he was working them now, in the Pat Pong.

"Dany, can you help? Do you know about these things? Can you help me out?"

"I've heard about them, but I can't help you, Yaron," he said, shaking his head.

"Dany, c'mon. I'll pay whatever it costs," I assured him.

"Yaron, you don't have that kind of money," he said, laughing. "Besides, you can't buy one because they're not for sale. The buyers are the people. The sellers are the people. The sick pricks who make them are the people. You've got to be in the loop—you have to already know, without having to ask.

"And the reason I can't help you is because I don't want to know," he continued after a short pause. "I've got enough problems. You want girls, you got 'em. Young, old, one or two or three at a time, no problem. I can get boys if you want! But snuff movies—that's something else. That's a very specialized field run by some very, very heavy people—people I don't want to know."

"Dany, can you help me out with a name—a contact?" I asked him.

He shook his head. "I don't know," he told me.

I reminded him of our friendship so many years ago, and he nodded. He remembered.

I gave him my room number at the hotel and asked him to call if he thought of anything that might help me. Then I left him there, sipping his drink. He looked tired, and I knew that I had touched him. All I had done was remind him that we had been friends a long time ago in a neighborhood in Israel. And I knew he was thinking about that now as I left him. Thinking about all the time between then and now. I wondered if he regretted what he had become. And I wondered if he would call me.

By the time I got back to my hotel, there was a message from Dany.

That's how I met the man I'll call Don Swinborne.

I called Dany back immediately and he gave me a little background on Swinborne: British national based in Hong Kong.

He had been in Thailand for a few weeks to do some business and was leaving today. He would talk to me if I wanted to go out to the airport. I asked Dany what kind of business Swinborne was in. Dany read down the list: prostitution, drugs, stolen goods—nothing big-time. Dany added that Swinborne had a reputation for talking too much.

"One more thing, Yaron, I told him your name was Ron—"

"Ron what?" I asked.

"Ron nothing—he didn't need a last name."

"Thanks, Dany. I owe you one."

"Sure, Yaroni. Remember me in your will." He laughed.

I hung up.

Don Swinborne didn't need a last name.

On the traffic-choked way out to the airport I thought about this, and how I would approach this Don Swinborne. I decided that the best way to go about things would be to get right to the point. Whatever business ventures he and Dany had been involved in together, they hadn't been selling lemonade to Sunday-school teachers, that much I knew for sure. This Don Swinborne, on whatever level, to whatever degree, was a criminal, like Dany. And I had learned a few things about dealing with his type over the years.

A reality of the criminal mind is that it comes with built-in blinders. Criminals, from petty thieves to syndicate empire warlords, all have one thing in common: they are not into small talk. Everything has to revolve around the next hustle, the next big deal—and you can be sure that it will be a big one, because if it's not, why bother?

These people do not discuss politics. They don't talk about their favorite books or what music they like. They talk about the deal—what's coming up, who's going to get it, and where it is coming from. You don't talk to them about anything unless it is directly connected with the business at hand—otherwise, they don't want to know you. They are, in fact, some of the most goal-oriented people I have ever met. Once they get a whiff of something they want, they go after it until they have it. On the other hand, once they have it, that's it—game over, and on to the next hustle. Because that's the addiction there—it's the hustle. People think that gangsters are in it for the money, and they are, but it is deeper than that. Once they have the money, once they've got the prize, it's gone. They don't like running things—that's not their business. Their business is taking something for everything it is worth—squeezing it dry and then leaving it for dead. These guys are good at getting things. They're good at figuring out the angles, and they're good at making huge sums of money. But they're not good at keeping it. I had yet to meet one who could hold on to his winnings and maintain them.

And Don Swinborne was no different.

3 DON SWINBORNE

He was a hustler. I had him pegged as soon as he rose to meet me in the airport restaurant.

"Hi'yer, mate," he greeted me, holding out a lumpish hand tipped with manicured nails, and smiling.

I shook his hand and looked him over as we sat down: late forties or early fifties, dark brown eyes, and the chubby, sly, good-natured face of a Cockney cabbie. He spoke with a heavy British accent, and he began talking as soon as we sat down.

He immediately began telling me about his various criminal activities. He sat there trying to impress a man he didn't know from Adam with a résumé of hijacked warehouses, stolen gold, and an international fencing operation. And why not? I was a friend of Dany's, wasn't I? Dany had vouched for me, and that was good enough for Don. Besides, if I was a cop, talk was bullshit and nobody could prove anything.

That was the other thing I had learned about the Don Swinbornes of the world. Talk was the hustle—if it worked out and there was a cut to be had, so much the better. If it didn't, they

34

had three or four deals going at once anyway, so by the time they realized that you had been bullshitting, they more than likely barely remembered talking to you in the first place. The only rule I had was, never go back. Never bullshit the same people twice. If they saw you again they might ask what happened to the deals you had talked about, and they might start checking you out. That, I didn't need. And in my adventures thus far, I had followed my one rule and it had served me well.

Don had spent the last six months in Asia, hustling in Hong Kong, Thailand, and wherever else in Southeast Asia he could smell a deal.

"And it ain't easy, I'll tell you. These fucking chinks don't know how to do business in a civilized way, right?" he told me, waving his hand to indicate the entire non-Western world and making his heavy gold bracelet jingle.

His attitude toward the Asians he dealt with was that of a colonial master toward his infantile subjects. He called them chinks, or sometimes, waxing eloquent, greasy yellow bastards. Of course, it was due mainly to this dismissive attitude that he was not doing better in the neighborhood he had picked to ply his trade. Despite his ongoing lack of success, however, he seemed convinced that he would be able, somehow, to use the "stupidity" and "greed" of the Chinese, and the Asians in general, to his advantage. Which brought him to his latest scheme.

"White women, Ron, that's what these greasy yellow bastards want—white women. They want to feel bigger than the white man—Christ, who doesn't? And what could do that for them? White women. They want to fuck the white man's women."

Apparently, in many of the smaller brothels in Hong Kong and elsewhere in Asia, a small number of Western women were the big moneymakers.

"Now," Don went on breathlessly, "if I could only arrange for a couple of shipments of young healthy white women to arrive at some of my friends' places in Hong Kong, Singapore—places like that—I could really clean up."

Don looked at me, waiting for some response.

"And they don't even have to be lookers, ya know—these chink bastards don't care, so long as they're lily white," he assured me.

Dany had told Don that I was into porn, that I was looking for some special stuff, but he hadn't indicated what, exactly, and he hadn't said any more than that. I realized that Don had drawn his own conclusions and decided that I might be able to help him out with his "shipments."

I didn't tell him otherwise. I did better than that. I told him I was interested and that we could probably do business. I bullshitted him. Sure, I would have to check it out with some associates back home, but it sounded like a good thing. And yeah, I knew women who needed money. Women who might like to take a trip.

"And where would they be taking a trip to, exactly?" I asked him. The more I talked, the happier he looked. He thought he had hooked a live one and now all he had to do was reel me in. I let him get excited. I wanted him excited when I hit him with what I wanted.

"Well, do you know a place called Subic Bay?"

"American navy base—Philippines, right?"

"It is right now, but it won't be much longer. Yanks are pullin' out—gettin' thrown out, more likely. Place is gonna close down —ya see?"

I didn't see immediately—but I didn't tell him that. I just looked at him. "Tell me about it," I said finally.

The place had a name, Don said. It had a reputation. And because of that, with the Americans gone, Asian tourists would come flocking by the thousands, especially if there were glowing white birds there to welcome them. According to him, Subic Bay would become the Las Vegas of Asia. They could have gambling there too. These chinks love to gamble, he told me.

"Confidentially, I have friends working high up in the Philippine government, working on licensing for all this as we speak," he told me with a conspiratorial air.

His eyes were glowing with the prospects. Don Swinborne was the quintessential small-time hustler with delusions of grandeur. He didn't want to run a couple of white girls out of some dingy apartment in Kowloon; he had visions of thousands of women, a gambling empire, and millions and millions of dollars.

In the end, however, he didn't have the money to pay for a cup of coffee. The big money would come in the next day, or the next year. But it was always out there waiting for him, if he could just figure out how to get hold of it—if he could just figure out the angles.

He got excited and chummy when I told him I would pick up the tab for dinner. He got even more excited when I told him there was something he could do for me.

"No problem, just ask," he told me grandly, lighting a cigarette.

"I'm in the market for some films—snuff films, to be exact," I said easily.

Don Swinborne considered the glowing tip of his cigarette for a moment and laughed. "Is that all? I don't like that sickie stuff myself, but—"

"I'm working for some very rich people who like that kind of stuff—it's not for me," I told him. It occurred to me suddenly that it might be better that way. I was a hustler, he was a hustler.

"Righto, mate. I don't give a damn who gets their kicks how. You do something for me, I do something for you. Me, I'm a straight businessman. I don't deal in that shit—but I know a guy who does."

All gangsters consider themselves businessmen. Whether they are hijacking truckloads of TV sets or running white slaves into Asian brothels, it is all business—whatever the market will bear.

"Yeah, I know this guy, has a place in the Pat Pong. Nice bloke, bit of a wildman, if you know what I mean—ex-CIA, that kind of stuff. Been living in Thailand since that ruckus in Vietnam died down."

"Yeah?" I wasn't sure I believed him. It was all a little too Joseph Conrad for me. "Can I meet him?" I asked.

"Sure, I could arrange a meeting. He's into a lot of things you might be interested in, Ron. He's got this place that's kind of old hat—Ping-Pong balls, razor blades, that kind of thing. But he's got businesses on the side. Runs sex tours and the like, and he can get any kind of film you want, Ronny. Little boys and animals, and little girls and priests—all that sickie shit. And if you want a snuffer he can even make one to order for you. You tell him what you want, how old, and what you want to happen to them. You pay for it and you pick it up. Nice little operation he's got going—wouldn't mind a piece of that myself," he finished.

"You all right, mate?" Don asked, looking at me sideways.

"Yeah, I'm all right. I'm just still a little jet-lagged out, that's all," I told him.

He looked at me, narrowed his eyes for a moment, and then smiled. "Right. Long trip," he said.

"Yeah, it is, too long to waste much more time here. This guy sounds good, this CIA guy—when could you arrange for us to meet?" I plowed into him. Enough of this bullshit, I thought. I wanted to go back to my room and take a shower, call Mikhal, and be rid of this lowlife.

"I'll give you his name and address. I won't be there—but I'll call him and tell him you're coming, all right?"

"Good, thanks," I said, shoving the paper into my pocket. I stood up to leave.

"Hold on, mate. What about our business?" he asked, looking up at me.

I asked him for a number where I could get hold of him. I told him I would check things out and see what I could do. I made him understand that I could get the women if things worked out. I also told him that if I got a film, I might let him in on a little of the finder's fee.

"Right, mate," he grinned. "Good doing business with you."

I shook his hand.

"See you soon," he called at my back as I walked out of the restaurant.

4 THE BAMBOO HUT

The name that Don Swinborne had written down for me was William McCall, and the place he ran was called the Bamboo Hut.

The Bamboo Hut was a classic Pat Pong dive—all glitz and gut-thrumming music. Inside was a small stage surrounded by tables and chairs; the place was filled with loud, drunken Americans, Europeans, and Australians. I stood by the bar, gave my eyes a minute to adjust to the swinging, multicolored lights, and checked the place out.

Compared to the Bamboo Hut, the Hotel New Orleans had been a haven of peace and tranquility. The Hotel New Orleans was for locals—Thai gentlemen who took their pleasure seriously and relatively discreetly. The Bamboo Hut was for suckers.

They had one thing in common, however. The same little fish that swam in the fish tank at the Hotel New Orleans were here too, although at the Bamboo Hut they were allowed to swim free. The girls circulated among the tables, naked but for bikini tops with numbers pinned to them. The women were pretty in

40

their fragile, small-boned way. And they all had a smile pasted on their faces. I got the feeling that when those girls were rotten in the grave their smiles would still be there, gleaming and eternal.

I pounded my hand on the bar, getting the bartender's attention.

"Hey, pal, I want to see the owner," I told him.

"I the owner. What you want—you no happy?" he asked.

"No, I no happy—and you're not the owner. I want to see William McCall."

Onstage, a girl shot Ping-Pong balls from her vagina.

The bartender glanced quickly and unconsciously at the end of the bar. I looked as well and caught a glimpse of a man who had to be William McCall. He was leaning on the bar with the air of a man at home—and he could only have been an American. He was fairly tall and powerfully built. He was balding and had on a pair of bifocals that gave his strong-jawed, cold face the appearance of a killer grandfather. He wore a gray shirt and loose khaki pants. I took all this in in less than a second and looked back at the bartender.

"No William McCall here—you no happy, you leave, yes?" he told me.

"No, I want to speak to this McCall guy and I want to speak to him now. You tell him I'm here, would you?" I peeled a bill off my diminishing roll and thrust it at the Thai. He took it, stuffed it in his pocket, and shook his head. "No McCall here," he told me simply.

Then I felt a presence behind me and I knew it was he. It was McCall.

"Listen, buddy, when I pay for action I expect some action. Now you go get your boss and do it quick," I told the bartender, biting off each word like a man making a doomed attempt to control himself.

The presence behind me moved to the bar, on my left side. I

turned my head and looked into a pair of bifocals. A cold voice asked, "How's Don doing these days?"

I knew immediately that he had seen me as soon as I walked in—and he had known who I was. He had been waiting for me to come to him. Now I was there.

"He's good," I told him.

"Yeah? He's good, huh?" he asked. He held out his hand.

I nodded. He moved close to me while we shook hands. He squeeezed my fingers—his grip was enormously strong—and whispered in my face, spitting out each word individually, "That motherfucker has got to go, you know what I mean? That son of a bitch has a big, big mouth. That motherfucker has big, big problems because he is too damn light with his mouth—you know what I mean?"

While he spoke he continued to tighten his grip on my hand until I was in real pain. He stared into my eyes and I looked back at him. He had gotten to me, that was for sure. And he knew it. He released my hand and looked out at the bar.

William McCall was the real thing. This guy was no small-time asshole—he was no Don Swinborne. This was a man I would have to deal with—on his level. It was his game.

Another girl was onstage. This one shot arrows from a small contraption inserted between her legs. Her aim was flawless as she popped balloons held by delighted customers. She looked like she was about thirteen years old.

"Look, buddy," he said out of the side of his mouth, without even looking at me. "I don't know who you are. I don't know what you want. I don't know you, and I don't know this fuck Swinborne. I do know one thing, though." Here he turned to me and looked knives into my face. "I don't want any business with you—is that clear?"

I got mad, and that was a mistake. This guy had threatened me—this scumbag had touched me. And I wanted to touch him back.

"You listen to me, you fuck," I told him. I am a great believer in swearing. Whenever I find myself in a jam I start swearing. I swear hard and heavy and with great conviction. It's usually more a reaction to fear than anything else. I have to admit, though, that it usually does the trick.

"I don't know what this fucking bullshit about squeezing my fingers was. I don't give a fuck about you or about that fucking son of a bitch Don Swinborne, but I'll tell you one thing, you bastard: I am not here to fuck around. I don't give a fuck if you have product or not. You don't touch me like that again—is that clear?!"

I jabbed my finger into his chest and nearly knocked him off his stool. After allowing myself to get angry, that was my second mistake. I should not have gotten physical. Two big bouncers came over and stood next to me, waiting for a signal from their boss. They had short bamboo sticks in their hands. I was wondering what they thought they were going to do with those when one of them pulled his stick into two sections and revealed the glinting edge of a razor-sharp knife.

We faced each other silently for a moment and then McCall said, very casually, "I don't know who you are, but I am a businessman. I run this bar and I pay my taxes. I don't know what police agency you are working for, but you either get out now or I throw you out, all right?"

I had blown it. I had been acting like a cop, old instincts taking over. He had seen right through me.

"McCall, listen to me, give me two minutes," I pleaded suddenly as the bouncers started to close in. McCall signaled to them and they backed off a step. Then he nodded at me.

I gave him the works. I made stuff up as I went along and just babbled it out as it came to me. I was in a bind. I had a rich client—a German guy. He wanted some movies—the kind McCall could get. A big deal going with some Iraqis and some Japanese, and he asked me to get him a film, and . . .

The upshot was that my supplier was dead and I had already told my guy that I could get the films. Now I needed them bad. McCall listened to me with the air of a bored professor. I was babbling. He let me run out of steam and then smiled at me.

"That Don will really talk to anybody, won't he?" he said finally.

"I don't know him. I just met that guy, but I'm legit," I began.

"That's the problem, isn't it? I don't know you, you don't know anybody. Listen, son, when you know what you're talking about, you come back to me, all right?"

Then he touched my face. He put two fingers on my cheek and pushed hard, swinging my head around to face the stage.

A new girl was onstage, smoking a cigarette with her vagina.

The bouncers closed in, took me by either arm, and escorted me to the door.

As I stood there rubbing my face, the Pat Pong glistened and chattered, incense from a nearby shrine filling the air with a delicate, alien odor.

The place where William McCall had left his mark burned as though I had been branded with hot metal.

Before I left Bangkok, I saw Dany one last time. He had tried to hide it, but when he heard what I had done he was terrified that I had tried to pull a fast one on McCall. He asked me again and again if I had mentioned his name or if there was anything that I did or said that would have pointed McCall in his direction. I assured him that there was not. I don't know if he believed me. In any case, he clammed up tight after that. He offered me the services of the Hotel New Orleans for the night —which I refused—and then suggested that I leave Bangkok on the next available plane. I told him I had already booked a flight.

5   I S R A E L

It took me a while to unwind when I got back home. I had run up against it in Thailand and come up with nothing. However, the trip had accomplished two things. I had the beginnings of a cover; I would take on the persona and big talk of Don Swinborne, adding to it where necessary as I went along. And more than that, I had my feet back under me. I had gotten ahead of myself in Bangkok and I had made a few mistakes. But I had also learned a few things about whom I was dealing with and gotten a couple of ideas. There was only one thing missing; I needed a direction.

But I knew one thing for sure—there was no sense beating my head against the wall trying to think of one. Whatever I had to do next would come to me—it always had before. If I thought too hard about where to take things, I usually ended up with a headache. I had to let it come to me. I had to sleep and eat well for a couple of days and let my brain work on its own without any interference from me.

Besides, I knew what I had to do—I just didn't want to do it. That's when Luke came through. Luke was a friend of mine.

He was also a crime reporter for *Achochront,* Israel's largest-selling daily. I had called him, among other people, before I left for Bangkok. On my second night back in Israel, he called me back.

"Yaron, remember a couple of weeks ago you were asking about those sickie films?" he asked me, yelling over the phone. Luke couldn't say anything quietly.

"It was last week," I corrected him.

"Whenever. Listen, I've turned up somebody you might like to meet."

"Yeah, who?"

"This guy, name's Nisim Simantov."

"Simantov?"

"Yeah, Russian guy. He's into all that shit—girls and guns. You know how these guys are," Luke told me.

"Yeah," I said.

I knew how those guys were, and so did everybody else in Israel. Ever since the Soviet Union had collapsed, Israel had been inundated by immigrants from all parts of the old "dark empire." Most of these were good, law-abiding citizens who wanted only one thing, to be in Israel. With them, however, had come part of the problem they were trying to escape. The Russian mob was working its way into every crack in Israel. And they were good at what they did. The new mobsters from Tbilisi and Kiev and Moscow were all well educated, computer literate, and ruthless as hell. They were proving to be a real thorn in the side of Israeli law enforcement, and at the rate they were expanding, they were threatening to become a thorn in the side of the world at large.

"Would he talk to me?" I asked.

"Why not? He'll talk to anybody who wants to deal. You want to meet him?"

I thought for a minute. It occurred to me that it might not be such a good idea to play around in my own backyard. After my little adventure in Germany, I had become something of a sensation. On the other hand, Israel being what it was, my fifteen minutes had been up before I had time to piss out the champagne from my welcome-home party. In a very small country surrounded by extremely hostile neighbors, all it takes is one little border skirmish or a car bomb and you are yesterday's news.

"Yeah, I'd like to meet him," I told Luke.

"OK, I'll set you up. But if you get a story, you cut me in on it, all right?"

"Sure, Luke, sure," I told him.

I spent that night at home with my family.

▌ ▌ ▌ ▌

I met Luke the next day around noon in the lobby of the Tel Aviv Hilton, on Yarkon Street. He came in, shook my hand in his quick, slightly nervous way, and told me that Simantov was out front in his car. He would know who I was.

I thanked him and went outside. As I stood there, bright sunlight reflecting off the Mediterranean, I scanned Yarkon Street for Simantov's car. I was expecting something big and imposing. I was expecting the typical, childish flash of the average small-time gangster.

"Hey, over here," a voice called.

I looked around trying to locate whoever was calling me.

"Over here." *Bang-bang-bang*, a hand slapping sheet metal.

It was a station wagon that had obviously seen better days. I walked over to it, crossing Yarkon Street in the direction of the sea.

"You Ron?" the small-featured guy at the wheel of the station wagon asked. I had told Luke to tell the guy my name was Ron.

"Yeah, you Simantov?"

"Who the hell else would I be?" he asked, laughing. "You

want to talk, get in," he said, jerking his thumb at the passenger-side door.

Who the hell else would he be? I thought. Simantov hit the gas and we took off.

He was from Georgia, the old Soviet satellite, now an independent republic. He was an affable guy. He had had some business with Luke in the past, and he ran a low-level porn-and-prostitution racket in and around Hod Passage. And he had the edge. It's the edge that lets you know that a person is not to be messed with. There was some big shit behind Simantov. I didn't find out until much later just how big it was.

"So what you want, porno?" he asked me as we sped up Diznogf Street.

"Something like that," I said noncommitally.

"You really into porn business?" he asked.

"I'm into a lot of businesses."

"That's what Luke say. Good man, him. He told me you move things." He turned to me and grinned big. "You know how to move things, Ron?"

The tires screeched around a corner as he pulled the steering wheel around, swearing under his breath.

"That depends on what kind of things—and for who," I told him.

"What you care for who—for you, that's who! I'm talking of guns, ammunition—can you move big shit like that?" he asked.

I looked at him and he pulled the station wagon to a screeching halt. We had arrived at Hod Passage.

"C'mon, we talk, I do business," he told me.

I nodded and got out.

For the next half hour I followed him into one porn store after another as he talked to the people behind the counters, collecting money from some and just chatting with others. In between, as we walked, he told me that he could get me anything I wanted. All I had to do was tell him.

"I'm looking for some very special films," I told him.

"What kind of films?" he asked.

"I'm looking for snuff films."

He laughed, looking into my eyes as if trying to read my mind. "I know you from somewhere?" he asked suddenly.

"I don't think so," I said calmly, hoping that he hadn't recognized me. I never found out if he had or not.

"Shit!" he said, looking at his watch. "C'mon, I have appointment."

He took off at a run, not stopping until he had entered yet another porn store with the emblematic "Eros" in Hebrew above the door.

I went into the store with him. He went straight to the counter and without introduction began berating the clerk. They spoke Russian, so I didn't understand what they were saying, and I couldn't have cared less anyway. That was his business. While he yelled at the clerk I picked my way along the shelves, picking up various video boxes and examining them for the names of the production companies that had produced them. Most of the stuff was pretty tame boy-girl stuff. Toward the back of the store it got a little harder, and at the very back was a locked case. In the case was the store's small collection of the real thing.

There were boxes with pictures of old women urinating on men and young women having sex with various animals. There was one whole side devoted to boxes with pictures of what looked like prepubescents engaged in various sex acts. The girls, many of them with no discernible breasts or pubic hair, wore headbands with the number seventeen written on them in red. That was the first time I saw those headbands. I had no idea then how often I would see them in the course of my investigation. I only wondered if the headbands really fooled anyone. The girls were obviously much younger than seventeen.

I moved down the case, trying to see through the glare created by the fluorescent lights. I wiped a smudge off of the glass —and then I saw it.

Tellall.

Shit, why did it have to be Tellall?

I stared at the tiny letters in the lower right-hand corner of a box bearing a photograph of a woman using what looked like an eel as a dildo.

Why did it have to be Tellall?

"Hey, Ron, you want go?" Simantov called to me from the counter. He was counting bills while the clerk stood cowering off to the side. "I almost ready."

"I'll wait outside," I told him, edging away from the glass case.

I walked to the door and just before I exited the store, I heard what sounded like a slap and a yelp. I didn't look back.

"You want snuff movies?" Simantov asked me when he rejoined me outside.

"That's what I'm looking for," I told him.

"Why? Is bad shit," he said simply.

"They're not for me—I work for someone."

"Who?"

"None of your business who—do you know where to get films like that?" I asked.

"Luke knows you want that?"

"Luke knows nothing. I told him I was looking for something that was not easy to find, and he mentioned you."

"That's it, snuff movies?" Simantov asked. "Only business?"

"I'm into all kinds of business. Right now I need these films," I told him.

"Me, I in other business—guns, you know?"

"What about the shops, all that?" I asked.

He waved his hand dismissively. "Bullshit—I move guns, weapons, you know, yeah."

It had worked with Don Swinborne. I didn't see any reason not to go along with this guy too.

"Well, my people might be interested in doing that kind of business, but first I need the films."

"You move guns?" he asked.

"I can move anything for the right price," I told him.

Again he laughed. "You got balls big? Huh?"

He then went on to tell me that he had a couple of big orders to fill—did I want to do some business?

"Always," I told him.

Then he winked at me. "You know a lot of people, right?"

"I know people."

"You know anyone interested in red clay?"

I had no idea what he was talking about, but that didn't matter—this was the hustle. If he asked, I knew. If he wanted it, I could get it.

"I know people who are interested in just about anything. Right now I know people who are interested in some very special films."

"Big bullshit—nothing, porno. Guns better, yeah?"

Well, money talks and bullshit walks. I told him that if he could find a film like that for me, maybe we could do some business. He pulled up outside the Hilton. My ride with Nisim Simantov was over and it had been a big waste of time. I thanked him for the ride and started to get out. He grabbed my arm.

"You really think you move red clay?" he asked.

"I told you, I can move anything."

He laughed again and nodded. "OK, Ron—we talk, yeah?"

"Sure," I told him. "We'll talk."

I had no idea what red clay was then, and I never could have known how that casual hustler's promise to move some would come back to haunt me.

■ ■ ■ ■

Tellall, the name I had seen on the back of the bestiality video at the Eros shop, was the production name used by a guy I had heard about, whom I will call Jürgen Dauer.

And Jürgen Dauer lived in Germany. Jürgen Dauer was a neo-Nazi.

I knew that there was my best bet, now that I had screwed up in Thailand. However, the last place I wanted to go was back to Germany. I actually didn't even consider it at the time. There was no way I was going back there—not for all the tea in China.

I had a lot of reasons. Some of them were good, some of them were not so good. The main one, of course, and the one that nobody could argue with me about, was that I didn't want to get killed. Not a bad reason, really.

The worst reason was that I was afraid of getting killed— which is not the same thing.

So I put it out of my mind. I didn't mention it to Mikhal. I didn't mention it to anybody.

Just then Elie came running into the office crying. She tried to climb into my lap, tugging on my shirt and whimpering about some hurt she had suffered at the hands of her brother. Then her brother came in pleading innocence.

I snapped. I yelled at the kids and told them to work it out or I would work it out for them. I stood up and put Elie on the ground. Mikhal came running in at the sound of my voice. She picked Elie up and held her close, quieting her.

"What is the matter with you?" she demanded, glaring at me.

I had no answer for her. Every nerve in my body was buzzing. It was as if I were made of electricity and shooting sparks in every direction. I mumbled something about being tired, walked past my wife, and went outside. I went to talk to Assaf. He was an old friend of mine from my days in the Israeli police force. He was still a good friend of mine. He worked for the government.

He waved me into his office and told me to sit down, offering me half of the sandwich he was eating. I shook my head.

"Well, then, Yaron, what can I do for you?" he asked, smiling.

I had had something to ask him. I could've asked him if I didn't know the answer already.

So I asked him something else.

"Assaf, what do you know about something called red clay?"

"Not much. What do you know about it?" he asked me.

"This scumbag I was talking to asked me if I knew any— anything about it. Other than that—nothing."

"You didn't ask?"

"He thought I knew—I mean, the guy was into arms smuggling—so I assumed it was some kind of weapon."

"Well, you're right about that—it's supposed to be some kind of portable thermonuclear device. *Kaboom!*"

"Oh, is that all? Why 'supposed to be'?"

"Because as far as anyone knows it doesn't really exist. It's supposed to be the size of a carry-on bag."

"You think it doesn't exist?" I asked him.

"I think anything is possible in a world like this one," he said, shrugging.

"Including snuff films." It wasn't a question.

Assaf nodded. "What you're looking for?"

"Yes."

We sat quietly for a moment. We are old enough friends that we do not have to talk to feel comfortable.

"What would you do?" I said, breaking the silence so suddenly that Assaf looked a little startled. "What would you do, Assaf, as a policeman, if you walked into a room of men watching one of these films? What could you do?"

Assaf took a deep breath, straightened up, and put his hands together on his desk.

"As a policeman?" he asked.

"Yes."

"As a policeman I would surely confiscate the tape. I suppose I would hold whoever I found, check them out, arrest whoever I could, check out the film to make sure that it was actually what it seemed."

"But what if you knew in your guts that it was real?" I insisted.

"You didn't ask me about my guts, Yaron. You asked me what I would do as a policeman, and frankly, I'm not sure. Could you prove that it was really murder? If you could, then, maybe, but —if you couldn't?" He stopped speaking, letting the question hang in the air.

"Nothing. You could do nothing," I said finally.

"If we could prove it, catch who made it—then, kidnapping, rape, murder, yes. But as far as I know there are no laws on the books prohibiting men from gathering together to watch a movie with horrible special effects. That's what I can tell you as a policeman."

I nodded. He had answered my question. I didn't have to ask him how he would feel as a man, as a human. I had known him long enough to know that if he ever did stumble into a snuff film showing, very few of the audience members would ever forget his handsome face.

"You wouldn't want to tell me who this guy with the red clay was, just for future reference, would you?" he asked, changing the subject.

I shook my head. "Scumbag, nobody—probably just testing me. I was just interested in what the hell it was."

Assaf looked hard at me. "You want to tell me anything else?"

Yes, old friend, I thought. I want to tell you that I am going crazy.

I didn't say that, however.

"I just—this latest thing with the movies is getting to me a little, I guess. I just snapped at the kids. It's getting to me already."

Assaf looked at me and smiled gently. It suddenly struck me as very funny that I was spilling my guts to him—as if he had nothing better to do.

"So, what are you going to do about it?" he asked me.

"I don't know," I told him, spreading my hands out on his desk. "I really don't know."

■ ■ ■ ■

That night, after the kids had been put to bed, Mikhal came into my office and closed the door.

"Yaron, what is wrong with you? You're yelling at the kids and you won't talk to me. What's the matter?"

I pulled her onto my lap. "I think I'm just tired, Mikhali," I told her.

"Don't give me that. You tell me what's bothering you."

I looked at her. At first I hadn't realized it, and then I had denied it. I couldn't deny it anymore.

"Mikhali—I know where to get these films. I have known all along," I told her.

"So go and get them," she said.

"They're in Germany," I told her.

She didn't say anything for a minute.

"Are you sure you could get the films in Germany?" she asked finally.

I told her that I was not 100 percent sure but that I knew it was a good lead.

"So, what's the problem?" she asked.

"What's the problem? What's the problem? People in Germany want to kill me, that's the problem. That's not enough for you?" I asked.

She patted my cheek. "Oh, it's enough for me, Yaron. It's

more than enough for me. If you don't want to go, don't go. You don't have to fight anybody else's battles, Yaron."

"I had the dream again last night, Mikhali," I whispered. I had dreamed about the girl in the film. "I feel like I have to do this."

She stood up and walked away from me. She was angry and she was trying to control herself. Mikhal does not get angry often. When she does get angry it hurts me in my soul.

"Why, why do you have to do anything? Who made you a superhero, Yaron? You are my husband and the father of our children—not Superman. You don't have to save the world—and you couldn't, even if you wanted to. The world will go on without you. Do you think if you get one of these films that that will solve anything?"

"It might."

"And it might damn well not! You've been neglecting your family and you've been neglecting the work you can do right now—journalism, remember? It pays money—money that we need. Because I don't know if you've noticed, but we eat like other people, and pay the same bills as other people. And we wear clothes and . . ." She stopped and looked at me. "And you're going to go, so go."

"It won't take long, I swear," I told her.

"I know, I know, I know."

The next morning I took my kids to the beach and watched them swim. When we got back to the house I closed myself up in my office and started making phone calls.

I called a couple of airlines and found a flight leaving in two days at a very good price. Then I called a professional man I knew. A man schooled in various martial arts, a man who was a friend and a companion and someone I could count on and trust.

If I was going back to Germany, I wasn't going to be there by myself.

6 THE TEAM

A year before, I had testified in Germany about my findings concerning the growing threat of the neo-Nazi movement. That's how I had come to know Ako Reinhardt.

Ako Reinhardt is tall and good looking, with jet black hair and an honest, good-natured face. He works out a lot, but he is not overgrown and lumpish. Rather, his muscles are long and elastic. His reflexes are fast and his mind has been shaped by years of meditation and discipline. He was a champion kick boxer for several years running. He is a good man and he runs his own private security firm.

He and his men shepherded me around Germany during the time I was giving testimony there, and I felt as safe as I have ever felt in my entire life.

Also, during that time, Ako and I had become friends. Ako and his number one bodyguard, Andreas, a former aikido champion of Germany, had never let me down, and I knew that they never would. They were men I could rely upon and trust. They were men like myself. And I knew that at a moment's notice they would be there for me. All I had to do was call.

"*Schade, Yaron, kann's nicht tun*"—sorry, can't do it—Ako told me when I called him at his office in Berlin.

I stared at the telephone. "What do you mean, you can't do it?"

"Well, yeah, sure I can do it—but I need a couple of days. I'm on a job right now."

"But, Ako, I already booked the flight."

"Sorry, Yaron, I can't do it."

"So when can I get you?" I asked him.

"This guy goes back to the States on Monday. I'm all yours then—me and Andreas."

"All right, Monday. I'll meet you in Saarbrücken in two days." I would change my flight.

"Good, yeah, OK. See you then. Nice to talk to you again." Ako hung up. I could see his handsome face grinning. I knew there was no sense in trying to get him to drop his other gig and meet me earlier. He would've just told me that when the time was right, he would be there.

■ ■ ■ ■

Two days later I flew into Paris, rented a car, and arrived a few hours later on the French-German border in the not very interesting town of Saarbrücken.

Ako and Andreas were due to meet me the following morning. I decided to use some of the time until they arrived doing some good old-fashioned legwork. I found what passed for the red light district and went from one sex shop to the next.

Nobody had any snuff films, however, and nobody even wanted to talk about them. Not surprising, really. Most of the people who worked in those places were just that—workers. They were usually immigrants trying to get by. I didn't meet any of the heavies by walking up to the counter, and in any case it would have been naive to think that I would. One thing I had learned, however, was never to count out the accidental. There was always a chance that I could run into the guy who knew— or the guy who knew who knew. That is what detective work amounts to a lot of times, no matter what it looks like on television. A lot of it is just walking around and asking dumb questions, hoping for a dumb answer.

When I got back to the hotel I took a shower, lay down, and fell into a troubled sleep. I was awakened by the telephone ringing. I rolled over and picked it up. The man at the desk informed me that I had visitors. I jumped out of bed and started to pull my clothes on. Suddenly there was a furious knocking on my door.

"All right—hold on a minute!" I shouted, jumping around with one pants leg on and one off.

There was a bit of laughter from the other side of the door, and then the pounding began again, even more furiously. I pulled my pants up, buttoned them, and stalked to the door.

"Who the hell is it?" I demanded, pulling the door open.

It was Ako and Andreas. They stood in the hall grinning at me. Then Ako stepped forward and grabbed me in a huge bear hug, which is not an easy thing to do. I shook my head and rubbed the sleep out of my eyes.

"What the hell are you guys doing here so early?" I asked as Ako passed me over to Andreas, who patted me on the back and cheeks.

"Well, good morning, sleepyhead," Ako said in German.

"English, please," I told him. It was too damned early for German.

"If you like," Ako said easily. His English was at least as good as mine. "But you know, it's not so early," he informed me.

"No—it's eleven-thirty. We are actually a little late," Andreas added, laughing.

"Well, what are you guys doing here so late, then?" I growled at them good-naturedly. I was determined to growl as long as I could. Their good spirits were a little annoying that early in the morning. Besides, I had really overslept—which I never do.

They stood there staring at me for a couple of seconds. "So, come in. Close the door and sit down. I'm going to go and— brush my teeth or something," I mumbled.

Andreas beamed at me. "Nice to see you again, Yaron," he chirped.

"Yeah, right," I responded, disappearing into the bathroom.

"So what are we going to do, Yaron?" Andreas asked from the other room. "Ako won't tell me."

I pulled my toothbrush out of my mouth and answered him, looking in the mirror. I looked like hell.

"We're going to see a man about a film!"

■ ■ ■ ■

Jürgen Dauer's shop occupied a busy corner in a sleepy suburb of Munich. The sun was shining through clouds—big white clouds that alternately hid and then revealed the sun, casting hard, cold shadows on the ground.

The three of us—Ako, Andreas, and I—sat in Ako's sedan, waiting for Dauer. I had seen him once at a neo-Nazi rally I attended the year before. He had been pointed out to me, but we had never been introduced. I didn't think he would recognize me.

While we waited, Ako and Andreas joked with each other, blowing off steam.

If I hadn't worked with them before I would have doubted their professional capabilities. They seemed too carefree, too unconcerned with the job at hand to be able to protect me, or anyone else for that matter. I had worked with them before, however, and I knew that when the time came, their entire concentration could be focused with pinpoint accuracy on any task set before them, whether it was simply to watch and wait or to act. I was not worried about them.

I scanned the quiet streets looking for a man who not only, by all accounts, had had a hand in making the snuff films that I had seen, but was also a neo-Nazi. A man who knew the men I had uncovered.

"Ow! Hey, what the fuck?" Something hit me in the back of the head. I turned and looked at Andreas. He grinned sheepishly.

"Sorry, Yaron, but your big head got in the way," he told me in German.

Ako reached back and grabbed him by the jacket. "I'll tell you what's going to get in your way, little brother," Ako warned him jokingly, holding up his large fist and shaking it.

I shook my head. I had worked with these guys before. Just keep telling yourself that, Yaron, I thought.

And there he was.

Every muscle in my body tensed. Jürgen Dauer—medium height, late fifties, brown jacket, light brown sweater over a khaki shirt, neatly ironed pants. He approached his store with his hands shoved deep into his jacket pockets and a green leather hat pulled down over his eyes.

I considered for a moment whether there was any chance that Dauer might recognize me. I didn't think so; we had never actually been introduced. If he knew my face from somewhere but couldn't place me, so much the better. If he did recognize me as Yaron Svoray, well, I had Ako and Andreas backing me up. If he decided to start something, we could probably finish it for him.

I reached for the door handle and had just cracked the car door when Ako touched my shoulder. Just a touch, and I knew that all playfulness was gone. I glanced back at Andreas. He sat ramrod straight in the backseat, waiting for instructions.

■ ■ ■ ■

It was twenty-five past four when I entered Dauer's store.

I asked him to sell me some snuff videos and he stonewalled me for ten minutes. Andreas was outside, window-shopping. Ako was inside, looking the shop over, pretending to examine a succession of lenses. I pushed Jürgen Dauer until he finally threatened to call the cops if I didn't leave his store.

The engine was already running when I got into the car. Without a word from me, Ako hit the gas and we got out of there. I looked back once as we pulled away from the curb, and saw Dauer watching through the window. We pulled around the corner and waited exactly four minutes. Andreas appeared, and we drove back to our hotel in silence.

■ ■ ■ ■

We got to the hotel, went up to the room we had taken for the night, and I had a fit. I was pissed.

"Yaron," Ako began quietly. He was standing by the window looking out between slightly parted curtains at the street below. He drew the curtains together and turned to me.

"Yaron, listen. Let's get in my car and go to my house. We could be there in three hours. We can relax there—have a nice meal—and you can figure out what you want to do next, yes?"

I sat up on the bed. Across the room Andreas opened his eyes.

"I'll tell you what, why don't I pay you guys off? You go to your house and wait for me there. I'll get there on my own, later."

Immediately, I knew I had made a mistake. It was a mistake to talk to Ako as though he were nothing more than a hired gun. He had earned respect from me, and he expected it.

He made no protest, however. He just looked at me and said stiffly, in his best formal German, "Yaron, I am here to see that you are safe. While I am doing that nothing else matters. You are in my charge and I will not leave you until you are out of my charge—and that will not be until I have made certain that you are no longer in need of my services."

I looked at him silently for a couple of moments. I do not enjoy leading people into trouble—and that was where I was headed.

"Ako, I'm sorry. I didn't mean it like that. You know I appreciate what you do for me, otherwise I wouldn't call you. It's just that I am thinking about doing something that could be totally stupid. I am going back to pay Jürgen Dauer another visit—but he's not going to be there, because I'm going after business hours. You understand? I just don't want you guys involved in any deep shit that you don't need to be involved in—that's all."

Ako smiled, and Andreas stood up and laughed as if that were the funniest thing he had ever heard in his life.

"What's so funny?" I demanded.

Ako walked over to me and clapped me on the shoulders. "You are, man. Deep shit? Every time I get near you I am in deep shit. You think I was big hero back home for working with you a year ago when you were traveling around Germany telling everyone how nasty we Germans were? Give me a break, man," he finished.

I was speechless. I had never even considered that aspect of my last trip to Germany. Ako and Andreas had been on the magazine covers with me. They had always been at my side. I had left Germany finally, but they had stayed. Shit.

I wanted to tell him that I was sorry, but I knew that he would just tell me that it didn't matter now. What mattered now was now.

I nodded and laughed. Then I went into the bathroom and splashed water on my face. When I came back out, Ako and

Andreas were looking at me expectantly. I did not disappoint them.

"So this is what I want to do . . . ," I began.

■ ■ ■ ■

Jürgen Dauer was not security conscious.

It took Ako all of three minutes to pick the lock on the back door of Dauer's shop. He used nothing more complicated than a piece of wire, listening for the tumblers in the lock to catch one by one and fall into place. A cheap alarm system that Ako had noted while he was in the store with me was easily bypassed through the quick reconfiguration of a few brightly colored wires.

"*Scheiss,*" Ako grunted quietly as he cracked the door.

"What? What's the matter?" I whispered.

I could barely see Ako grin in the darkness. "I'm getting slow," he whispered back.

I shook my head, pushed the door open a little wider, and slipped inside. Seconds later, after a short, hissing conversation with Andreas, Ako came in after me and closed the door. We were in.

Ako pulled out a flashlight that he had prepared earlier. He had equipped it with an ingenious hood made out of cardboard. The hood blocked the light so that only a very diffused glow illuminated an area of about six inches around the bulb and no more. There was light in the darkness. We went to work.

Dauer had two machines for dubbing and editing videos in the back of the store. Besides that, there were stacks and stacks of neatly organized videos along all the walls. They seemed to be arranged by date, as there were no titles. I pulled one down at random. There were no markings at all to indicate what might be on it—it might have been a bar mitzvah, but I didn't think so. I moved down the stacks of videos looking for something that might tell me exactly what I was looking at when I heard Ako hiss from the other side of the room.

I crept carefully across the cluttered studio and joined him where he was investigating the contents of a file cabinet he had discovered.

The files were dated in the same style as the videotapes along the wall. What they contained was much more revealing, however. Each file contained a manila envelope, and each envelope contained eight-by-ten glossies.

The subjects in the photographs were obviously not professional performers. They were either too fat or too skinny or too old to excite anyone but those personally involved. So here were Jürgen Dauer's amateur efforts.

In the drawer that Ako had opened, the photos showed people in various states of undress, engaged in pretty run-of-the-mill sexual acts. All of the participants had funny looks on their faces, as if they weren't sure they should be doing what they were doing but were doing it anyway. They were more pathetic and desperate than sexy—bored people trying to recapture sexual energy they had lost, and hiring Jürgen Dauer to help them.

The next drawer down had a little more of what we were looking for. It was a little more hard-core: leather, S&M, bondage.

I reached down to open the next drawer and it wouldn't budge. I pulled again, harder—nothing. It was locked. That was it! I knew suddenly that that was it. What I was there for was in that drawer. Ako shined his light on the lock.

I pulled on it again, hard—nothing. I felt like I could pull the damn thing apart. Ako nudged me aside and put his piece of wire to work once more. I was sweating as I watched him work his wire into the lock in the feeble glow of the modified flashlight. I could feel it sitting in there—waiting for me.

Then we heard it. *Knock-knock-knock.* It was the warning that we had agreed upon beforehand. Andreas, standing watch in the shadows outside, had seen something or heard something, and he was letting us know that it was time to move.

Ako began to scramble the wire around in the lock. He put his head down close to it and listened. Dauer's back door had almost had a welcome sign on it—the lock had been so easy to bust. This one, on a damn filing cabinet, was giving us real trouble—and we didn't have time for trouble.

"C'mon, Ako, c'mon," I urged him.

"I almost have it," he whispered calmly. There were times when his Zen discipline, which usually annoyed me, came in real handy.

There were another three taps on the back door.

"Got it!" Ako sighed.

We pulled the drawer open.

Nothing.

Son of a bitch!

There were the same files, but this time there were no envelopes. I scrabbled through the green hanging dividers, but there was nothing there. Then, at the back, taped to a divider, was a date. I tore it out of the filing cabinet and raced over to the wall of videos on the other side of the room. I had assumed that the dates on the photos in the other drawers corresponded with the dates on the videos. I ran my finger down the video boxes looking for a match.

"Yaron, it is time to go," I heard Ako call quietly from the other side of the room. The dates ran down in perfect order. I was almost there. Months, weeks, days—I was almost there. I almost had it.

"Yaron," Ako called again.

And my finger fell into an empty space. It had been there, and now it was gone. Where the video matching the date in my hand should've been there was only an empty space.

I stood there motionless while it sank in. I could hear Ako urging me to hurry, but only vaguely, as if from a great distance. Then I felt a hand on my arm.

"We really have to go—now, Yaron," Ako commanded.

I let him lead me away, my body slack with disappointment. It was only then that I realized what I was doing: that I had broken into a shop in Germany; that, in fact, had I been caught, I would've been counted as no more than a common burglar, at least until the German police found out who I was. Then it was anybody's guess what might be done with me. It was crazy. I was crazy. It was crazy.

Suddenly an idea hit me. It was a long shot, but I had nothing left but long shots. I couldn't go away like that. I had risked so much, was risking so much, I couldn't . . .

I pulled away from Ako and leapt over to the video dubbing machines. I jammed my hand into the slot—nothing again. I moved to the second and—there it was.

"Ako, shine your light over here," I commanded.

He resisted. "Yaron, it's over—we have to go now."

"Get that goddamn light over here!"

Ako came over and shined the light on the machine. I searched for what seemed like years until I found the eject button. I pushed. There was the sound of a machine responding to electrical commands. A whirring and then *click*. A tape appeared. I wrenched it from the machine and grabbed Ako's arm to hold it under the light. There was a date on the tape. I checked it number by number with the date in my hand. It was a match.

"We got it!" I hissed triumphantly. "We got the son of a bitch!"

Ako didn't respond. He didn't have time. At that moment Andreas poked his head in the door and told us that it was getting light. Two cop cars had already passed on their morning patrols. "C'mon—now. Let's go!"

I didn't need any more urging than that. I had what I had come for. Ako and I bounded for the door and out into the alleyway behind the shop. Andreas had the car running and ready. We leapt inside and Andreas took off before we had the door closed. As we came around the corner, a police cruiser passed us, going in the other direction, and turned onto the street we had just turned off.

"What the hell took you guys so long?" Andreas demanded as the sedan sped up and we flew in the direction of Munich.

Ako ruffled his hair. "What's the matter—were you worried, *Junge?*"

"No, I was just wondering. It's almost time for breakfast— *und ich habe einen grossen Hunger.*" (I'm really hungry.)

Ako laughed. I looked at the sky and for the first time I realized that the sun was almost up. We had been hours in the shop of Jürgen Dauer. I patted the lump under my jacket where I had stuffed the video. It had been worth it.

■ ■ ■ ■

First came the sounds. There was automatic-rifle fire and men shouting. The image on the television screen flickered in bars of color, then cleared. The camera had been on auto-focus; that much was evident from the momentary fuzziness of the image as the camera swooped and dove toward each new scene. It was also obvious why whoever made the film had left the focusing of the image up to the camera: there isn't a lot of time to measure distances and get a clear picture in a war zone.

There were loud shouts in a language I didn't understand. The camera swung around to show a village. Although it was hard to estimate because of the flatness of the video image, the village looked to be about a hundred yards away. It was obviously Europe. I knew it was somewhere in the former Yugoslavia. The village was a picture-perfect Middle European village with a church steeple rising above a huddle of whitewashed, sloping-roof houses. It looked like a place that would've been mobbed by tourists—if it weren't for the plume of smoke rising out of the middle of it. There was an explosion. The camera shook, and another plume of smoke climbed up to the sky from somewhere on the other side of the church. The camera swung around again. This time, as the auto-focus did its job, men in uniforms came into view. They crouched and ran, firing from time to time. I didn't recognize their uniforms. At that point they could've been Croatian or Bosnian or Serbian; what was clear was that they were intent on entering the village—and that the village was putting up resistance. A bearded face then loomed into the image and screamed something, pointing in the direction of the village. The camera swung around yet again. When the image cleared, a man was running toward the village. Another man appeared ahead of him, running between two buildings. The first man raised his rifle and fired. The second man hit the ground and lay there.

Then a huge howling went up from very near the camera, to judge by its loudness. Suddenly a whole group of men went running and firing into the village. There might have been a whole platoon—it was hard to judge because the camera kept flying around trying to get everything, and consequently it got very little. Finally the camera operator aimed his camera at the village again. There was more automatic rifle-fire and another explosion. A voice made some comment and laughed. There was a *click,* and the image flickered and dissolved into a screen of static and snow.

"What the fuck is that?" I demanded of no one in particular. I was sitting with Ako and Andreas in Ako's house. We had driven straight there from Dauer's shop.

"It looks like someplace in Yugoslavia," Ako said.

"No shit—yeah, it looks like someplace in Yugoslavia. But that's not what I just risked my neck to get!" I raged. I couldn't believe it. I had thought for sure that I had gotten what I wanted, that finally I had gotten a snuff film, when really all I had gotten was some home movies of Yugoslavian bastards playing John Wayne.

Then I realized something. "Play that last bit back," I told Andreas. "What was that last thing the guy said—was that German?" I asked Ako.

He shrugged. "I wasn't really listening."

"Well, listen this time," I told him.

The image reappeared. It was German; the guy was speaking German.

"What'd he say?"

"He said something about saving the batteries—that's all."

Andreas hit the mute button so we could talk. I told them that I was sorry, but that was it for me. The disappointment was too much. I had just put these two guys in a situation with potentially far-reaching consequences for all of us, and I had come up with nothing. Not only did I not have a snuff film, I did not even know what I did have.

"I know how we can solve that," Ako offered.

"What? Solve what?"

"I know a guy who volunteered in Croatia for a while—he just got back. I could try and get him over here to have a look at this thing and tell us what it is," Ako explained.

I looked at the silent, snowy screen and shrugged. "Why the hell not?"

Ako went off to make a phone call. I could hear him talking to someone in the other room when suddenly another image appeared on the screen. The scene had changed. The camera was no longer moving frenetically. The battle was obviously over. Instead of soldiers rushing into a firefight, there were three guys standing around a bare room. They had their shirts off and they were smoking and laughing with one another, obviously talking about the day's fighting.

"Oh shit, Andreas, turn that shit off," I said, waving my hand at the screen, wanting to make the television and the last forty-eight hours disappear.

Andreas pointed the remote control at the television and was about to switch it off when something changed. "Stop, don't!" I yelled, grabbing the remote away from him.

Two young women are pushed into the room.

The image suddenly flickered and slowed, dissolving for a moment, then . . .

One of the women is taken by the arm out of the room. The other remains. She looks around and closes her eyes, her head drooping.

The image flickered again. It dissolved again, but this time, when it came back, it was distorted. Only the sound was clear. The sound of women screaming and men laughing. The image flickered a final time. The German voice of the camera operator swore heavily—that much I got. And the image died.

"Son of a bitch, no! No, no, no, no!"

"I can't believe it," Ako said. He had seen the last part. He had come back into the room and I hadn't even noticed.

"What the hell was that?" I whispered, looking at Ako and Andreas. "What the fucking hell was that? Who were those guys? Regular army?"

Ako shook his head. "I don't think so. I didn't recognize the insignia."

"So where the hell is your friend? Is he coming?"

"No, he's not around—won't be back for a week."

I laughed. "Well, I'll tell you what—I'm not staying in Germany a week to see this guy, that's for sure."

"I couldn't let you stay anyway, Yaron. Shit, you've already robbed an honest German shopkeeper. By the end of the week you'd be the most wanted man in Germany," Ako lectured me, laughing.

"Yeah," I agreed. But I wasn't laughing.

7 ISRAEL

Yaron, it's for you!" Mikhal called from the other room.

I had heard the phone ring—let the fucking thing ring all night. What the hell had I done? It was unbelievable. Breaking and entering—trespassing—burglary! Take your pick. Un-fucking-believable.

"Yaron, pick up the phone," Mikhal called again.

Something had happened to me in Germany. I had gotten out of control and let myself be swept into a ridiculously dangerous position. I had also endangered my friends. It made me shudder to think what might have happened if I had gotten caught by the cops while I was in Dauer's store. I didn't even want to think what might've happened if I had gotten caught by Dauer and a couple of his friends.

I picked up the phone. A man from the States wanted to give me the dates, times, and places for a speaking tour that had been arranged for me. I wrote them down carefully, grateful for the distraction.

By the time I hung up I felt better. This was work, money-making work for my family. It was something else to concentrate on, and it would give me some breathing room. I would go on the tour and consider new directions for the investigation —or whether I wanted to continue it at all.

8 AMERICA

In the words of Pastor Niemoeller: 'When they came to take the communists, I did nothing. I was never a communist. When they came to take the Catholics, I turned my head. I am not a Catholic. When they came to take the Jews, I closed my eyes. I did not know any Jews. When they came to take me, there was silence—there was no one left.'

"I thank you for coming—and I thank you for listening. Good night."

I stepped down from the podium as the applause began and the lights in the auditorium came up. I was exhausted. I had been speaking to up to four different audiences a day for weeks, and now it was finally over. It was my last night, and I couldn't have been happier. Soon I would be home with my wife and kids. We now had a little money in the bank—life would be easier for a while.

But things are never as simple as that. There was something else—something that was not quite right.

I had gone through the entire speaking tour with a small hole in my stomach. It was a black hole that would not be filled.

And no thoughts of my family or the good things in my life or happinesses past or present seemed to be capable of filling it. I could ignore it for a time and concentrate on other things. But the only time when my awareness of the hole disappeared completely was when, at about the same point in each of my lectures, I spoke about the snuff films I had seen in Germany.

The peace was usually short-lived, however, because that part of my story was usually greeted with horrified disbelief. I was never called a liar, but there were always a few questions during the Q&A session after my lectures that made it clear that, while people were willing to accept the anti-Semitism and the hatred and the lust for naked, unrestrained power of the neo-Nazis, they were not ready to accept snuff films as the very plain evidence of it. I couldn't blame them, really. If there is real evil in the world, those films are a manifestation of it. And it is difficult for people to accept real evil and look it in the face.

There is no longer a concept of true evil as a thing that exists unalloyed, with no part of it good or redeeming. We are taught now that there is no true good or true evil, only varying degrees of each. An evil with no element of good (and I can see no good in the image of an eight-year-old girl being slaughtered) cannot be classified and therefore must be rejected.

So my audiences would sit in dumb silence as I told them what I had seen. And afterward they would erupt with questions concerning the authenticity of the films. "Couldn't they do that with special effects?" was one I got a lot. I would have to admit that was true; it could've all been faked. It was easier to believe that than to admit that it was real.

"But you have to understand," I would say, "the psychology of power that is at the heart of Nazism, or any other fascist doctrine. It isn't that they want to see the blood and be scared and go home like you would if you went to some horror movie. Watching those films is for them a methodical affirmation of their goal, which is absolute power. The slaughter of the girl is tangible evidence of power over human life, and their watching it is their participation in the exercising of that power . . ."

I would go on like that for fifteen minutes sometimes, trying in vain to convince people who still, as the clock ticked down, would ask me, "But it could've been faked, right?"

"Yes, it could've been," I would respond. "But it wasn't."

"How do you know?"

"I know," I would tell them. "I just know."

Then I would usually say good night.

■ ■ ■ ■

Thank you, Yaron—thank you," Rabbi Mandelbaum, the local rabbi and cosponsor of my lecture along with a radio station in Miami, said to me, taking my hand in both of his and shaking it gently.

"Thank you for having me," I responded, greeting in turn a representative from the radio station.

"Can I get you anything?" the rabbi asked.

"Something to drink?" I was always dry after a lecture.

"Yes, sure, I'll get it." The rabbi disappeared for a moment and then reappeared with a glass of orange juice. I made small talk with the rabbi and the radio guy for a couple of minutes and shook people's hands. I was congratulated and told how enlightening and horrifying my talk had been. I listened and chatted with a smile pasted on my face, but I was a million miles away. I wanted to go back to my hotel and sleep, and then go home.

"Mr. Svoray, can I talk to you for a second?" a woman asked.

I looked around, and the rabbi and the radio guy were gone. They had gone away to take care of something, and I had nodded and excused them without even noticing. I was sitting with a glass of orange juice in my hand, and a woman in her thirties was peering at me with some embarrassment. She was a large woman with tired brown eyes and a silver crucifix suspended on a leather thong around her neck.

"Mr. Svoray?" she asked again.

I nodded. "What can I do for you?" I asked, wishing my hosts would return. I had no wish to talk to this woman about her next-door neighbor the Nazi war criminal or her postman the grand dragon of the Ku Klux Klan. After every lecture there were always well-wishers and certified loonies clamoring for my attention. One look at this woman with her unkempt appearance and slightly crazy eyes and I classified her as the latter.

"Mr. Svoray, I heard you speak and—"

"Did you enjoy the lecture?" I asked pleasantly, hoping to deflect her before she got started, or at least until my hosts returned to tell me that my car was ready and to run interference for me.

"Yes, I did. But I wanted to tell you—those films you were talking about. I know about them."

I stared at the woman. She didn't want to talk about Nazis. She wanted to talk about snuff films. I didn't know what to make of it.

"What do you know about them?" I asked.

She grabbed and held the crucifix around her neck. It was a touching, childlike gesture on so large and obviously badly used a woman.

"I just know about them, that's all," she said quietly.

I couldn't believe what I was hearing.

"I was in one of them films—they killed a girl. I was there—right there," she continued in an urgent whisper.

I was about to respond when the rabbi finally reappeared and stepped in, taking me by the arm. "Well, you'll excuse us now, Miss . . . ?"

"My name is ———." I'll call her Liz Lopez.

"Well, Ms. Lopez, Mr. Svoray has an early flight to catch."

The woman shrugged sadly. I didn't know what she thought I could do for her, but I had to find out if this was for real or not.

I detached myself from the rabbi and asked if what she had said was true. Had she really been part of a snuff movie? She answered me in a rapid-fire whisper. "Yes, Mr. Svoray, I was in one of them movies. I myself am a victim of snuff porn—did you know that? All those other people in there think that stuff isn't real—but I know it is. Won't you please talk to me for just a little minute?"

I wrote down the name of my hotel and told her I had a little time before my flight left. If she wanted, she could come and we could have breakfast together and talk.

9 L I Z

The next morning at eight-thirty, Liz showed up at my hotel room with a friend who was never introduced by name.

I showed them in. They were clearly intimidated by the basic luxury of my room. Liz brushed her hands along the wallpaper and then looked at her fingertips. She looked up and saw me watching her and looked away quickly. I ordered breakfast from room service. We were practically silent until the food arrived. As we sat down to eat, Liz looked at her friend and then looked at me, and then started talking as she ate.

She told me about her father, who had sexually abused her, and her mother, who had known of the abuse but had done nothing to stop it. She told me about her brothers, who had raped her when she was ten. She told me about running away and hooking on the streets of Memphis at fourteen. Then she met some biker guy, a member of the local Hell's Angels chapter, when she was sixteen. He was all right to her. He always had drugs and he could protect her—even if he did beat her up some of the time.

By the time she was sixteen, she had been around the block a couple of times, so she didn't really mind that the gang got the idea to make porno movies when money got tight. It was usually her and a couple of other girls who hung out with the gang having sex with one of the bikers—no big deal, really. It was just sex.

She must've noticed me glancing at my watch because she started speaking more quickly. She told me that the people who bought the films that the gang made were members of the Dixie mafia, a crime syndicate that operated throughout the Mississippi Valley—an organization made up of government officials and police officers.

I decided to force her to get to the point, if she had one.

"Well, listen," I told her, "that's all pretty interesting, but what did you come here to talk about, really? I don't have the time or the resources to investigate some Dixie mafia, even if I wanted to, which I don't. I have a radio interview to do before my flight. Do you have a story to tell me, or not?"

"Yes, Mr. Svoray, I do," she said. She looked like she was going to cry, and her friend patted her shoulder and rocked her a little bit. I felt bad about talking to her so harshly, but sometimes people need to be pushed.

"All right, so tell it," I urged her.

"Well, there was this girl who had been hanging around for a couple of weeks—she was a runaway, I think. She was real pretty—long blond hair—real pretty. And one day we were supposed to make a movie—all three of us, me and that girl and my guy—"

"Listen, if you're not going to talk about what you came here to talk about, let's just forget it, all right?" I said, cutting her off.

She looked at me and looked through me as if I weren't even there, and she said in a monotone, "That's when we made the first movie."

I knew what kind of movie she was talking about. I didn't interrupt her again.

"Anyway, we were supposed to make this movie, and this guy Jerry—we called him Jerry the Jew on account of the fact that there aren't many Jews in the Hell's Angels—did you know that? Anyway, this Jerry guy's making the film—we didn't have any video cameras back then, just a little Super 8 camera Jerry just held in his hand that he filmed with. Well, they brought that runaway girl in and put her down on the bed naked, and Jerry tells me to start licking. I knew what to do 'cause we done that scene a bunch o' times. I was supposed to be licking her, and then Jerry hollers and my guy comes in, and he acts real surprised that we're doing it, and I pull his pants down and he makes the other girl, you know, suck on him—you know.

"So this time I'm licking the girl and Jerry hollers and my guy comes in, but this time there was something different going on. My guy comes in but I don't look up, really, 'cause I'm not supposed to until he says—I think I saw something in his hand, but I'm not sure now. Anyhow, my guy comes in and he's all mad. He's yelling 'cause he's so high, ya know? And Jerry was all excited and he was yelling, 'Do it, man, do it!' And he's laughing. And then my guy, instead of making me pull down his pants, he goes over to the other girl and grabs her by the hair —grabs her and pushes her head backwards so she's hanging half off the bed. Then he takes this big ol' knife and he starts to cut her. He cut her throat and there was this gargling sound and—that girl was dead."

Liz stopped talking and looked out the window.

I asked Liz if she wanted anything else. Liz shook her head. It was all I could do—ask if she wanted anything else to drink or eat. I had no idea what to say to her or how to react to her story. But I knew it was true—I knew it deep in my guts. I knew from the way she had told it, without inflection, without emotion. Someone lying about something like that would have tried to make a show of it, would have tried to show me with gestures and draw me into her story, but Liz knew there was no way to do that. She lived that story alone. No one could ever live it with her. And she would live it alone for the rest of her life.

"What do you want me to do, Liz? How can I help you?" I asked finally, breaking the silence as gently as I could.

The woman wiped her hand over her face. Her shoulders tensed. Then she drew a deep breath and slumped a little in her chair. She had probably learned a long time ago that there was nowhere to run.

"I don't know exactly," she told me. She told me that she had read about me in the *Miami Herald*—she was very proud of the fact that she read the newspaper every day from cover to cover. She told me that she was going to junior college and learning a trade.

"I don't know what you could do—I just thought you should know about it. That's all." Then she looked at her watch and stood suddenly. "I have to go now—I have a class in a half an hour. Thank you for—for listening to me, Mr. Svoray. I'm sorry to take up so much of your time."

I wanted to know more, but she had to leave. She had told her story and she could no longer stay in the room. She had left her story now with me. She had classes to go to—she had a life to make some sense of, however she could.

I watched her and her friend—the friend who was never introduced and to whom I had not addressed one word—walk out the door of my room.

I stood in my doorway watching them wait silently for the elevator. Liz tilted her head as the dial above the elevator doors counted up to my floor. Then she turned suddenly, as if against her will, and approached me again.

"Mr. Svoray, I think I remembered something," she told me. She was trembling a little. Her friend stayed by the elevator. It arrived and she held it open.

"What is it, Liz?" I asked.

"That guy—Jerry—Jerry the Jew? I think his name was John Sillman. I'm sure it was, and I think his father lived in California."

"Do you know where?" I asked.

"Los Angeles, I think—somewhere in Los Angeles. He was a big deal in the meat business. He had a packing plant or something. I remember because they always used to say that Jerry was good with knives 'cause he worked butchering animals since he was a kid. Maybe you could find Jerry if you wanted to," she said.

I shoved my hand deep into my pocket and came up with a handful of bills. She looked at me as I put the money into her hand. She said thank you. They got in the elevator.

As the metal doors slid together, the last thing Liz had said to me repeated itself again and again in my head.

"Maybe you could find him if you wanted to."

Well, Los Angeles is a big town.

But maybe I could find him if I wanted to.

10 LOS ANGELES

Mikhali?"

"Yaron—what are you doing? Where are you?" There was tension in her voice.

"Mikhali, I had to go to L.A. for a few days."

"Yaron, what is going on? You were supposed to be home yesterday."

"I know, I'm sorry. I'm in L.A. I have to check something out."

"What? What do you have to check out?"

"A story—I have to check out a story." I told her about my meeting and subsequent conversation with Liz.

"But I thought you were through with that," she said.

"So did I," I told her.

"When will you be back?"

"Soon, Mikhali—soon. Give my love to the kids. I love you, Mikhal—don't forget that."

"I'll try not to," she said—then she laughed.

I hung up and stared out the window of my hotel room at the glass-and-steel skyline of Century City. I had found John

Sillman. That had been the easy part. His father was still in the meat packing business. With his father's name I had gotten a friend of mine, a computer whiz making a million in Silicon Valley, to do me a favor. Everyone is on a computer somewhere; you just need to punch the right button.

■   ■   ■   ■

I arrived at John Sillman's house, a block back from the beach in Venice, California, early the next morning. It was a typical California morning. The sky overhead was bright blue despite the smog line lying heavily on the horizon. Sillman's place was a small blue-and-white cottage with a front lawn badly in need of watering and a small droopy palm guarding the front door.

When the door opened I was surprised to see a woman who looked to be in her early seventies or thereabouts. She ushered me in. The inside of the house was as innocuous as the outside —and quiet.

Where was the evil biker—the maker of snuff porn and the killer of women? That was the next surprise. The man whom the elderly woman took me to and introduced to me as John Sillman was a frail invalid lying in a large bed in an undecorated bedroom. He was dying of AIDS, and he never even asked who I was.

John Sillman was dying and he wanted to talk. All day long he spoke easily of his days with the gangs, of the fast life of crime and drugs and women. He was neither ashamed nor proud of what he had done. He had done things, and that was it.

I was somehow not surprised at all when he told me that that was his old life and that now he was a believing Jew and a solid member of the local synagogue.

"I am making a peace with my God by speaking to you about this stuff," he announced grandiosely on more than one occasion. I didn't tell him that I thought that if there was a God, peace with John Sillman would probably be the last thing on his omnipotent mind.

"But I'll tell you what—whoever told you that I was behind the camera instead of in front of it most of the time was wrong. I was never very good with those things. And I was too drugged up to care most times anyway," he told me.

I asked him point-blank, "Did you ever make a snuff porn movie or were you ever involved in one?"

He looked at me for a moment and then started rattling off a list of crimes he had been involved in, from transporting stolen goods to murder.

"Did you ever murder anybody on film?" I pressed him.

His gears seemed to stick at that one. He wanted to confess, but he wanted to confess on his own terms.

Finally, he said, "Yeah, I might've—I don't remember, really. We had a lot of parties where we filmed each other with women . . ."

He continued on in the same vein and I let him. He told me about gang rapes and using and abusing women. He said he remembered some guys in the gang doing snuffs.

"When was that, John—where?"

I would ask for specifics and he would clam up. He would wander over other things that he wanted to talk about. At one point the old woman who had shown me in came in and said good night.

"Who is that?" I asked him when she had gone.

She was his mother. He was being taken care of by his mother and he was a good Jew, and I wanted to smack him. This feeble little skeleton on the bed was a man who had caused so much grief and so much pain, and he still had a mother who would take care of him.

"John, do you know anyone who could help me get a snuff film?" I asked him again.

This time he went silent for a minute. He closed his eyes and I knew he was deciding something. Then he opened his eyes and indicated a duffel bag lying near the foot of his sickbed.

"Hand me that," he said. He could barely move.

I put the duffel bag on the bed next to him and he fished a small leather pouch out of it. He pulled out a worn address book and read me off a phone number.

"Call this guy. He'll talk to you. He'll talk to anyone as long as they pay," he told me.

"Does he know about snuff movies?" I asked.

"Yeah, he knows about it. Pay him, he'll tell you," he wheezed.

I thought for a minute that his repeated mentions of payment were some kind of hint. But I wasn't going to give this asshole anything. As a journalist I should've been objective, but AIDS or no AIDS, the thought of this man wreaking so much havoc in the world and then turning good Jew at the end revolted me.

He must've sensed that that was how it was because he didn't ask. When I finally left John Sillman that night, I was ashamed to find myself thinking that, when the end came for him, I hoped it would not be peaceful and it would not be easy. I was ashamed but I thought it nonetheless.

11 CARLOS

I met with Carlos in a park on the east side of Los Angeles. The park was a patch of green grass surrounded by graffiti-covered concrete embankments tucked under a freeway interchange.

He had agreed to meet me easily enough once I had offered to pay him for his time, as John Sillman had instructed me. He had told me on the phone to wait for him at the park. I waited almost two hours.

When he finally showed, stalking across the grass in his baggy khakis and bandanna, swinging his head slowly to the left and to the right, his hands shoved into his pockets, I was surprised at how young he looked. You wouldn't have thought he was any older than eighteen or nineteen. His face was delicate, with a thin nose and high, Indian cheekbones. He was short and wiry, with black hair and suspicious light hazel eyes, which were continually darting around, not in a nervous way—in an observant way. He didn't miss anything. He couldn't afford to.

Carlos was a killer, and vengeance can be swift and terrible

88

on the streets of east Los Angeles. Every car that passes holds a potential threat, or as he put it with his first words to me, sizing me up, "A guy could get popped out here."

"A guy could get popped anywhere," I replied, holding out my hand and hoping it was the right answer.

Carlos looked at my hand and then shrugged. "That's right, man; that's fucking all right." He took my hand. So far so good.

"So, what you want?" he asked. He didn't look at me, he looked at the street. In profile I noticed that he had incredibly long eyelashes. His eyes were beautiful and gentle-looking in an attitude of concentrated watchfulness.

I decided not to risk things by getting into a long complicated story I might not be able to get out of. "I'm looking for some snuff movies—videos," I told him.

He turned and looked at me. "Snuff movies—what the hell is that 'snuff' shit?"

"Movies with sex—porno movies where someone gets killed at the end, you know what I mean?"

Carlos's eyes blazed suddenly and his delicate nostrils flared. "That's what that fucking *cabrón* told you I got, fucking killer movies—that's what he told you?"

"No, man—no," I assured him quickly. I was walking the edge with him. For all I knew he had a gun on him, and we were on his turf. "No, man. He just told me that if I wanted something, you were the man to see. I just said I needed something and he told me Carlos, man—he's the one, you know? He's the one for anything," I rattled off as quickly and as calmly as I could.

The young Mexican, veteran of a hundred street battles, seemed to calm down. He looked me up and down again.

"All right," he said finally. "Who the fuck are you?"

I told him my name was Ron Smith.

■ ■ ■ ■

Yo, man, I was working both sides of the street, you know what I mean?" Carlos asked me loudly. Then he laughed and forked up a bite of *carne asada*.

We sat in a small Mexican restaurant that he had taken me to. I was the only non-Mexican there.

"I was in the fucking navy—the fucking U.S. Navy—at the same time I was still in the gang. You know what I mean—that's a crack-up, right? It was great, you know? In the daytime I was this good fucking sailor, and at night I would hang with my bro's. And I could push any shit in the fucking navy. I was a good sailor too—I got a certificate at my mom's house for some shit; I forget. But those fucking *blancos* would buy any shit." He laughed again.

I imagined this hard boy/killer working the ranks of the U.S. Navy, pushing bad drugs on farm boys from Wisconsin and then laughing in their faces. The navy never had a chance.

"So what the fuck you want? Stuff movies—what you call 'em?" he asked suddenly, sipping from a wax-paper cup of Coca-Cola.

"Snuff movies," I told him.

"Oh, yeah—that's it, snuff. Shit. I don't even have a VCR!" he crowed, cracking himself up again. He didn't say anything after that for a couple of minutes, and I decided to draw him out again.

"You're not in the gang anymore?" I asked.

"Fuck, no—I'm alive, right? I'm too old for that shit."

"Well, tell me about it. What's the gang life about?"

He kind of sneered at me then. The corner of his mouth went up a little and he nodded. "What kind of business you into again?" he asked.

I told him I was a middleman. I got things for people and I took my cut along the way.

"And you're from where?" he asked, smiling broadly.

"All over," I told him.

He laughed out loud then and asked for another Coke. I gave him some money. He walked to the counter, ordered, and came back with his chest puffed out and his chin held way up. He sat down opposite me and pulled back the sleeve of his flannel checkered shirt, exposing an intricate, obviously homemade tattoo.

"You know what that shit is, man?" he asked.

I had to tell him that I didn't.

"That's the fucking sign; that's your fucking outfit, man. You know how you get one of those?" he asked, looking me straight in the eyes.

"With a pin and some ink and a lot of time to kill?" I asked levelly, staring right back at him.

He burst out laughing. "That's fucking funny, that's funny, man—you should be on television or some shit. No, man—you got to pop somebody, man!" He made a gun with his fingers and blew an invisible enemy's head off.

"That's what the gang shit is, man—a bunch of kids popping kids. That's what was great about the navy. You get to mess with them big ol' fucking *pistolas!*"

"You popped a lot of people?" I asked.

"I don't know—who the fuck knows? I just—you know, I was hanging with the bro's but I wasn't in. I'm from Georgia, you know, I ain't from this shit here. I came from Georgia when I was a kid 'cause my dad was all the time beating my ass and shit, so I left, man. I left and I made it out here, and I was hanging with them and they tell me one day, "You want to be in?" and I go, "Yeah," so they go, "You gotta pop somebody," so I go—I was all fucking messed up, you know—I was like, "Give me a fucking piece and I'll pop somebody right now!" I wanted to kill somebody, you know. I just wanted to be in, and nobody mess with me then. So they give me this piece-of-shit little gun, like a revolver or some shit, and they tell me that they was across the street, these other guys, flying colors in this restaurant. So I go, "Who you want me to pop?" and they go, "Anybody with the colors." They thought I was crazy, man, but I walked over to that restaurant and I walked in, and those guys didn't even look at me. They just thought I was another skinny-ass wetback. So they didn't see me and I just walked up behind the guy I chose and pulled out the gun. I tapped the guy on the shoulder, and he turn around and *blam!* Right in his fucking face. My hand was, like, an inch from his face—*pop, pop,* into his face. Then I put the gun back in my belt and I ran."

And that was it—Carlos was in. His life as a killer and a member of the gang had begun. I was shocked at first by the nonchalant attitude with which he recounted his killings and his fights. I was shocked until I realized that Carlos lived in a small world bound by other rules than the ones I recognized. What I saw as anarchic savagery and blood lust he saw as a set of rigid codes that had to be respected because death was the penalty for ignoring them. It was twisted but not incomprehensible. Carlos's code dealt with honor and respect and rights of territory. It was understandable because it was familiar. It was the same code that the rest of the world played by, but on a much smaller level—and at a much faster pace. Nations played the games that Carlos and his bro's had played. But nations counted their lifespans in centuries. Carlos and those like him counted their lifespans in days.

Death was always around the corner. And that corner was just down the block. They all knew they would get it, probably sooner than later. Life was lived hour by hour, and pleasure was taken where it was found. It could've been a day of three square meals, or half an hour watching television without having to look behind you, or half a night in bed with one of the young girls who hung around the gang. The way Carlos described a good day seemed to me to be petty and thoroughly ridiculous. I could only imagine how the rest of the world seemed to him, when he'd lived over half of his life with a gun to his head.

I was so fascinated by the stories he was telling that I had forgotten all about why I was there, until he brought it up himself. He was telling me about the young women who hang around the gangs. He talked about women in general and how for him and his boys any woman who walked through their territory was fair game.

"It's about respect, man. You're mine, you don't come and go as you please—you respect me," he told me. "And if you don't, you get it, *pop-pop*. You get it, man. That's what happened to that girl when that guy filmed us popping her—like those movies you looking for," he said.

"What? What happened?"

"You a nosy fucker, aren't you?" Carlos snorted.

"I told you, I'm looking for—"

"I know what you looking for. I'm gonna tell you. There was this guy hanging around a couple of years ago. I was in the navy then—like a part-timer, you know?" He laughed. "So I never met him, but he was, like, hanging around saying he was going to make a documentary and put us all on television and shit. First he was just filming guys talking and hanging out, and they didn't care, but then he was, like—he wanted to film sex and shit—and that's it. And the girls doing stuff, you know? Well, there was this girl hanging out who got in trouble—she was making trouble and talking big, you know? So they decided that they had to get rid of her to teach the other bitches to stay in line, and this guy asked if he could film it. He was, like, 'You could all have a hundred bucks,' and shit, and then everybody was, like, 'You know it!' So they let this guy come along and they took that bitch—I forget her name; Lisa or some shit— and they took her out and they did her good! My bro told me about it, man. They all fucked her and they beat the shit out of her and then they fucked her again, and this guy was filming the whole thing and trying to tell them what to do. So they did that, and then they were going to leave her there, and the guy goes, 'She still alive. You better kill her or she might tell on you,' which they didn't think of that. So one of the guys was going to pop her and the guy goes, 'Why don't you cut her?' Right? Like we ain't no fucking old wetbacks, man—nobody use a knife anymore—but he's like, 'Cut her, cut her.' He said he would give more money, you know?

"So one of the guys gets a knife, and the rest of them hold the girl down while she screaming and shit, and this guy sits on her tits and he stabs her in the throat, and that film guy is getting close-ups and saying do this and do that and cut her here and there—he was fucking weird, man, you know?"

I looked at Carlos, expecting him to laugh. I looked into his eyes expecting to see some glint of understanding of the horrible irony of what he had just said, but there was none.

"And that fucker said we was—they was gonna be famous, you know? Be on TV and shit. They told him if anything happened because of that shit they would kill him and his family and shit. We saw the video—I saw it too, later. It was pretty funny, everybody making faces at the camera and that girl wiggling around and shit. But they were never on TV."

"Carlos," I asked finally, "can you get me a copy of that film?"

"No, man—I don't know where it is. I wasn't there, remember?"

"Yeah, I remember. What about the guy, the film guy? Do you remember his name? Do you know where I could find him?"

Carlos looked at me, narrowing his eyes. "If I did get you a film of that shit, how much you pay?"

"Whatever it costs," I told him.

"No man, what would you pay?" he asked again.

"Ten thousand dollars," I said.

"Man, you must want that shit bad. But listen, man—what are you, really?"

He caught me totally off guard. "What do you mean? I told you—"

"I know what you told me, and you a bad liar. What the fuck

is your game, man?" He said it calmly. He wasn't threatening. I guess he figured he had nothing to worry about from me. I figured I had nothing to lose. I told him I was Yaron Svoray, a journalist from Israel.

He nodded. He didn't give a shit. "I knew it, man. You ask too many questions. You like a cop or something. You should drop that other shit—it don't suit you."

We sat in silence for a moment and then he asked, "You really from the Holy Land?"

It seemed that Carlos, like John Sillman, had recently gotten religion.

I told him that I was from Israel—yeah, I was from the Holy Land. For a while after that we talked about Jesus and the church and the Bible. For the first time in our conversation I felt as though we had a common reference point. We talked philosophy, as far as Carlos understood it. We established a common reference point apart from guns and violence and macho posturing. Carlos knew his Bible, and I lived near the places in which stories he had heard from his grandmother had taken place. He asked me about Jerusalem and Bethlehem, and he listened to me describe those places with the wide open eyes of a child. I really think that he doubted whether those places really exist at all. To him they were like places in some Steven Spielberg movie, unreachable and impossible.

"Carlos, can you help me with this stuff? Can you get that film guy's number or something for me?" I asked him during a pause in the conversation.

He nodded. "I'll have to make some phone calls. You stay here, I'll be back," he said simply. He walked out of the restaurant and disappeared. My first thought was that he was never coming back. I almost left right then, convinced that the whole story had been a big put-on. He hadn't bought my act from the very beginning, and he had been stringing me along, taking me for what I was worth until he got bored with the game and made his exit. I was also shaken by the fact that the first time I had really tried to use the Ron Smith story, a twenty-four-year-old street kid had seen right through it.

I waited forty-five minutes. An hour. I waited until the hope started to drain out of me, and just as I was finally starting to convince myself that I was being stupid to wait for Carlos, he came back.

"Yo, you still here," he said, smiling and sitting down opposite me.

"Yeah, you told me you could get it. I waited," was all I said.

Carlos shrugged and handed me a piece of paper with a name and a number scribbled on it. I laughed.

"What are you laughing at?" he asked.

"This is about the thousandth time since I started that somebody has given me a scrap of paper like this. If I put 'em all together, they'd probably tell a story all their own," I told him.

Carlos laughed then too. "Well, that's how they do it in the movies, right?"

"Right," I agreed. I pulled out my wallet and gave him the sum we had agreed upon. Carlos took the money and shoved it into his pocket.

He got up to leave without saying anything, and then stopped at the door. "You know, you really better work on that Ron Smith shit or it ain't gonna fly, you know?"

"Thanks for the advice," I said.

He walked out of the restaurant and disappeared into the night of the east side of Los Angeles. Thanks a lot, I thought, looking down at the name and number on the paper—thanks a lot.

The name on the paper was Lorenzo Conti. And the area code preceding the phone number was from San Francisco.

I would be heading north.

12 NEW YORK

I never made it to San Francisco. I called the number and was informed by a female voice that Lorenzo Conti didn't live there anymore. He had moved to New York. I asked if she could give me his number, and she wanted to know who the hell I was.

I told her that I was a friend of his who owed him some money. It's the oldest trick in the book. She gave me the number in a weary monotone and then said, "You see that son of a bitch, you tell him to send a little of that money my way. He still owes me his last month's rent!"

I assured her that I would, and hung up. Then I dialed the number she had given me. When a male voice answered, sounding sleepy, I asked if Lorenzo was there.

"Yeah, this is he, who are you?" he asked.

"This is Lorenzo Bennet? You don't sound like you, man," I said.

"Well, that's because this isn't Lorenzo Bennet—this is Lorenzo Conti. What number were you calling?"

I read him his number, changing one digit.

He read me back his number correctly.

"Wow, and you're Lorenzo too—what are the odds of that happening?" I asked.

"Not very high!" Lorenzo Conti yelled into the phone before slamming it down.

Bingo!

Ten hours later I was halfway to Newark International Airport, and Lorenzo Conti was probably telling one of his friends about the funny phone call he had gotten in the middle of the night.

■ ■ ■ ■

I know New York. I spent a lot of time there in my student days, and I loved it almost as much as the other city of my youth—Paris. Not in the same way, of course. Paris is a city that one falls in love with at first sight. New York is a city that one hates at first sight and slowly learns to respect, and finally to admire. As someone once told me when I compared New York unfavorably to Paris, many years ago, Paris is beautiful because it was built by kings who had nothing better to do; New York was built by poor bastards from all over the world and corrupt bureaucrats lining their pockets at the poor bastards' expense. You have to love a city like that. New York will either kill you or not, but it is up to you—make of it what you will.

I planned to make as much of it as I could. My first stop after checking into the Hyatt next door to Grand Central was to go out and find some things to make my outside match my inside. Inside, I was determined to be Ron Smith, middleman extraordinaire—outside, I was determined to look the part. I spent the whole day looking for a uniform. I remembered from my days in the army and the police that nothing made you feel more official than a uniform or a badge—a tangible outer symbol of purpose—and the shit to back it up.

For Ron Smith's uniform I thought about a suit at first, and then discarded the idea. Ron Smith was casual; no problem. Besides, I rarely wear suits and I have found that the best thing to do when I am undercover is to stick with what I know and who I am as closely as possible. It cuts down on unnecessary bullshit that could very easily come back to haunt me. I ended up with a navy blazer with gold buttons, a linen shirt, slacks, and loafers. A thin gold-chain bracelet completed my uniform. When I looked at myself in the mirror, I realized that I looked more than anything like Don Swinborne, and that pleased me. It meant that I was internalizing the role that I was taking on. The changes were subtle but effective. I felt more like Ron Smith. All I needed was a badge.

I decided that Ron Smith's badge would be money. Money to throw around and wave in people's faces and bully people with.

I called Mikhal from the hotel to tell her what I was doing. It was a bad conversation; she sounded more upset than the last time I had talked to her. She told me that the kids were getting anxious, not having seen their father in such a long time. Every night they asked when I was coming home, and Mikhal didn't know what to tell them.

"And people keep calling for interviews and speaking engagements, and I don't know what to tell them. What are you doing, Yaron?"

"I'm doing what I'm doing, and I'll be done when I'm done," I told my wife.

There was a silence on the other end of the line. I was sure Mikhal was wondering whom she was talking to. I was sure because I was wondering the same thing. I had been overtaken by an inexplicable surge of anger and frustration. I had not spoken loudly, but the harshness of my tone had been unmistakable, and I immediately apologized.

"Yaron, what's going on out there?" Mikhal asked, her voice full of concern.

"I don't know, Mikhali. It's the world I'm dealing in now—I guess it's beginning to affect me a little," I told her. "I'll be back soon. Tell the kids that Daddy misses them, all right?"

"All right, Yaron."

"And don't worry about the money. It's going to be all right. I'll get it all back, OK?"

"OK—yes." That was all she said. She said it and she meant it. She wouldn't worry. But there was the slightest touch of doubt in her voice, and I felt an incredible need to reassure her, to know that she knew everything was going to be all right.

By the time I hung up I felt a little better about things—I felt like hell. So I did what I always do when I am away from home and feel like hell. I made phone calls. The first and most important one went like this . . .

Ring-ring-ring.

"Yeah, hello?"

"Yeah, hi, is this Lorenzo Conti?"

"Yeah, who the hell is this?"

"Right. My name is Ron Smith. A friend of mine gave me your number. I'm looking for some films, right? He said you might be able to help me out."

Click—dial tone.

Mr. Lorenzo Conti was going to be harder to get to than I thought. I decided to leave him alone for a while and call him back later. After all, Ron Smith had a lot of shit to take care of in New York.

I leafed through my black book until I found the number I was looking for. Scott was an old friend of mine from when I had lived in New York years before. He was now a freelance journalist, like me. I thought he might know something that could help me out—and if not, at least we could get a drink together and talk for a minute.

■ ■ ■

You don't remember that? No shit? Didn't I send you a clipping?" Like all journalists, Scott thought very highly of his own work and was totally surprised that I had not seen the article in question. It was an article on the pornography racket in and around New York that he had done a couple of years before for the *Village Voice*.

"No, I didn't see it. I don't read the *Village Voice*. I don't live in New York, remember?" I told him.

"You telling me that you can't get the *Voice* in Israel?" he asked, half joking.

"I wouldn't use that rag to clean up dog shit," I told him, laughing.

He hit me on the shoulder. "All right, all right—enough. Anyway, I did this piece. There was nothing as heavy as what you are into now, but there might be some people I could put you in touch with."

I sipped a cream soda. Scott had come to meet me at Katz's Delicatessen. He lived downtown, and I loved Katz's. Pastrami-and-brisket combo on a roll with cream soda—nothing like it.

"Yeah, like who?" I asked.

"What? Is this business, or pleasure? If all you want to do is pump me for information, old buddy, forget it. I got my own work to do," he berated me good-naturedly.

"This is definitely business," I told him.

"Man, Yaron, when did you get to be such a hard-ass?" He laughed.

"I don't know. It's New York, I guess—it does something to me."

"Don't it, though? Listen, I got a number back at the office. A guy you are really going to love. We can walk over there later and I'll get it for you. Just eat now, all right?"

"No problem," I told him, taking a huge bite of my sandwich.

Scott had eaten only part of his sandwich and had left the rest on his plate. He watched in awe as I silently devoured what was left of mine and then washed it down with some more cream soda.

"You're disgusting," he said finally, grimacing.

"Nothing like it," I told him happily, wiping my face. "Nothing like it in the world.

"So, why am I going to love one guy in particular?" I asked.

"He's a kook—name's Reginald Smith. Runs a bank up in Connecticut," Scott told me.

"Sounds real kooky," I said sarcastically.

"He's also into some very heavy shit—the kind of thing you're looking for."

"And he'll talk to me?"

"That's the thing, he'll talk to anybody. He's a smug son of a bitch. He's close, according to him, with some mob guys up in New England. He feels protected, you know?"

"Yeah, I know," I told him.

■ ■ ■ ■

When I got back to my hotel later that night I put in another call to Conti. I got an answering machine. I left a message that I thought might get his attention. I told him that if he would see me—just come talk to me—I would be happy to pay him for his time. I didn't wait around for him to call back. As he had promised, Scott had given me the number of his banker guy up in Connecticut. He had then put in a call to the guy himself. Reginald Smith had told Scott that he would be happy to talk to me.

13 REGINALD SMITH

You know, of course, that you can't use any of this."

Reginald Smith was a respected member of the community. He had a wife and a couple of kids.

"Why not?" I asked.

"Because the consequences could be dire if you did."

"Dire for who?"

"Well, not for me, at least," he told me, leaning back in his executive chair and puffing a cigar.

He was one smug son of a bitch.

"So why am I here?" I asked.

"Because I am a clever man, but what good is it if no one knows about it, eh?"

"You want to confess?" I asked, looking at him steely eyed.

He leaned forward in his chair. "I want to inform," he told me.

"So, inform me," I said.

He started talking.

"I was raised very strictly by religious parents, so of course as soon as I got out on my own, I started experimenting. I didn't use to have this spare tire around my waist, and I used to have hair—which really makes a very big difference with the ladies."

"I'd been going into New York for a while, going to the Hellfire and Plato's Retreat. I wouldn't do it now. AIDS everywhere and all that kind of thing.

"And then I met a woman. I was a speaker at a financial convention in Rhode Island, and afterward I met this woman in the hotel bar and we chatted, and one thing led to another."

"You were married then?" I asked him.

"Yes—second wife. But I am only a man."

I nodded agreement, silently urging him to continue.

"So it happened she enjoyed pain. And I enjoyed it as well."

"Getting or giving pain?" I asked him.

"As I said, I am a man, and man's natural instinct is to dominate women, don't you agree?"

I looked over his shoulder. His office walls were lined with certificates of achievement, diplomas, and letters of thanks from various community organizations and charities.

"We indulged ourselves for a while. She liked being hit, hard. Not just little taps; everyone likes that a little. No, she enjoyed being slapped and manhandled. It was really very good—we had some wonderful sessions. And then I found out—she's a Pugliese!"

"What's that?" I asked.

"The Pugliese, the family, with a capital F. They're the mafia, they run Rhode Island—you've never heard of them?"

I had to tell him that I hadn't.

"In any case—that disturbed me at first, but she said it didn't matter, and I finally met her uncle and her father, and I suppose they didn't mind having a bank manager in the family because, really, they were very nice people—even when I stopped seeing Annalise."

"You stopped seeing her. Why?" I asked.

"Between you and me, she wasn't the best-looking woman in

the world. And after a while I began to feel that her tastes were kind of coarse—not sophisticated. There was no finesse in what she wanted; she wanted brute force, and I became bored after a while.

"I still received Christmas cards from her after we broke up, though, which said if I ever needed a favor to call them. We all stayed friends. Annalise and I still write, and the rest of them —her father and uncle—we're friends."

"What do you mean by 'sophisticated'?" I asked.

"Well, there's more to it than just slapping someone or pushing them around and calling them names. It's a whole world of —options, you know?"

"I don't know. Tell me."

"I first got into it by answering an ad in the back of a magazine in Boston. I went to a seminar where there were other people like me, and they talked about the joys of bondage and discipline and S&M, and it was all kind of folksy and New Agey —until people started drinking. Then it got a little wilder and I —well, I was an ace student." He laughed.

I didn't ask him what he was an ace student of. I could do the math.

"I spoke to the people who had organized it and asked them if there was another level, another step to this thing, something harder. They got back to me about a week later and told me about something that sounded really interesting. I went to a basement apartment in the East Village and I got to do anything I wanted. I had on leather pants and vest, and there were women there, submissives, who I got to whip and cane until they bled. They had their vaginas pierced, and their breasts, and then at the end of two days and nights of this, they showed three snuff movies." He stopped talking and looked at me, waiting for me to react.

"What did you think of them?" I asked straightforwardly.

"I couldn't get them out of my mind. I masturbated every

time I thought of them. They were stimulating, and I wanted to see some more. I had to, it was like a drug—I had crossed the limits. It was something that's hard to explain."

"Did you see any more?"

"I have a deal. I talked to some friends of mine," he told me.

I could tell by the look on his face which friends he meant. Family with a capital *F*.

"They said they could get me as many as I wanted, but they were a little expensive—so we worked out a deal." He stopped and raised his eyebrows at me. He knew I wanted to know what kind of deal he had made, and he was daring me to ask—to become an accomplice.

I bit. "What kind of deal?"

"I'll tell you what—are you staying in New York for a couple of days?"

"A couple of days, maybe. I have some business to take care of. Why?"

"Because if you come back up here in two days, I'll show you what kind of deal we made—we're having a meeting."

"What kind of meeting?"

"A meeting of friends with mutual interests." He was getting coy.

I stood up and shook his hand. "If I'm still in town tomorrow I'll give you a call—how would that be?" I asked him. I suddenly felt like I had to get out of his office as fast as I could.

I left the bank without putting on my overcoat. The cool air revived me and made me feel good again. During the hour-and-a-half drive back to New York, I listened to the radio and tried to think of nothing at all.

When I got back to my hotel, there was a call from Lorenzo Conti. The offer of money had done it. He wanted to meet with me.

14 LORENZO CONTI

At first glance you might've taken Lorenzo Conti—not his real name, but the name he gave me nonetheless—for a professor at some small New England college. At second glance you would've noticed that his houndstooth coat was frayed and shiny and his gold-wire-rimmed glasses were scratched, and you might've taken him for a professor who had lost his tenure for drinking too much. But he wasn't a professor. Lorenzo Conti made porn movies, and it didn't look like business had been very good to him lately. The first thing I did was slip him $200 when we shook hands.

His watery blue eyes opened wide when he saw the money. "Hey, thanks, man—that's good, thanks a lot," he gushed.

"For your time," I told him.

"Yeah."

"On account," I added.

"Yeah, no problem." He stuffed the money into his coat pocket.

Lorenzo Conti was a happy boy.

He had asked me to meet him in the lobby of the Chelsea Hotel. For some reason he felt safe there.

"Nothing can happen to me here," he told me when I asked why he had wanted to meet there.

"What could happen?" I wondered out loud.

He glanced around the room, laughing nervously. "I don't know. You know—things can happen, to people. People could get grabbed or arrested—you know."

"Why would anyone want to arrest you?" I asked.

He touched his nose. "I can smell things like that, man—I can smell that shit, you know?" He laughed again, a little too quickly. Then he added, peering at me through his ruined glasses, "So, who are you again? I mean, what are you—what do you want?"

"I told you all that over the phone, Lorenzo," I reminded him.

He clapped his hands together and sat back in his chair. He began to enjoy our meeting. "Well, tell me again. Why not?"

I told him again. I went full on Ron Smith. I told him where I had come from and what I was doing. I told him about my worldwide network of connections and the wealthy—maybe too wealthy—people to whom I was connected.

I watched him swallow it piece by piece as I fed it to him. He had been careful at first, but he wanted to believe it too much for it not to be true. I was sure he was thinking that his ship had come in, and now all he had to do was tie it off and ransack the hold.

"So, can you get me what I'm looking for?" I asked him finally.

His suspicions returned. He didn't like direct questions. Direct questions demanded direct answers.

"Yeah, I can get you any film you want. The question is, who's buying?"

"I told you, I'm working on behalf of certain people who—"

He cut me off, waving his hand. "Yeah, yeah, well—yeah, but you know, you gotta be careful."

"Look, I don't have time for this. Either you want to deal or not—if not, I got other things to do," I told him angrily. I stood up to go, but he waved me back into my seat.

"No, no, OK. You know, you gotta be careful—can you appreciate that? Right? Sit down—we'll talk."

I sat back down and waited for him to start. He ordered a Bloody Mary, took a sip, and leaned forward in his seat. "How about—you want to see a movie being made?"

I froze. Was this idiot actually asking me if I wanted to see a snuff movie being made?

"You want to?" he asked again, raising his eyebrows.

"Sure," I said. "Sure—let's go."

"OK, good—just let me finish my drink first. All right, then, we'll go, all right?"

I nodded and leaned back in my chair.

Forty-five minutes later, I pulled my rental car up to the curb outside a warehouse in the Williamsburg section of Brooklyn. One block away, the East River shone metallic gray between the large brick ruins of industrial New York.

We got out of the car and Lorenzo led me to the front door of the warehouse. It was unlocked, and we walked into a small room with a stairway on one side and a freight elevator on the other. The first thing I noticed was a strange sound that seemed to come from all directions at once. It sounded as though the building were a giant beehive. It was a buzzing, whirring sound that could drive someone crazy if he were exposed to it for too long. It was just audible, so that I strained to hear it and discover the direction from which it was coming, only to have it fade away before I could pinpoint it or even decide what it might be.

"Fourth floor," Lorenzo said.

I started toward the stairs and Lorenzo laughed his nervous

laugh. "I don't take the stairs, man," he told me, pushing the button to call the elevator. There was a mechanical clicking, and then the abused hum of the ancient elevator making its way grumblingly down to us.

After a couple of uncomfortable minutes the elevator finally arrived, and we got in, Lorenzo pulling the safety gate closed behind us and yanking expertly on the pull cable that operated it. We began to ascend, and as we passed the second floor, I saw what the noise was that had troubled me when we first entered the building. Climbing slowly, we passed the closed gates of a sweatshop in which perhaps a hundred women were hunched over sewing machines in the ceaseless glare of fluorescent lights. The sound I had heard was the sound of industry, the whirring of the sewing machines worked by Chinese women for pennies an hour, turning out the latest must-haves for a fashion-conscious world.

Between the elevator and the sweatshop there was a large gate, locked and barred. Near the gate a big, tough-looking Asian man stood guard. He didn't even glance at us as we continued to climb, until the women and their ceaseless, thankless labor were out of sight and only the sound was left to remind us that they existed at all.

We passed two more sweatshops on our way to the fourth floor. They looked exactly like the other ones, except that in the last one the women were on a break. They sat at the machines motionlessly. Some of the younger ones stretched, but no one talked. Then a bell rang and the women went back to work.

"Poor bastards," Lorenzo said.

"The land of opportunity," I responded cynically.

"Yeah," Lorenzo agreed, yanking on the cable and stopping the elevator in front of a clean gray metal door.

"Here we are—everybody out," Lorenzo announced.

He pulled the gate back and pushed the door open. We stepped out of the grimy elevator and into an antiseptically clean white room about the size of a basketball court. The ceilings were at least twenty feet over my head. At the far end was a glassed-in room—a control booth for sound, it looked like—suspended from the ceiling and reachable by a flight of stairs. What I noticed first was the activity going on under movie lights just below the control booth. A woman with short dark hair, in her early twenties, sat in a director's chair. She was naked and surrounded by three men, whose penises she took in her mouth one after another, while masturbating two of the men at the same time. Above her, on a ladder, the cameraman angled for an overhead shot, while a man who I assumed was the director crouched nearby, looking thoughtful and saying something quietly that I didn't catch.

The second thing I noticed was that the sound of the sewing machines was gone. The room was completely soundproofed.

The people making the movie didn't even glance around as we quietly approached them. However, when we were still a good twenty feet from the action, a big burly guy in a shiny tracksuit inserted himself between us and the set, folding large arms across a larger chest and barring our way.

Lorenzo nodded to the man. "Hey, Jimmy," he greeted the goon.

"Hi'ya, Lorenzo," the goon replied, looking me up and down and sideways.

I wondered what the hell in me had inspired such trust in Lorenzo that he had brought me to this place. And finally I put it down to mutual desperation, feigned on my part but 100 percent genuine on Lorenzo's. He wanted to show me that he was a man on the inside, someone that a big wheel like Ron Smith could deal with.

"Can we go up?" Lorenzo asked the goon.

"Sure, go on up," the goon told him, jerking his thumb in the direction of the control booth.

We skirted the action by the same twenty feet and climbed

the stairs into the booth. A guy at a sound board nodded a greeting at Lorenzo, and we looked down on the scene being played out below. The brown-haired woman was now bent over the chair. One of the men had entered her from behind, while the other two masturbated in her face, putting their penises in her mouth and rubbing them on her cheeks.

"So, what d'you think?" Lorenzo asked me, grinning.

"What do you mean, what do I think? You think I haven't seen this shit before?"

"No, no, I just—"

"What? Look, I need the kind of films we were talking about —not blow jobs that I could get at home, right? So, can you get me the films here? Is that why we are here?" I demanded.

"No, I just—I thought you wanted to see the business. And anyway, I don't run things, you know—I just work for people. I just shoot the film. The guys who run things are—maybe—you want to meet somebody?" he offered, trying to placate me.

"Meet who?"

"Meet my boss," he told me. He turned to the guy at the sound board and asked him if the man I will call Ed was around. The guy nodded without looking at him.

"Yeah, well, Ed is here—you should meet him." Lorenzo reached over and thumbed the switch on an intercom.

Suddenly I felt trapped. The elevator was the only entrance I had seen, and therefore the only exit. I didn't know who the players were in this game, but I knew that Lorenzo was not one of them. He had his own reasons for believing in me and trusting me. Two hundred reasons already in his pocket and the hopes of more where those had come from. I had the distinct feeling that whoever Ed was, he was not going to be as hard up —or as eager to please.

"What are you talking about? I'm talking to *you*. If we're going to make a deal, let's make it."

"Don't worry about it." He waved his hand at me as a deep voice barked from the intercom.

"Yeah, who is it?"

"Ed, it's Lorenzo. You want to come up in the booth for a minute. There's somebody here I want you to meet."

"Yeah," the intercom barked again and went silent.

A second later Ed joined us in the control booth. He was in his early forties. He was dressed casually, in an expensive white linen shirt, khaki slacks, and loafers with no socks. He walked right up to me and shook hands without waiting for an introduction. His grip was strong and his eyes never left my face as I told him who I was and what I wanted. He didn't frown or smile. He listened, searching my eyes. He didn't believe me or disbelieve me; he listened, taking in the information I was giving him and weighing it on some hidden scale.

"So, what I'm doing is looking for some very unique films. I got Lorenzo's name from a friend of mine, and here I am," I finished.

Ed continued looking into my eyes for a good ten or twenty seconds after I finished speaking. I smiled, meeting his gaze. Suddenly he turned to Lorenzo.

"You got anything for him?" he asked the filmmaker.

I knew immediately that Ed was a dangerous man. Here was a man who would never act out of anger. Ed's potential for violence was cold—ice cold. He would weigh the facts, make a decision, and then strike. For men like Ed, the act of violence is never an end in itself. What is more important is the message it conveys.

Lorenzo looked startled. Ed had turned his cold eyes on him now, and Lorenzo could not take it. He looked anywhere but at Ed as he babbled something about how he thought Ed should meet me.

"Why did you think I should meet this man, Lorenzo?" Ed asked. He used Lorenzo's name every time he spoke to him, pounding him into the ground with every word.

"I—I thought we could do some—some business, that's all," Lorenzo stammered.

"We? Who is 'we,' Lorenzo?" Ed demanded. It was as if I had disappeared. "I'm making a movie here, can't you see that? I don't know who this guy is. I don't know what you're talking about. What is this shit?"

Suddenly Ed turned back to me and without intonation asked my name again.

"Whatsamatter—you want to see my fuckin' driver's license?" I asked him. Lorenzo looked like he was going to collapse any minute. He had also, over the last couple of minutes, acquired a strange nervous tic. Every couple of seconds he touched his ribs, pressed for a minute, and grimaced.

Ed responded to my offer of proof with a barely perceptible shake of the head. He turned back to Lorenzo.

"Listen, Lorenzo, why don't you go home and take your friend with you. You know I don't do any of that sick shit—you know that, don't you, Lorenzo?" he said, spitting each word out individually and punctuating his little speech with hard jabs of his finger into Lorenzo's chest.

Lorenzo went white as a sheet and could only nod. Ed left the booth without a word to me, and after a few seconds Lorenzo had regained his composure to the point that he could just barely whisper, "Let's get out of here."

We walked down the stairs and across the studio in silence. Lorenzo looked like he was going to break into a run at any second, but I walked casually, looking around like a tourist as we made our way to the elevator. It wasn't easy. Ed was a man who inspired real fear. He emanated power—the power of life and death—in a way that was unmistakable. It was in his eyes and in the way he carried himself.

As we waited for the elevator, I saw Ed at the far side of the room talking to a guy who looked our way and then back to Ed. I didn't like that. The worst thing about Ed was that you never doubted that if he wanted you, he would get you. His arms were long but his hands were clean; he was someone who would surprise you in an alley or as you left your house for work, and that would be that—game over.

The elevator finally arrived, and four minutes later we were back out on the street.

We stood in front of the building. The sun had come out, making the sagging buildings and broken, pitted streets look even more pathetic. I hadn't said a word to Lorenzo all the way down. Now he stood by the door in the sun mumbling something like, "Shit, I should've thought of that. Shit, shit." Now I turned to him.

"So, what's the story? Are we going to deal or not?"

Lorenzo reacted violently. He pushed me away from him. "You get away from me, all right? I don't want to know you. I don't want to talk to you—just stay away from me!"

Startled by Lorenzo's sudden outburst, I just looked at him for a minute, wondering how I should react. I started to say something and my tongue caught on my teeth. The guy whom I had seen talking to Ed before we got on the elevator came out of the building, looked our way, lit up a cigarette, and turned his face into the sun. Lorenzo's back was to him, but he saw me looking and turned around.

"Oh shit, oh shit, oh shit," Lorenzo started repeating like a mantra.

I looked into his eyes and said, "Relax, Lorenzo, relax, all right? You did good. If Ed doesn't want to deal, no deal."

"Yeah, that's right, no deal, right," Lorenzo repeated after me.

"Look, this is for your trouble." I pulled out a hundred and stuffed it into his breast pocket. "Now what do you say we go get a drink?"

Lorenzo pulled the bill out of his pocket, looked it up and down, and then put it back. "OK, yeah, let's get a drink—shit, I could use one."

"Yeah, me too," I agreed.

We got into my car and drove back into Manhattan.

■ ■ ■ ■

Lorenzo drank single-malt scotch and I drank ice water—about a gallon. My throat was parched. "Son of a bitch," Lorenzo kept saying over and over. "Son of a bitch, son of a bitch, son of a bitch."

He told me that what he had done was a big mistake. Ed was a link between the various filmmakers and some very bad boys; he told me that taking me to the studio and talking to Ed in my presence was a big no-no. He was really afraid—afraid for his life.

It didn't help that the guy who had been sunning himself in front of the building where I had met Ed was now standing across the street, having been joined by a big blond guy.

Son of a bitch.

I wanted to know more, but I had to be very careful with Lorenzo in his agitated state. At any minute he might decide that this was just not worth it and bolt.

So I trod carefully and got him back on the subject by asking him about how he got into film in the first place. He told me about film school and then getting into porn movies to make a quick buck. And how now quick bucks were getting harder to find. There was some kind of battle raging between the different crime syndicates that ran the porn industry, and the little guys like him were feeling the squeeze. He looked out the window at the guys who seemed to be tailing us.

Son of a bitch. "I broke a big rule, man. Not only did I trust you, but I introduced you to Ed—shit."

I followed Lorenzo's gaze out the window. The two guys were just standing there across Bleecker Street—not looking at us, not looking at anything.

I didn't know if they were there just to keep an eye on us—and if so, what for?—or if they were there to do us some dam-

age. I didn't believe they were after *me*, in any case. As far as I
was concerned, Lorenzo was the one who had to watch his ass.
Even if they thought I was an undercover cop, it wouldn't do
them any good to mess with me. Lorenzo, however, was nothing
to them.

"I think it's time we got out of here," I said.

Lorenzo nodded, still looking out the window.

We got in my rental car and went west to the Henry Hudson
Parkway, then north toward the George Washington Bridge. I
couldn't be sure that we were being followed and I was probably
overdoing it, but I didn't feel like taking any chances. Besides,
I felt that the real threat was minimal, while at the same time I
was finally getting into the action—things were popping, and I
could feel the adrenaline rushing through my body as I swerved
in and out of traffic up the West Side of Manhattan.

And more important, Lorenzo started talking. I imagine that
it was the general excitement plus the couple of drinks he had
had that loosened his tongue. Whatever it was, by the time we
were crossing the George Washington Bridge and halfway to
New Jersey, he was telling me what I wanted to hear. He was
telling me about making snuff pornography.

He told me that he had been sickened at first. Some guys,
mob types, had come to him in his studio and asked him if he
wanted to make some money. He always wanted to make some
money, so he said yes. And he did it. By the third or fourth film
—he didn't remember which—it was just another job.

I pulled into the parking garage of a Holiday Inn just off
Route 4 in West Orange, New Jersey, and told Lorenzo to get
out. We walked into the lobby bar and sat for a while, keeping
our eyes out for the two guys. I didn't see them. Lorenzo ordered a drink, threw it back, and ordered another. I still didn't
see the two guys, and I have to admit that I was a little disappointed. I hadn't done much to lose them. I told Lorenzo that
whoever those guys were, they weren't pros.

"Oh yeah, they're pros—fuckin' A, man, believe me! I know."

I asked what he meant by that, but he didn't answer. Instead he started trying to justify his involvement in the making of snuff porn movies by telling me that people see things that are just as bad on the news every day. He talked about car accidents and shootings and slashings and torchings. He told me about a video series called *Faces of Death,* which showed executions and home videos of vacationers being mauled by bears. He wanted desperately for me to agree that snuff movies were pretty much the same thing.

He wouldn't go into details about the films he had made. If I tried to push him, he got quiet and would look around nervously, sipping his drink. He didn't want to tell me what he had done. He wanted to tell me his rationale why what he had done was not such a big deal. He wanted me to agree with him that a newsman's taking pictures of a car accident was the same as his shooting a film of a murder. In his mind, death was death, whether it was dealt by a drunk driver in a speeding car or by a man with a knife. Whether it was on purpose or by accident, the result was the same.

I couldn't answer him as I would've liked to. Ron Smith agreed with him to a point. I could only sit and listen and wonder what kind of life had led him to such brutal indifference. I shuddered inwardly at the thought that Lorenzo was not alone, that there were Lorenzos all over the world, and that that same brutal indifference runs through everything, just under the surface, just out of sight. It's not a new thought, but it's a terrible one. The absolute realization of a world stripped of conventions and without pity flashed upon me in a terrifying moment of utter, horrible clarity—and left me empty.

I interrupted Lorenzo in mid-rant and stood up. I told him that I thought we had done a good job of losing those guys. Lorenzo laughed. I think he was having fun with the idea that he was in some spy movie. We drove back into the city. I dropped the car off at a parking garage on Essex Street, and Lorenzo invited me up to his place.

His apartment was a small studio in Alphabet City, in the East Village. The only furnishings were a mattress on the floor, a couple of wooden chairs, and a night table with some dirty magazines on it. All the way up three flights of stairs he had been telling me about all the porn stars he had done, bragging about bedding down with the best girls in the business. I was getting tired of listening to him and tired in general. As he closed the door behind him and switched on the light, I decided to cut to the chase.

"Lorenzo—can you get me any snuff movies?" I asked.

"No, man—I mean, I don't have any," he told me, shrugging his shoulders. "Would you believe it, though, three years ago I was running my own gig? I had a stack of films," he told me, holding his hand about five feet from the ground, indicating the height of the bygone stack.

"So, what happened?" I asked.

"Well, I got into some real deep shit with Ed and his friends —you know? I mean, the deal is simple. I make the movie. I do mostly amateur stuff, new girls, fresh faces." He laughed. "You'd be surprised how many fresh faces turn out to be hookers."

I nodded. I had examined row upon row of porn videos all claiming to be filled with new girls' first times on film. It was amazing how many times you would see the same fresh face over and over again.

"So, I make it, I bring it to Ed, I get paid—that's it."

"What about snuff films?" I asked.

"If I get one of those, same thing."

"How often do you get them?"

"Not very." He didn't elaborate. "But I used to do all kinds of films. I was going all over the place—Detroit, Seattle. That was cool, yeah, that was good. Sometimes I even got girls who really had never done it before."

"How about east L.A.?" I asked.

He looked at me warily for a moment and then smiled slyly. "Yeah, I did some stuff there," he said.

"Do you pay the girls to be in your films?"

"Sometimes. Not if I can help it. But yeah, sure, if they're good."

"Where do they come from, your actresses?"

"At first I put ads in papers and stuff, for models, you know. But once you're in this line of work for a while, you get to know a certain kind of people—and they get to know you. You'd be amazed at how many girls would do just about anything to be on film. Mostly they're strippers, though, like that—girls who are already taking their clothes off somewhere. You tell them that this is their big shot, and they go for it."

I nodded. "So, Ed tells you what to film, and then you do it and bring it to him."

"No, no, I do what I can. I make a movie—I'm kind of freelance, you know. But when I have something, I bring it to Ed and nobody else. He pays me. If I bring him one or a hundred, he pays me and gets the product—the master tape and everything else. One time I tried to go around him, deal on the side, you know? Check this out."

Lorenzo lifted his shirt, revealing a deep ugly scar running up the side of his body from his waist to his armpit. I remembered Lorenzo's nervous tic during his confrontation with Ed and his very real fear afterward.

"Man, I don't do that shit anymore—you understand what I mean?"

For some reason we started laughing. There was nothing funny about the situation, but we laughed. It was a release of nervous tension and we laughed like kids. I thought I was going to pee my pants, I laughed so hard looking at Lorenzo pointing at his scar and guffawing like it was the funniest thing in the world. Eventually the laughter subsided and I asked him again: if I got him enough money, could he get me a film?

He said he might be able to but he would have to make a lot of phone calls and talk to people who might be cool or might not be. He asked me how much I would be willing to pay, and I told him I would pay the price, whatever it was. He told me to call him in the morning and I promised that I would. And I left him there with another $100. Lorenzo Conti was having a good night.

I was walking down the stairs when it suddenly occurred to me, more out of instinct than anything else, that maybe going out the front door was not the best idea. When I got down to the first floor I looked behind me down the shadowy hallway and saw a door leading to the back. I went through the door and ended up in a long empty courtyard shared by Lorenzo's building and the two next door. Lorenzo lived in a building just a few buildings down from the corner of Avenue D. The back door to the corner building was open, and I went through it, emerging onto Avenue D, around the corner from Lorenzo's. I walked up Avenue D, found a cab, and asked the cabbie to take me back past Lorenzo's place. As we turned onto Lorenzo's block, I pulled myself down in the back seat, trying to make myself as small as possible. I just wanted to make sure that I wasn't getting paranoid—or that I was. I just had to know whether my hunch was a good one or all this shit was really getting to me in a bad way.

As we passed Lorenzo's building, I saw a dark blue Honda Civic parked across the street and ducked down, mumbling something about dropping my keys. In the Honda was one of the guys who had been following us. It really shook me. I had the cabbie drop me off at the parking garage where I had left my car. I paid him off, paid the attendant at the garage, and tore out of there. I got back on the Henry Hudson and drove north. I had no idea where I was going; I just had to chill out and get my thoughts together. I was sure that those guys were not interested in me as an individual. After all, they had already dealt once with Lorenzo's double-dealing. They didn't know me, that's all. I didn't figure into their universe, and they were trying to place me. I still had no sense of immediate physical danger, but it is always a very fine line with people like that, people who could do what they had done to Lorenzo.

I remembered laughing almost hysterically at Lorenzo's vicious scar. The thought sickened me.

I got off the Henry Hudson and looked for a phone booth. I was tired of talking to criminals. I wanted to talk to somebody on my side.

15 SERGEANT PETE EDWARDS

I first met Sergeant Pete Edwards of the NYPD years before, after a lecture I had given before the members of an organization for Jewish policemen in New York City. The organization is called Shomrin, after the Hebraic word for "guardian."

Pete is a career cop. He has served with New York's finest for over twenty-eight years, having joined the force after a tour of duty in Vietnam. He is a family man. He has two daughters. One is still at college and the other is married with children. Both of his daughters live within five miles of the home he shares with his first and only wife.

Pete Edwards is bald and happy, with bright, smiling eyes and a funny story for every occasion.

For most of his career, Pete Edwards worked Homicide. Then he was transferred to a special squad working exclusively on cases involving missing children. Pete Edwards has seen a lot.

I sat across from him in his kitchen, in Queens. His wife was in the other room watching television. I told him my whole story up to that point, including my hasty retreat from Lorenzo

Conti and the people behind him. He listened quietly, nodding his head from time to time. At one point he got up and asked me if I wanted a beer. I asked for some ice water. He grimaced, popped a beer for himself, and set a glass of water down on the table in front of me just as I finished speaking. I took a long drink and then asked him, point-blank, what the cops were doing about it all.

"About what all?" he asked.

"About snuff films, about pornography, about the whole stinking mess," I told him.

We sat in silence for a moment, listening to the television in the other room. Finally he reached out, put his hand on my shoulder, and looked me full in the face.

"How could a fella with all your experience be so naive?" he asked me.

Naive?

"I'm not naive, Pete, just practical. Forget snuff films for a minute. What about plain old porn? Do you know how much money that industry generates? Is anybody from the government overseeing it, making sure all the taxes are paid? Is anyone investigating who runs the show? Is anyone looking into pornography's ties to organized crime?"

Pete put his hands up. "Whoa, whoa, hold on a minute there. It's me, Yaron, all right?"

I settled back in my chair. "Sorry about that," I said quietly, sipping at my water. "But these are real questions that nobody seems to be able to answer," I told him.

"First of all, porn is not illegal. Whether it should be or not is another question, but it is not. If you ask me if the people who make porn are good, tax-paying citizens, I would say probably not. Is the mob tied in? Probably. Is it a horrible business that takes advantage of people and generates all kinds of bad things, from drug abuse to kidnapping? I'd say, probably. But it is not illegal."

"But—" I began.

Pete cut me off. "As for this snuff film business, this is a whole other thing. All of it—kiddie porn, hard-core, prostitution—they're all tied together. You add this snuff porn into the mix and what was already overwhelming becomes even more so—and that's the problem. Policemen don't work well with 'overwhelming.' You know; you were a cop once yourself. Policemen work with specifics. We don't look at big pictures, just our little piece of it." He paused then, looking silently at a spot somewhere over my head.

"C'mon, lemme show you something," he said suddenly. He got up, told his wife he would be back in an hour or so, and ushered me out to his car.

■   ■   ■   ■

This is kiddie porn," Pete told me.

Two detectives, one man and one woman, seemed to be buried under a ton of paperwork at the end of a narrow hallway in a precinct house somewhere in Manhattan.

The woman, slightly overweight, with an extremely harried expression on her face, didn't even look up. She was on the phone. The man, equally harried looking, with a Beretta handgun stuck in a holster at the small of his back, greeted Pete wearily, sipping from a large cup of coffee.

"Hi'ya, J.T. J.T., this is a friend of mine; he used to be a detective in Israel," Pete told the man, pointing at me. Pete then stepped away from me and spoke to J.T. quietly at his desk. Finally, J.T. turned to me and waved me over. He had wavy brown hair, and it looked like his nose had been broken several times.

"So, you want the long lecture, or the short one?" he asked me.

I looked at Pete and then back at J.T. "Give me the long one," I told him.

J.T. looked disappointed. Then he pointed to two huge racks

of folders in front of him. On one side the folders were light brown; on the other side they were light green.

"The green folders there, those cases are still being worked. The brown ones are the ones that we frankly don't think will ever be closed—lost causes. We get between twenty and twenty-five calls a day. People misplace their kids. Kids misplace themselves. Kids are kidnapped, stolen; they run away. They have a bad day at school; they come home late; whatever. It ends up on our desk, and this is what it looks like—a big pile of paper it would take a bulldozer to shuffle through," he told me in a cop monotone tinged with exhaustion.

"And this is just the beginning, Yaron," Pete jumped in.

I got the long lecture. They told about parents killing children and children killing one another. They told me about mothers getting high and throwing their children out tenth-story windows. They told me about children being raped by their parents and children arriving at the hospital covered with cigarette burns or with all their teeth broken. Then J.T. outlined for me how difficult it was to follow up on just one case, not to mention thousands.

"Sure, you have a victim," he told me. "You have a victim; some guy kills his own kid in a fit of rage. But by the time you get him to trial, get him through the whole process, and then, maybe, through some miracle, he goes to jail, he won't stay there. He'll get out soon enough, and the kid is still dead, a statistic. End of story."

J.T. stopped talking and regarded me silently, a disgusted look on his face.

After a moment I asked him if he knew anything about snuff pornography. He shook his head and reached for his cup of coffee. "I don't know anything about it and I don't want to know," he told me. I asked him how long he had worked in his particular department. He told me with a cynical laugh, "Too long."

Pete cut in again. "He's got so much shit on his table, you think he goes around looking for more?"

I told them both that as far as I knew, children and teenagers were the main victims of snuff pornography.

"Have you ever even heard about it?" I asked them both.

J.T. answered. "Sure I've heard about it. But I've never seen one and I hope I never do. I've seen too much of the real thing, up close and personal. I don't have to look for it; it looks for me."

"And there's no way to find any of the animals who do these things? There's no way to stop that?" I asked, indicating the rack of brown folders.

J.T. looked at me, smiling thinly. "I'm not sure who you are talking about," he said.

"The people who kidnap and kill and hurt these children," I told him.

"Most of the people who hurt these kids, you won't find them in street gangs or in some mafia hideout," he informed me, shaking his head. "You want to find them, go look through their living room window. The hell of it is, you don't need a license to become a parent. You don't need anything at all," he finished.

The lecture was over. I thanked J.T. for his time, and Pete and I left him there with his partner, his pile of paper, and his day-old coffee.

■ ■ ■ ■

There, look over there. See those two guys?" Pete asked me, pointing across the arrivals area of the Port Authority bus terminal, at Eighth Avenue and Forty-second Street.

I had thought that the tour was over after we left the precinct house, but Pete had informed me that we had one more stop to make.

I looked where Pete was pointing and saw two clean-cut-looking Caucasian guys in their late twenties or early thirties. One of them had on a Dallas Cowboys T-shirt, and the other one sported a baseball cap with the words "Texas A and M" written across the front.

I didn't understand why Pete chose to focus on those two. The whole grimy, echoing mass of the bus station was filled with hustlers and drug dealers and junkies. Homeless people sat in the corners looking listless and exhausted, talking to themselves or staring glassy-eyed into space.

"What about them?" I asked.

"See what bus they're waiting for?"

I looked at the sign over the door, through which at least some of the passengers would get their first taste of the big city.

"Dallas?"

"Yeah. Let me tell you a story about those two sons of bitches," he began. "The bus from Dallas comes in, and people get off, and they're tired because they've been in a bus for sixteen hours, and they're hungry and they want to pee. And in amongst all these people, who were too poor to fly or take a train, there is always someone, some kid, running away from a small town or abusive parents. Or they're running *to* something —life in the big city, gonna be a star, all that crap. So some kid, a girl, kicked out of her home or run away from it, gets off the bus alone and nervous and a little scared, with everything she ever heard about how tough New York is running through her head. And who does she see? Lo and behold, those two guys looking all nice and neat. Well, those two guys plant themselves in front of her and start a loud conversation in a wide open Texas twang, and the girl hears it and it seems familiar. Then they approach her.

" 'Howdy. Where you from?' they ask, all smiles. 'Dallas,' the girl tells them. 'Well, this is your lucky day,' they tell her. She looks them up and down. She's not stupid. 'Why?' she asks, wondering who these two are and what they want. Are they going to rob her? Are they going to hurt her? Hell, no! These guys are friendly, and they tell her, laughing and joking, that they need someone from Dallas.

"The girl asks them why, and they tell her. It turns out that a friend of theirs has an apartment around the corner, and he's going away for a month, and he needs someone to take care of it. He doesn't want to lose the lease, you know. The girl asks again why they need someone from Dallas, and they tell her that their friend only trusts people from Dallas.

"She hesitates. Again, she's not stupid, but she is alone and nervous and a little scared, and these boys seem so nice and friendly, and they know all about Dallas. She goes with them. They take her to an apartment. It's big. There is no television or phone, and there are mattresses against the walls, but they tell her that their friend just moved in. 'It's not much,' they tell her, 'but it's free for a month, if you want it.' They tell her to decide right away because if she doesn't want to stay, they'll have to find somebody else pronto.

"She doesn't know what to do. She almost leaves. Then one of the guys hands her fifty bucks to buy groceries. Would they give her money if they were bad people? She tells them that she will stay, and the two nice boys leave, all smiles. She asks them what she is supposed to do right then, and they tell her to just hang around, they'll be back later to settle everything up.

"They come back a few hours later and wake her out of a sound sleep. They put the mattresses against the door and the windows and they rape her repeatedly. They beat her savagely and rape her again. For the next week she is left in the apartment with no clothes and very little food. They keep her half starved and in a constant state of terror, never knowing when they will be back to rape her and beat her again."

Pete stopped talking and took a deep breath. I couldn't believe what he was telling me, and yet I knew from the look on his face and the tone of his voice that it was true, every word of it.

"At the end of the week," Pete picked up where he had left

off, "they let her out. But she doesn't get to go shopping or look for a job. Within a week of her arrival in the big city she is out on the West Side Highway selling her body, with one of her new pimps wiggling his finger at her if she even looks in the wrong direction."

He stopped talking. That was the end of the story. I wanted to ask him why he didn't do something about it. Why he didn't go over and drag those two bastards away? But I knew the answer. I had been a cop once myself. There was no law against hanging around the bus station.

"So what do you do about it?" I asked him.

Pete swung his head around and looked into my eyes. "Too damn little, that's for sure. Too damn little," he told me.

Afterward, he drove me back to my hotel. I thanked him as I got out of his car, and he told me not to mention it. He told me to call him again if I needed anything else.

Up in my room I collapsed on my bed. The hopelessness of what I had seen in the last few hours had crept into me little by little, leaving me feeling lost. They hadn't wanted to talk about snuff porn, and now I knew why. The everyday viciousness was overwhelming enough as it was. There was no snuff porn industry. There was no conspiracy. The darkness was everywhere, everywhere.

I had to move. I had to act. I had to do something. Then I remembered Reginald Smith's invitation and I gave him a call. It was a little late, but I didn't think he would mind. I was right.

"Yes," he told me when I had gotten him on the phone, "the meeting is still on."

He gave me instructions and a time to meet.

16 THE VIEWING

The uniformed security guard at the gate asked for Reginald's name and the person he was going to see. Reginald told him. The guard nodded, jotted the information down in a registration book, and waved us on.

We were in a nice neighborhood: faux Tudor and Colonial architecture amidst large, stately oaks and elms.

I was going to see a snuff film.

As we drove, Reginald told me how things would work.

"You don't say anything—don't talk to anyone, OK?" Reginald admonished me for the third or fourth time. He stopped in front of a driveway winding back into some woods and examined the house number on the mailbox, checking it against his paper. He nodded.

"OK, this is it," he said. He backed the Cherokee up a little and drove into the driveway.

We proceeded down the driveway for about a quarter mile until we came to a very well appointed house with a single yellow porch light burning. There were a number of cars already parked in front of the house—we were not the first to arrive.

131

"No one is going to ask you anything anyway—but in case, you are my brother-in-law, from out of town, all right? You're here to hang out with me, OK?"

∎ ∎ ∎ ∎

There were nine men gathered in the living room. They all looked to be businessmen between the ages of thirty and fifty. They were dressed casually but neatly in pressed slacks, khakis, or clean blue jeans. There were no ties—this was a casual affair. It was a gathering of friends—or at least acquaintances with a mutual interest.

The men mixed and chatted in an offhand way. There didn't seem to be any real conversations—just small talk to pass the time. They looked at their watches a lot and drank heavily from a small bar laid out at one end of the room. They chatted and drank and glanced every once in a while across the room at a large color TV and VCR set up opposite the bar.

No one asked me anything about myself, and I volunteered no information other than my name. Reginald introduced me a couple of times, and I usually cut short the chitchat by going to the bar for some water or by simply looking bored and impatient.

There was an air of urgency in that room. The men in their button-down shirts, glancing from their watches to the door to the television, gave me the impression of a gathering of junkies more than anything else, with their ceaseless twitching and their thinly veiled lack of interest in anything other than what they knew was coming.

Watch—television—door.

The doorbell rang.

The host went to the door, opened it, and into the room marched a figure out of a comic book. He was a short man in his early sixties wearing an ill-fitting light suit that was probably expensive but on him rumpled and creased in an extremely unflattering way.

As the newcomer spoke quietly with the host, I realized what he represented.

I was looking at the face of the people behind the Reginalds and the Lorenzos. It was the face of the suppliers and distributors—and an idea began to form in my mind. I began to realize that I had been going about my investigation all wrong. I felt the first tenuous shreds of a new tactic begin to form in my mind as the host took a package from the old gangster and walked over to the VCR. He punched the television on. Men scrambled for their seats as the television went from black to snowy static, accompanied by a loud hissing sound, which the host quickly ended by stabbing at the volume button on the remote control.

I had been working from the wrong direction! As the lights went down and our host asked if everybody was ready, I went over all the contacts I had made so far and realized how a subtle change of angle—the barest of geometric displacements—could turn the whole investigation around!

The lights went down in the room. The old gangster did not stay. He went into another room—the kitchen, I think. He seemed totally uninterested in what was about to happen.

Then I flashed. My train of thought was broken completely, and I was hurtled back to my experiences in Germany as the film began. I could smell the sweat in the air around me; the attention that the men focused on the monitor was laser-like. I had been here before. But that was Germany—those men had been neo-Nazis. And these men who sat alongside me were—what? Doctors, maybe. Lawyers, bankers.

Two men were having sex with a young dark-haired girl. She was not black—she was dark, Hispanic, South American.

The old gangster looked in once with a sandwich in his hand, made a gesture of disgust, and turned back into the kitchen.

The girl's head was hanging off the edge of the bed as the man on top of her ground into her. The other man pulled a knife and knelt down by the woman's head.

In a second it was over.

I heard the same sounds of finishing—light cough and deep breathing, the coy sounds of men ejaculating into their own hands—that I had heard when I was with the neo-Nazis. But how much worse and less understandable this was—this *pastime*. It may be difficult to grasp that one experience could be worse than another, but this was worse. With the neo-Nazis, there was organization, however slight—there was ideology. For the neo-Nazis the films served an alleged purpose. But this served nothing more than the sick fantasies of bored middle-class professionals.

I had thought of something before the film began, and slowly, the idea once again began to take shape in my mind.

What I had to do was become a seller—not a buyer! How, I wasn't sure, but I knew that that was what I would have to do if I was going to get a film.

As the lights came up and the men in the room arranged their clothing without looking at one another, the old gangster came out of the kitchen. Without a word he took the videocassette out of the VCR, put it back into the box, and then collected money from everyone present.

The price for the single viewing was $1,500 per person. I did not pay. Reginald waved me off, telling me that I was his guest.

Now I knew why these films were so hard to get and so expensive, if you found someone willing to sell. The old gangster was there to make sure that no copies were made. That videocassette was gold to the people who had possession of it —tarnished, bloody gold, but gold nonetheless.

The old gangster left, and the men in the room stood and began chatting again. They were perfectly normal-looking Americans. They could have been at a barbeque or mowing their well-tended lawns on a Sunday morning. Some of them looked a little flushed, but beyond that there was no sign that anyone had been upset by what he had just seen.

It's funny how a lot of times it's the small things that you notice. On our way out Reginald stopped to shake hands with someone, and the glint of metal on the man's hand caught my eye. It was a ring with a large stone, and I recognized it as a class ring. Ivy League? Who knows? I couldn't read it; the writing was too small.

■ ■ ■ ■

So, what'd you think?" Reginald asked me as he eased his car into the fast lane on the highway.

Instead of answering him I asked if he could get me in touch with the Pugliese family, or even the snuff film baby-sitter who had brought the tape.

"Yeah, I could," he assured me—sounding none too sure of himself. "But it would have to be done very carefully. You don't want things falling into the wrong hands and—or—or you don't want to get on the wrong side of those people." He stammered, peering at the red taillights of the traffic ahead of us.

"Do you think you could get me one of those films?" I asked him straight out. I didn't think he could, but it was worth a try.

To my surprise, he looked at me and shrugged. "Yes, sure I could," he told me nonchalantly. Then began the story I had heard before—the story I had been hearing all along. It would cost a lot of money—two hundred, two hundred and fifty thousand. Then he went on to explain what I had already surmised. That was the reason for the baby-sitter. He brought the tape, showed it once, collected the money, and left with the tape.

I asked him how many films he had seen altogether. He counted silently and then told me that he must've seen thirty-five or forty over the years.

"Were all the showings handled in the same way?"

"Pretty much. They come with the film, you watch it, you pay up, they take the film and leave," he told me.

I asked him if the audiences were always the same, and he told me that they differed. "It doesn't matter," he told me. "Whoever is there, is in. They've been introduced by someone or they've gone through the ads, one level at a time. They are in the circle of people who know."

I asked him if I was in the circle now, and he shrugged.

"It's not a circle like that. The people who run the thing don't care who watches the films as long as everybody understands the rules. You watch, you enjoy, you pay up and leave. No questions asked."

He stopped talking and then glanced at me for a moment. "And besides, if there were ever any trouble, everybody would get hurt. I mean, if there were ever any police or trouble like that, then everyone would get hurt—you understand that, right?"

I understood fine. In his insinuating way Reginald Smith was threatening me. But I shook my head. "No, I don't understand," I told him, playing dumb.

"You understand that nobody wants to get their hands dirty with this stuff, correct?" he asked. "This is something we do alone in the privacy of our own homes—we don't hurt anybody, right? If anybody tried to uncover this—if the police ever decided to make a raid or investigate this—the implications would be very far-reaching. You understand that, don't you?"

I nodded.

Reginald Smith had seen thirty-five or forty films. Thirty-five or forty bodies.

As we pulled into the parking space next to my rental car, behind the bank where Reginald worked, Reginald said, "I know where you can get a film, no questions asked."

Whether it was a final gift for being so patient or just a way to get me on another track because he was getting nervous, Reginald told me that if I had the balls, I could go and talk to people at a Russian restaurant he knew in the Little Odessa section of Brooklyn.

"What do you mean, 'if I have the balls'?" I asked.

"What I mean is that dealing with those gentlemen, from what I understand, is not like dealing with the old-timers like the Pugliese," he told me.

"What people are you talking about?"

"The Russians—the Russian mob. I mean, the Pugliese run a nice, smooth porn business—a nice, smooth everything business. But the Russians don't understand a handshake like the Pugliese do. One of the Pugliese guys, if you make a deal with one of them, that's it—he'll do what you need, and you do what he needs, and their word is as good as gold unless you cross them. But the Russians, you have to make sure you get the merchandise up front—that's all. Once they get their hands on the money, they are gone." He snapped his fingers.

I asked Reginald if he had a name for me. He said he thought he remembered someone telling him to ask for Oleg—Oleg Bulganin or something like that—but that was all he knew.

I thanked him. We shook hands like gentlemen. I got into my rental car and pulled out of the parking lot. The sadness that had crept into me continued to grow as I got on the freeway and headed south for New York City.

I shook my head in disbelief. Thirty-five or forty films.

17 TRANSFORMATION

I knew what to do now. I had to be a seller. It was a small shift in attitude with big implications. Like some medieval alchemist I had to make myself sympathetic to the devil before the devil would condescend to do a little business with me.

I found the restaurant that Reginald Smith had told me about—the Samovar. It was on Brighton Beach Boulevard in Brooklyn, a mile, maybe a little more, from the world-famous Coney Island amusement park, or what was left of it. That part of Brooklyn had certainly changed over the years. Coney Island bears little resemblance to the grainy photographs of its heyday at the beginning of the century, and English is no longer the first language spoken by people in Brighton Beach—Russian is.

I had to knock on the glass door a number of times before it was answered. The restaurant was not yet open. When I was finally allowed in, I asked for Bulganin. A guy in a tracksuit asked me if I had an appointment. I told him that I didn't but that Bulganin would be happy to see me. He shrugged and led me to the back of the restaurant and up a flight of stairs.

A small, crowded office. There was a guy sitting behind a desk at the far end of the room. Three other guys in tracksuits and gold chains lounged around on folding chairs.

I went right for the guy behind the desk. He suddenly began to carry on a hushed conversation in Russian with a blond guy sitting next to him. He didn't look up at me. He didn't seem to notice my presence at all. It was gangster time. It didn't seem to matter whether they were Israeli gangsters or Italian mafiosi or small-time little pricks running a Johnny-come-lately sideshow out of a restaurant in Little Odessa. It was always the same—a game of chicken and nerve, with little men surrounded by tough guys who were anxious to please. It didn't bother me and it sure as hell didn't scare me. I know a show when I see one. They had let me in and they weren't going to do anything rash if there was money to be made.

I gave him three minutes, then I stepped up to the desk. I rapped on the old wood, scarred by cigarettes, with my knuckles and said, "Hello, I'm Ron Smith. Pleased to meet you."

The guy behind the desk glared at me. "What do you want?"

"I want to talk to Oleg Bulganin about some business. Are you him?"

The blond guy leaned back in his chair. "I am Bulganin. What you want?" he asked me, grinning.

This was it: bluff, counterbluff. These guys had no idea who I was, and that was the only thing going for me. I didn't think that either one of these guys was Bulganin. They were his welcoming committee. I would meet Bulganin later, once—and if—I got through his men.

And there was only one way to do that. I had to do it the same way I had always gotten to the people I wanted to talk to in the course of my work. I had to lie through my teeth and make it stick, and to make it stick, I had to be Ron Smith the dealer. I knew that as far as these guys were concerned, just by walking through the door I had made an impression. At that point they couldn't have cared less who I was. If I was a cop, it didn't matter; they weren't doing anything wrong. If I was one of them, it mattered even less. There was only one way to deal with a situation like this: I had to go straight at them, make sure that they got the idea that I was not someone for them to fuck with, and then dangle something in front of them. I knew I didn't really have to show them anything, just make them think that there was a big deal to be made and if they wanted a piece of it, they would have to treat me right.

"You're Bulganin?" I asked Blondie.

He nodded, still grinning.

"I don't think so. People told me that Bulganin was good looking, and I think you are too damn ugly to be him," I told him, grinning back at him.

He took this in, rose from his chair, and began screaming at me. "What you say, you fuck? Fuck you, you stupid fuck," and so on.

I shook my head and yelled louder than he. "What in the hell is the matter with you?"

Blondie stopped and stared at me, dumbfounded.

"I mean, Christ, I come in here to talk business, and you play bullshit games and then scream at me. What is the matter with you people?"

Blondie looked at the guy behind the desk while the others in the room fidgeted and cast questioning glances at Blondie. The guy behind the desk held up his hand.

"What you want?"

"I want to talk to Oleg Bulganin about a business deal," I told him.

"What kind of deal?"

"I need something, and I was told Bulganin could get it for me. Are you him?"

"No, but I know him. What you need?" he asked me.

I gestured at Blondie. "He isn't going to start yelling again, is he?" I asked.

The guy shook his head. "No, what you want?"

I looked around the room and then back at the guy behind the desk. "I'm looking for a film where girls get fucked then they get killed," I told him.

Blondie burst out laughing.

"How you know Bulganin?" the guy behind the desk asked me.

"Friend of mine, Nisim Simantov," I told him, the lie rolling as easily off of my tongue as the truth ever did.

The guy behind the desk considered for a moment. Did he know Simantov? Probably not. Did it matter? Definitely not.

"Listen, I have people who are willing to pay a lot of money for those kinds of movies. If you can't get them for me, don't waste my fucking time," I told him.

"How much money?"

"Two hundred and fifty thousand dollars for a good one," I told him.

Blondie laughed out loud for the second time.

"All right, fuck you guys. You don't want to do business, fine with me," I said, turning for the door. Halfway across the room one of the guys sitting around the room moved to intercept me. I lowered my head a little, ready to plow into him if I had to. I was Ron Smith the dealer, ready and willing to take my business elsewhere.

Then the guy behind the desk called out to me. "How much money?"

I turned. "Two hundred and fifty thousand."

"You have money?"

"Of course I have the money. You think I'd come up here just to fuck you guys around? I'm not stupid." A small play on their vanity.

"With you?"

"I just told you I wasn't stupid. Christ almighty, of course I don't have it with me," I told him, laughing.

The guy behind the desk laughed with me. I had him. He

said something to Blondie, who marched out the door with a killer glance at me.

"Wait one minute," the guy behind the desk told me.

Ron Smith the dealer waited.

■   ■   ■   ■

The Russian bathhouse in the East Village, in Manhattan, is a converted four-story tenement building on Tenth Street between Avenue A and First Avenue. It doesn't look like much from the outside. It is owned by partners who have a running feud. If you buy a membership of ten visits at a time, you get a discount—but your membership is good only every other week, depending on which partner was in charge the week you bought it. It caters to old Russian and Ukrainian Jews, who have lived in the neigborhood since the first socialist rallies and riots in Tompkins Square Park—a couple of blocks away—toward the end of the last century.

On the other hand, the old babushkas and *lazars* and *yonahs* are no longer the majority in that part of Manhattan and haven't been for years. Now and for a long time past, leggy models in leather pants make their homes there. They share blocks with squatters—their faces tattooed and their hair matted—who stand outside the restaurants on the recently gentrified Avenue A and panhandle for quarts of Midnight Dragon malt liquor. Young stockbrokers and advertising executives have recently moved into the neighborhood, hoping to soak up a little of the seedy glamour that is rapidly diminishing with every co-op sale; Internet cafés are springing up on every corner.

In other words, it is New York, and the bathhouse reflects the subtle, ever-evolving chaos of the neighborhood in which it is situated. I like the neighborhood. It reminds me a little of the neighborhood I grew up in in Israel—tough but comfortable. A real neighborhood.

On this particular trip, however, I wasn't there to soak up atmosphere. My man from the restaurant, his man Blondie, and I walked in, paid our money, and went downstairs to the Russian heat room to meet with Bulganin and some other people he knew who might be able to help me out. I talked and sweated for two hours, pouring buckets of freezing cold water over my head whenever the heat got to be too much. The conversation was a good one.

When I left the bathhouse the sky was still overcast, except far in the west. The sun was going down over New Jersey, streaking the sky orange-red under an otherwise unbroken gray pall that promised more rain before the night was finished. I thought about getting a cab and then decided to walk uptown. I felt like a million bucks. I had bulldozed my way through to Bulganin and gotten back out. I had a list of contacts given to me by Bulganin and his cronies in exchange for a promise to deal them in later and do whatever business I could do with them next time I was in town. It was no skin off their teeth; they didn't have what I wanted, but they knew who did, and I made them think that they would see something for it down the road. All of the names on the list were in Europe. I didn't know whether they really didn't know anybody for that kind of thing in the States or they just didn't want me playing right in their backyard. In any case, it didn't matter. I had names and I was just as happy to get as far away from those guys as I could.

My new strategy seemed to be working. The subtle shift in attitude from buyer to seller had given me the balls to do what I had done. From now on, I had a much better idea how to handle things.

I was in.

I would go to Europe as soon as possible. I was finished in the States, and in any case I thought it best to remove myself as soon as possible from Bulganin and his people. They were erratic, and though I had no proof of it as yet, I got the feeling that they were trigger happy. They were not the mafia, with hundreds of years of dark traditions and codes of honor. It made sense. If they had survived and flourished under the Soviets, they had done it by wile and cunning and by being even more bloodthirsty than the KGB—and more dangerous. They were certainly more dangerous now, if what I had heard was true. With the breakup of the Soviet Union, many highly trained Soviet operatives and agents had suddenly found themselves out of work, or working for nothing. These were people with intensive weapons training and training in surveillance and counterintelligence. Suddenly, their skills were of no use to the struggling Russian Federation—or the struggling Russian Federation was unable to afford them the perks and luxuries that their skills had once commanded.

So they went to the people who could afford them—the mob.

It was not a pleasant thought. The mafia, made up of hungry street kids and half-ignorant bosses three generations away from a peasant village somewhere in Sicily, was bad enough. A mob made up of men trained in the tactics and ideologies of the Cold War, with access to weapons and technologies developed during that struggle and the know-how to use them effectively, was really not a pleasant thought at all.

I walked through Times Square and just floated in the flashing lights and crowds, feeling anonymous and powerful, lost in the swirling masses of tourists and street hustlers crowding the sidewalks. I was in. In what, exactly, only time would tell.

18 SPECIAL AGENT MITCHELL

I had one last stop to make before I left for Europe.

I had come to know special agent Clint Mitchell through a series of phone calls we had had after my investigations in Germany. At the time he had been heading up a special division at the FBI that tracked the activities of various far-right movements in the United States, and we had traded information concerning the links between certain American organizations (such as the Posse Comitatus, the Aryan Nation, and the Klan) and the neo-Nazis in Germany and elsewhere.

He had at first been skeptical of my information and of me, not necessarily in that order, but as my numbers began to tally with his, he came to trust me. We grew to respect each other, which was probably the most I could hope for.

Clint Mitchell (not his real name, but the name he goes by with outsiders) is everything that I am not. He is a company man and has spent the greater part of his adult life in the bureau. As far as I know, his street experience is minimal. His world is one of computer readouts, memos, and task forces. As a gatherer and organizer of information, however, he is, I believe, one of the best men in the bureau.

Information was what I wanted. I had called him from New York and told him what I was after. He had made time to see me. He had not seemed overjoyed about it, however, and he did not look overjoyed to see me when I walked into his office.

"As far as anyone in the bureau knows, there has never been a legitimate snuff movie ever found," he told me five minutes after saying good morning.

"There seems to be concern by various groups and individuals about these things, and the FBI has investigated," he continued after a moment's pause. "So far, not one has been found. Furthermore, most of these groups and individuals are considered by the bureau to be neither trustworthy nor legitimate. Does that answer your questions, Yaron?" he asked me.

"But I've seen more than one with my own eyes. Snuff movies made in the United States," I told him. I was sure he could not continue the company line in the face of an eyewitness.

He frowned, clasped his hands on the polished wood of his desk, and took a deep breath. "What can I tell you? My information is different," he told me. Special agent Clint Mitchell likes his information neat.

I asked him if I could speak to someone investigating organized crime. He laughed and told me that half the bureau was doing just that. I asked him if I could meet someone working on pornography. He smiled and reluctantly took me on a tour.

I met two or three more agents. I got no more information than I had gotten from Mitchell; and more than that, I was made to feel as if I were stepping on toes asking the questions I was asking. The agents I met looked at me through slitted eyes and answered my questions in monosyllables.

How much of this noncooperation was simply the inherent distrust of any bureaucracy toward outsiders, I couldn't tell.

But I was starting to understand where other people got their conspiracy theories.

If it wasn't a cover-up, their stonewalling sure made it seem like one.

So much for the FBI.

19 LONDON

Three days after my meeting with Mitchell, I was in London. I had called ahead to Ako and Andreas. Neither one was on assignment at the moment, and they agreed to meet up with me in London. They were waiting for me at Heathrow when I arrived.

The first name on my list was a man I'll call Bill Webster.

I made contact with him and told him that I was new in town, wanted to do some business, and had been told that he was the man to see for anything you needed done in London.

I told him where I had gotten his name and number, and he asked if he could call me back. I gave him the number of a voice mailbox I had taken in London. Two hours later he called me back—his voice friendly.

"Right, what about tomorrow?" he asked.

"I'd like to get this going today if I can," I told him.

"Sorry, no can do. Got business. I could meet you tomorrow, though," he told me. Tomorrow it would have to be. No sense pushing it this early in the game. He told me to meet him in Victoria Park and gave a location near a café not far from the entrance to the Central Zoo in London—and a time, 10 A.M.

"All right, see you then," I said.

"Right. Cheers, mate." He hung up.

I hung up slowly and then went to Ako and Andreas's room. They looked at me expectantly as I came in.

"What's up, Yaron?" Ako asked.

When I told them that I had arranged a meeting for the next day, they looked a little disappointed.

"So what are we going to do now?" Andreas asked.

"We're going to have a run-through—check out the location and walk through as much of it as we can," I told him.

On the way to the park I outlined how I thought this whole thing would go. It was cold but not freezing. There was snow on the ground, but the sun was out and it felt warm on my back. I was glad that Bill had unwittingly given us time to prepare a more formal welcome for him than we might have been able to put together on the spur of the moment.

I went to bed that night confident that the next day would bring real, tangible results.

■ ■ ■ ■

I'll get out here," I told the cabbie. He pulled his vehicle over to the side of the road. I paid the fare and got out.

As the cab was pulling away from the curb, I slipped on a patch of ice and went down into a puddle of slush, soaking my jacket and one leg of my pants. The time was nine-fifteen—the day was just beginning.

The weather had gone bad overnight, and it was much colder than it had been the day before. The sun was hidden behind a thick layer of uniform gray clouds, and a freezing rain was predicted for later in the morning.

At 9:25 I was in position. A wind had kicked up, and I shivered as I looked toward the coffee shop and saw Ako sitting in the window.

Andreas was also in position, playing his role to the hilt. He was a photographer, snapping photos of the park in winter.

We were in position. We were ready. And I was freezing to death. I knew that Bill and his colleagues would be cautious dealing with an unknown quantity like myself. I had gotten there early and prepared myself to stay there while they checked me out. What I had not counted on was this change of weather or just how long this waiting game would take. Soon I began to shiver as the water on my pants froze, bleeding the warmth from my body.

By ten-fifteen there had still been no action. The only other humans in the park were a couple of homeless people who had a fire going in a trash can about a hundred yards away. I watched the flames rise as they warmed their hands over it and I envied them their small comfort.

Ten-thirty, and nothing. People had begun coming and going hurriedly through the park, but no one I had seen so far had struck me as the type I was looking for.

Andreas had moved to another part of the park. He was checking his camera and changing lenses methodically. He was going about his business convincingly, but I knew he was mentally calculating his range from me with every step, so that at a moment's notice he could be at my side, ready for action.

Action that I was not getting.

At 10:45, an older man arrived on the scene. He looked in my direction and then he stopped and pulled out a map or pamphlet of some kind and began to examine it intently.

Somehow I was sure that this was Bill's scout. It was something about how he held himself. Checking Andreas's position, I walked toward the guy. He glanced up in my direction once, and then, as I approached him, folded his paper up, stuck it into the pocket of his heavy wool coat, and began coming toward me.

This is it. He's coming to meet me halfway. I began to sweat despite the cold. The wait was over.

I was close enough to see his dull gray eyes and bushy eyebrows and the lines in his face—laugh lines.

I stopped and looked at him.

"Good morning. Not a very nice day for a walk, is it? Can you tell me which way to the entrance to the zoo?" he asked pleasantly, his eyes glinting.

It was he—I knew it was he. He stood there waiting for me to say something, daring me to react.

Finally I raised my arm and pointed. "It's over there," I told him. "On the other side of the café."

He nodded. "Cheers—stay warm," he told me with a smile. And off he went in the direction I had indicated, humming a little tune to himself, which I didn't recognize. I watched him walk away and gave the hand signal that we had decided on. Andreas saw it and acknowledged it.

It was time to pack it in.

I turned toward the café, and the older man with the map reappeared.

He walked straight up to me. "Bill'll meet you inside in a couple of minutes."

■ ■ ■ ■

I sat down at a table facing the door. Ako sat reading a German magazine he had picked up somewhere. Andreas was in the back, again fiddling with his various lenses and pieces of equipment, this time having planted some extra firepower in his camera bag for insurance.

Our British counterparts arrived promptly. Four men in their late thirties or early forties, they were dressed in a shabby, utterly ordinary way—like shop workers on their lunch break. When they stood before my table, a slightly built guy with a mustache and twinkling blue eyes held out his hand and introduced himself as Bill. After him, the guy standing next to him, with dark hair and a black-Irish look, told me his name was Adam and gave my hand a vigorous shake. Another guy, younger and a little less sure of himself, didn't say anything. The fourth guy I had recognized immediately—he was the older guy with the map.

Bill and his associates grabbed some seats and got down to business immediately. He told me that he had had to check things out, and that he had spoken to a friend of his who had told him that I was all right and that I was interested in doing business.

I cut him off in midsentence, waving my hand angrily in his face. "What the fuck was all this bullshit, waiting around in the park?" I demanded. "Why the big charade? Why did I have to freeze my ass off in the snow?"

Bill smiled. "I'm just not much interested in having to deal with local law enforcement or getting into any scrapes, you understand," he said gently, smiling a little.

I laid my hands on the table and spread my fingers apart, looking right into Bill's eyes, my face blank. "Frankly, I don't give a rat's ass about the cops, here or anywhere else. I don't have anything to do with local law enforcement anywhere. You understand that. I'm here to do business, nothing more, nothing less, so save the bullshit for somebody who gives a fuck. I'm clean—clean as a whistle," I finished, smiling broadly.

The gangsters looked at one another and then back at me. I felt good. I felt comfortable and in control. They didn't speak for a moment, and neither did I. I didn't have to. I wanted them to wonder just what kind of motherfucker they were dealing with.

Bill looked at his watch and then glanced at the door. When he turned back to the table, I caught his eyes again and asked him in a mock-conspiratorial tone, lowering my voice, "You guys waiting for something?"

Bill nodded. "Yeah, we're waiting for a friend," he told me. "You don't mind, do you?"

"Hell no. Why don't we make a fucking party out of this?" I said loudly.

And at that moment, Don Swinborne, my British contact from Hong Kong, loped through the door of the café and up to our table.

I have to admit that I was thrown for a minute.

"Here he is now. You remember Don, don't you, Ron?" Bill said.

I ran through all the possible scenarios that this unexpected encounter might entail, not the least of which was Andreas and Ako having to come, guns blazing, to my rescue.

"Hello, mate," I heard Don say to Bill casually, laying a hand on his shoulder briefly as he came around the table toward me. I stood up to confront him. At least I would not be trapped behind the table. If anybody on either side did open up, I wanted to be able to get out of the way fast.

Don approached me and looked me up and down, his eyes expressionless.

I held out my hand and smiled at him. "Hello, Don. How you doing?"

Don shook his head and pursed his lips together. Then he turned to Bill. "This is all I get?" he asked his friend.

Silence.

Suddenly Don swung back around on me, and before I could react, slapped my hand away and grabbed me in a huge bear hug, putting his arms around me and patting my shoulders, laughing and repeating over and over again, "That's all I get, Ronny? A fuckin' handshake—that's all I fuckin' get?" Then he stepped back and looked at me. "Business all right, lad? Things going good? You look good, you fuckin' bleeder!"

I sat down heavily, wondering if the Brits could hear my heart beating.

As soon as Don sat down and got himself a cup of coffee, we got down to business. His mood sobered appreciably as he explained to Bill and the others—not for the first time, I'm sure —what kind of business he and I had talked about in Bangkok and, basically, that I was a high roller who could put together deals that could work out profitably for everyone involved. Don was inadvertently giving me a refresher course on the conversation we had had in Bangkok—that was good. What was bad, however, was that I began to get the idea that Don had told them that the meeting we were having today was supposed to be about transporting women to the Far East—to Subic Bay.

"So, what about it, Ron? What do you think of Don's plan?" Bill asked me when Don had finished. It seemed that, without even trying, I had won their confidence to the point that they were soliciting my advice.

"He thinks it's a great plan, don't you, Ronny?" Don cut in before I could speak.

I sat back in my chair and twined my fingers together on my chest, raising my eyebrows. "I think it's a hell of an idea, and I think it could make us all very happy, if you know what I mean," I said cryptically. "Unfortunately, Don and I have some unfinished business, don't we, Don?" I added.

Swinborne turned to look at me. The smile dropped from his face and he ducked his head, the closest thing to an apology I would get from him.

"Right. I told you that McCall bloke was a bit of a loon. I heard what happened—fuckin' loon, that guy. He almost came after me, right. Just tryin' to set him up and he comes after me —fuckin' loon!" he said quickly, his voice lowered almost to a whisper. Now I knew why he had greeted me as he had. We were definitely on the same side.

"That's all right, Don. Shit happens," I told him.

The smile reappeared on his face and he nodded. That was it.

"So, here's the deal, you guys," I told the Brits when I had gotten their attention again. "I have some business I need to take care of—same stuff I talked to Don about last time we met. And until that's squared away, we don't have much time for anything else."

They looked at Don, who looked at me. When I didn't continue, Bill finally leaned forward and asked, "So what do you need, Ron?"

"I need snuff films, Bill. That's all, a couple of films for my employer in Germany. He wants what he wants—you know what I mean? But I need them right now, and I need good ones —not bullshit. If you can get me what I want, we can all make a nice chunk of change and start talking about bigger and better things," I told him, smiling as if I were talking about a new pair of shoes or a shipment of televisions.

The Brits looked at one another silently.

Finally I turned to Don and said, "So, what's the deal? Can you get me some movies? What is so difficult?"

Don opened his mouth but Bill intervened, leaning forward and saying, "We can get the movies. Have you got the money?"

I looked at him and laughed out loud. "No, Bill, I'm here fucking with you! Shit, of course I have the money!"

I turned and motioned for Ako to come over. He got up, rising about a head taller than almost everyone around him, and stomped over with a dangerous look on his face, making sure everyone in the café saw him.

He came over to the table and stood by silently, towering over the Brits in his heavy black clothing and steel-toed Ruhr Valley steelworker's boots.

"He holds the money. If you want to see it, ask him," I said.

They looked at Ako for a moment and then started saying things about how they trusted us, and if I said I had the money, then they knew I had it . . .

Ako looked at me and I waved him back to his place. He glared at me angrily and retreated to his table.

Bill nodded. "Yeah, Ron, sure, we can get some movies," he told me.

"So, how much is this going to cost?" I asked. Bill said he would have to find out.

"Fine," I told him. "So, how do we work this?"

"We'll get you what you want, but we're going to need a little down payment," he said.

Crunch time. I didn't know these guys. I didn't know where they were from or if this whole thing wasn't just a big scam. I did know one thing, however. If I was going to talk like a big wheel, I was going to have to back it up. I reached into my pocket and brought out a big wad of money, mainly twenties, that I had brought with me for just such an occasion. It was about $800. I threw it on the table like so many used tissues.

"There, that oughtta get you guys a ride home, right?" I asked. Adam made a move toward the money, but Bill was quicker; he shoved the wad deep into his front pocket with a satisfied grin on his face.

"So, when do we meet again?" I asked.

"Let's get together tomorrow—same place, same time, right?"

"Right," I agreed.

■ ■ ■ ■

A few hours later, as I lay on the bed in my room, leafing through a magazine, the phone rang. I picked it up and was surprised to hear Don Swinborne's voice on the other end.

"How you doing, mate? Surprised to see me today, right?" he asked.

"Yeah, it's a long way from here to Bangkok."

"World's getting smaller all the time, mate."

I agreed that it was.

"Ronnie, how about you and me getting together tonight?" he asked.

"Whenever, wherever, Don," I told him affably.

"All right, how about another trip to the coffee shop in the park?" he asked.

"You got it, Don. See you there." I hung up and looked out the window. One deep breath later, I was up and dressed and waiting for Ako in the lobby.

■ ■ ■ ■

I arrived at the coffee shop at ten minutes to ten.

By ten-thirty I knew that this wasn't going to work. Don hadn't shown, and I was furious. I was being jerked around yet again, and it didn't make sense. Ako was outside, sitting in his rental car. I had told Andreas to stay at the hotel.

At 10:45 I went out and told Ako to drive back to the hotel without me. He didn't want to leave me alone, but I needed time to think and cool down.

"What's going on, Yaron?" he asked.

"Don't ask me any questions, just go the hell back to the hotel, all right?" I barked at him.

I definitely needed time to cool down.

Ako finally drove off and left me alone. The park was silent and glistening with a new layer of pure white snow, which had fallen in a short flurry while I was waiting in the coffee shop.

Waiting for nothing.

I walked for a while, emerging through the trees at the entryway to the zoo, closed since five, blocked now by a knot of people. At that moment an ambulance swung around the corner and raced down the two-way road, its lights slashing out into the trees and twisting their shadows around me in shades of red and yellow. I quickened my pace as the paramedics jumped out of the ambulance, one of them fighting his way through the crowd while the other collected some equipment from a panel he had yanked open on the side of the truck. I approached the knot of milling onlookers and pushed my way through to the center of the small crowd.

There on the ground, a man was clutching his stomach with both hands, his face contorted with pain. One of the paramedics was standing by, receiving instructions and barking questions into a radio while the other one was futilely trying to stop the blood that was flowing from the wounded man's abdomen. The wounded man was uttering curses hoarsely and moaning, until finally he leaned back full-length on the wet ground, breathing raggedly, the gash in his stomach making a slurping sound with every short breath.

I stood looking on for what seemed like an eternity but what could only have been two or three minutes, and then walked away. I walked to the edge of the park, hailed a cab, and gave the address of the hotel in Swiss Cottage. I rode silently for a couple of minutes, barely daring to breath. This was London. I had been here before, more than once, but now it was a different place. This was London, and the man I had seen on the pavement, clutching his intestines and trying to shove them back into his own stomach, was Don Swinborne.

I leaned out of the cab and vomited. I couldn't hold it in any longer. The cold night air rushed at me as I hung my head out the window and emptied my insides of everything they contained.

The cabbie did not say anything. Without looking around, he held a pile of napkins over his shoulder so that I could clean myself up.

I will forever be grateful for that man's silence.

■ ■ ■ ■

When I got back to the hotel I told the kid working the front desk to prepare a bill for our rooms—we would be checking out. I then went upstairs to Ako and Andreas's room to tell them to get dressed and pack up.

They asked me what had happened. I just told them we were leaving.

Don's getting it was a perfectly simple matter. Don had seen an opportunity to make some money, and he had taken the risk of going behind his friends' backs to get it. Somehow his friends had gotten wind of it, and they had decided to teach Don a lesson. If he died, bad luck. If he lived—good for him. But either way, he wouldn't be going behind anybody's back anytime soon. Who had done it? What did it mean? These were questions that couldn't be answered right then.

And none of that mattered.

What did matter was that things had gone sour and we had to get out of there. I called Bill.

"Hello, who's there?" he asked in his thick Cockney accent.

"Bill, it's me, Ron. Listen, what's the deal with Don?" I asked.

"I don't know, what is the deal with Don? We were supposed to get together tomorrow, right?" he asked. He hadn't hesitated. I couldn't tell if he knew anything about what had happened or not. I did know that he was a professional, however. Whether he knew or not, he wasn't going to give away anything until he knew what was going on, and I sure as hell wasn't going to tell him.

I told him I just wanted to see if we could move ahead with the Subic Bay deal. He liked that. Then I asked him about our business. He reminded me that we had spoken only that afternoon and told me to be patient. I told him that I was going to have to leave town for a while so I wanted to wrap things up as soon as I could.

"Good then, Ronny. Good thing you called, because the thing is, I checked with some friends, and it seems the person I need is away for a while," he told me.

"What kind of a while?" I asked.

"Gone to Holland, something like that. Could be a week. But you leave it to me, Ronny. We'll get this thing sorted out, right?"

One thing I was learning was that time meant nothing to these guys. A day, a week, a month—it's all the same thing to a crook. If one of these guys tells you that he'll get what you want tomorrow and you get it a week later, you should consider yourself lucky. And even if you are dealing with someone who wants to play straight arrow with you, the guys he's dealing with will jack him around because they don't give a shit. Why should they? It's not their deal. We had thought that we were going to get what we were looking for in the morning. Now I knew for sure that it wasn't going to happen.

"Just let me know when you have something to show me, all right?" I told him.

"Right you are, Ron. Talk to you soon," he said.

"And give my regards to Don," I told him, hanging up the phone.

20 A M S T E R D A M

The three of us arrived in Amsterdam the following day.

The next name on my list was Horacio Lada, and it took three days, sitting in the Hotel Tucumara, Amsterdam, before I was able to talk to him.

In that time, I had a conversation with a member of the Dutch police, Captain Kass Van-Holit. He told me that there was no such thing as snuff films. "I have been a policeman for twenty-nine years. Believe me, if there were any such movies, I would have seen them," he told me.

I didn't feel like arguing with him.

Andreas drank too much.

Ako complained about the work he was losing out on.

Then I got the call. Horacio Lada wanted to get together.

■ ■ ■ ■

There was the knock on the door. As I went to answer it, I glanced again at the vent where Ako and I had installed the microphone. Ako and Andreas had taken the adjoining suite, where they would monitor the meeting that was about to take place. I had taken these precautions because I remembered very clearly the admonishments of the Russian back in New York when he told me about the guy we were in Amsterdam to see.

As we sat in the steam room, surrounded by hipsters and old Jewish and Russian businessmen, my Russian had wagged his finger at me and said, "This man—he can get what you want, but watch out for him."

I looked at him and asked, "Why—is he a problem?"

My Russian smiled and then said something in Russian to one of his men. The man addressed then went and filled a bucket with cold water from an eternally dripping tap in the wall.

"No, he's not a problem," he said, waving his hand and muttering something in his own language that made Oleg Bulganin and the others sitting around laugh quietly.

"He's not a problem. He's just a crazy motherfucker, crazy, crazy," my Russian said as the man with the bucket emptied it over his head, causing my Russian to sputter and spit as the cold water splashed over him and hit the concrete bench, flowing eventually to the drain set in the middle of the hard floor.

A crazy motherfucker.

I hoped that Ako and Andreas were listening and that they were both ready to intervene if things got hot. They were armed to the teeth, Andreas with his nunchaku and Ako with his all-plastic SIG-Sauer handgun.

When a Russian mafia guy tells you to watch out for someone, you listen.

I opened the door and immediately sensed trouble. The man standing before me had short brown hair, green eyes, a nose that had been pushed all over his face, several scars intersecting his eyebrows, and the thin-lipped, contemptuous sneer of a real punk. He came into the room without a word to me. I looked out into the corridor and saw that he was leaving three guys outside.

That was not good.

As I closed the door and turned to face him, he was looking around the room as if he owned the place.

"*Was willst du dann?*"—what do you want?—he asked, in German, spinning around to face me.

Without answering him I offered him a chair. He threw himself down in it and spread out his arms and legs. He had to take up as much space as possible.

"*Hast kein Bier?*" Got no beer?

He smiled like a lizard, shrugged, and jumped out of his chair. He was high, that much was obvious. Whatever it was— coke, speed—it was making him crazy. He walked quickly around the hotel room, went into the bathroom, turned on the faucet, and splashed away the beads of sweat covering his upper lip. He then walked quickly to the door, opened it, and whispered something to his guys outside.

Suddenly he swung the door shut, came back, and threw himself back in his chair. "What the fuck you want?" he asked, glaring at me, his pupils dilated, nostrils flaring.

"I'm looking for snuff movies," I told him.

"What the fuck is that, snuff?"

I told him, and to my surprise he pulled out a knife, laughing. He twirled the blade around in his hands like a drum majorette with a baton until his face started to redden. Then he opened his coat and slipped the knife back into the sheath under his right arm, breathing heavily.

My hand slid nearer to the pillow on the right side of the bed. I had a Beretta .22 planted there. The fun and games were over. I was prepared to fire if I had to. But I was going to have to wait until the last possible moment.

Suddenly I thought that the moment had come.

The guy went rigid after his show with the knife. He closed

his eyes, and a small smile played over his lips as whatever he was on hit him hard. My hand was about an inch from the pillow as, suddenly opening his eyes, he shoved his hand into his jacket. I counted seconds. My hand tensed. I waited for the glint of metal—I had to be sure. One, two, three . . .

"See that?" the guy said suddenly, pulling a roll of small foil squares out of his pocket and holding them so that they unrolled like a proud father's pictures of his son's first Little League game.

Condoms. The guy was showing me a roll of condoms!

My hand went numb and I fought the urge to collapse backward on the bed.

"See that," he said again, wagging the condoms. "That's what I use in one night, one fucking night," he told me. He threw the condoms on the bed and made yet another circuit of the room.

He stopped suddenly and took a deep breath. "I have to get out of here," he said.

"OK. Let's go out—wherever you want," I told him.

His eyes were totally lit now. He rubbed his hands together and muttered something in German. He went into the bathroom, washed his face, and collected his chain of condoms.

Then he smiled and walked out the door.

I took my Beretta from under the pillow and shoved it into my belt at the small of my back, covering it with my shirt.

■ ■ ■ ■

Not far from Dam Square is the world-famous red light district of Amsterdam. Nothing in this charming city of seven hundred thousand—not its placid canals, not the elegant facades of its centuries-old merchant houses—draws as many tourists as this small area along a few of the inner canals, known in Dutch as the Streets of Red Windows.

The narrow thoroughfares are thronged every night with the desperate and the lonely and the mad and the just plain curious. It is here that the prostitutes of Amsterdam conduct their business, in a manner more open and free of stigma than in probably any other place in the Western world. It is here that women from all over the world present themselves in storefront windows, bathed in red light, half naked, and unashamed. Once a prospective customer sees what he wants, he has only to knock on the door next to the window. A price is settled upon, depending on the services being offered, a Be Back Soon sign is put in the window, the curtains are drawn, and in ten minutes the woman is back—ready for business again.

■ ■ ■ ■

As Horacio Lada went for his third woman, I motioned Ako over and told him I thought we should end this little game, and instructed him to be on the lookout for an opportunity to do so. He was about to ask me something when Horacio Lada called my name. I looked and saw him waving me over to where he was about to enter one of the women's "offices."

"What do you want?" I asked him, walking over.

"Come, look at this," he told me, grabbing me by the arm and pulling me inside.

I was surprised by the cleanliness and the order of the small room. There was a queen-size bed covered with what looked like satin sheets. A lamp on a bedside table draped with a piece of transparent red material gave the room the warm bloody glow after which the Streets of Red Windows are named. Horacio Lada was talking to the woman whose room it was. She was pretty in a very Nordic way, tall, with blond hair, large breasts, and narrow hips. She stood with him at the other end of the room in nothing but a see-through baby-doll nightie. They spoke together for a moment and then he turned to me.

"She'll take both of us for the same price," he announced happily.

I glanced at the girl and she returned my look with a resigned raising of her thin eyebrows and a pursing of her lips.

"No thanks, my friend. Enjoy yourself," I said, giving him some more money.

I turned and walked outside. As I went to rejoin Ako and finish the conversation we had started, Horacio Lada popped his head out the woman's door. He called to one of his bodyguards, who threw his cigarette away and walked over to him. After a hurried conversation, the bodyguard returned and spoke to his partners, and one of them disappeared, to return a few minutes later with someone new in tow. He was a small-boned East Indian. He walked directly up to me and addressed me in heavily accented English.

"You got the money?" he asked.

I was startled into silence. Was this how it was going to go down? Here on the street? I looked at him.

"Do you have what I want?"

"Yeah, I got it—good stuff." He then produced a small glassine envelope. "Good coke—very good," he said.

Coke—what the fuck was this?

My friend's bodyguard stepped in at that point, motioning toward the window behind which his boss was enjoying himself.

"He want," he said simply.

It wasn't a snuff movie. It was, however, the opportunity we had been waiting for. This was where I could sign off, mad as hell, and stalk back to my room with Ako in tow, fuming about the bullshit way people did business in Amsterdam.

"He say you pay me," the Indian told me.

"Fuck off," I told him, glancing at Ako.

"What do you mean, fuck off?" the Indian asked.

He was then joined by another man, larger than the first guy.

"I mean, if you don't get out of my face, I'm going to knock it off," I told him.

I took a step back and looked at them, trying to decide whether to kick him in the knee or the groin. Ako came out of nowhere and laid the first guy flat with a solid punch to the side of the head.

The second man faced off with Ako. He held his hands in front of him and murmured something in his own language. Ako dropped back, shifted his weight, and let go with a roundhouse that sent him flying two yards onto his back.

Ako stood over the two Indian guys until they came to their senses. The bodyguards looked at us impassively as their boss rejoined them, having finished his fifteen-minute conquest.

"What the hell is going on?" he asked, pulling on the cuffs of his jacket.

"You want some coke, you buy that shit yourself—I don't have anything to do with that shit, you understand?" I told him. Ako came over and stood by my side as the two Indians got up off the street, shaking their heads, and began jabbering at each other in their own language.

"Yeah?" he said.

"Yeah," I told him. "You want to get laid, you fuck all the whores in Amsterdam, I don't give a fuck, but you buy your own drugs."

His three guys were squared off against Ako and me, and I wasn't sure how Horacio Lada was going to react. His expression changed so many times in the space of a half a minute that I didn't know from second to second whether he was going to shoot me or hug me. One of his bodyguards took a final drag off of a cigarette and flicked it at the Indians, who were trying to air their complaints in the face of overwhelming disinterest from all concerned.

Suddenly Horacio Lada took a step back and clicked his heels, and a big grin cracked his face. "I salute you, *mon capitaine,*" he said, putting the blade of his hand to his sweat-beaded forehead.

What a nut.

■ ■ ■ ■

It was four o'clock in the morning by the time I got back to the hotel. Horacio Lada had insisted on escorting Ako and me, along with his bodyguards, through the quaint, now-quiescent streets of Amsterdam.

In front of the hotel, Horacio Lada finally said, "So how many of these films you want?" He said it out of the blue, just like that. I was taken by surprise.

"As many as you have," I told him.

"Oh hell," he told me, waving his hand in front of him. "I can get as many as you want. The real hard stuff, kids, animals, *schlitze und dize.*"

"*Schlitze und dize, was ist's?*"—what is that?—I asked him. He had been speaking in German, and I thought it was some kind of new specialty.

"*Was Du willst,*" he told me. What you want. He ran his finger across his throat and laughed.

Then I got it. *Slice and dice.*

"*Na—ich könnte mit Arkan sprechen*"—I could speak to Arkan—he said, shrugging and pulling a face.

He looked at me like I should have known who he was talking about. I knew of only one Arkan—the same one everyone knew of. Arkan the Bosnian Serb paramilitary leader.

"You could talk to Arkan?" I ventured.

"Yeah, I'm a good friend of his. I was invited to his wedding. I know him and his wife. I would really like to fuck her. God, what I could do to her. You saw her in the papers?" he asked.

"Yeah, sure, a nice piece," I agreed. I had heard of Arkan's lavish wedding to a Serbian beauty queen and model. I had not seen any pictures, however.

"You know Malatesta?" my friend asked. The name he mentioned was not Malatesta; it is the name I have chosen to use.

I glanced at Ako leaning in the brightly lit entrance to the hotel. Then I looked back at the street. "I've heard of him," I told my friend. Malatesta was the supposed criminal master-mind behind Arkan, and the paramilitary leader's connection to very heavy people in Italy.

"He's a motherfucker; put up all the money for the wedding. Those Italian bastards know how to put on a show. I bet that wedding was full of pussy."

"You didn't go?" I asked.

He looked at me and shrugged. "No, I had business," was all he said. "I could probably talk to him in a couple of weeks," he added.

"I don't have a couple of weeks. Can you get them from anyone a little closer to home?" I asked.

He seemed to consider for a moment. "You know, you're all right. I like you," he said finally.

"I like you too," I said, smiling.

"I'll tell you what, there's going to be a get-together in a couple of days where they're going to show exactly the kind of shit you're looking for. You interested?"

I told him that I was and asked when it was going to be.

"Soon. It's a quick in-and-out, so nobody knows until the day before, where or when. I'll let you know."

I gave him my voice mail number and he gave me a business card with a number on it—no name, nothing else.

He shook my hand and called to Ako. "You're a good fighter—call me if you ever need another job."

Ako grunted.

■ ■ ■ ■

Ako, Andreas, and I hung around Amsterdam waiting for Lada to call. Finally, I did get a call, but it wasn't from Lada. It was from Bill Webster. He left a message on my voice mail telling me he had something for me. I called him back immediately.

He had a film for me and he wanted to give it to me cheap as a token of good faith. Ako and I left Andreas waiting for Lada's call and caught a plane for London. We were back within twenty-four hours, and three hours after that we had a video player set up and were watching the film. It showed some rough S&M. A woman was tied spread-eagle to a door. She seemed to strangle to death, her air cut off by a rope tied around her neck.

"It's no good," I told Ako and Andreas after the screening.

"What do you mean, it's no good?" Andreas asked. "It's horrible."

"It's bad, but it's nothing like what I saw in Germany. This is a two, maybe a three, tops. Her death is not intentional . . . anyone can see they didn't intend to make a snuff film," I told him.

They were disappointed and tired. I knew Ako wanted to go home and take care of some business, and I knew that Andreas was eager to go with him.

"I'll tell you what. You guys go home for a while."

"What're you going to do?" Andreas asked me.

"I'm going to wait for that nutball to call. As soon as I hear something, I'll let you guys know."

They nodded. We had dinner together that night and they left soon afterward. I stayed three more days. I was thoroughly sick of the stately old city of Amsterdam when Horacio Lada finally called and gave me instructions for his "get-together."

21 THE CHÂTEAU

My plane from Amsterdam touched down on the runway at Orly international airport, bounced once, hit solid ground again, and rumbled to a halt.

Customs was a snap. I strode through the arrivals terminal, picked up my small bag from the luggage carousel, and scanned the long hall looking for the Germans. We had arranged to meet just inside the terminal at two-thirty. I would brief them on what I needed from them, and they would disappear, trailing me unseen as I was taken wherever it was that I was going.

The airport was packed with people. Hurried footsteps echoed up and down the terminal as men and women rushed by me. High-pitched women's voices, the sounds of crying babies, and the grumblings of travel-weary businessmen, combined with the insistent, continual announcements of arrivals and departures, filled the terminal with a hum of white noise. Snatches of conversations flew by me, individual words registering for a moment and then fading, lost in the excited buzz of travel in the jet age.

Ako and Andreas weren't there. I looked for them and looked at my watch.

Two-forty-five.

I swung my head slowly, letting my gaze rest at one end of the long terminal before turning it upon the other end. The large windows, running the entire length of the terminal, showed a sky grayed over by thick uniform clouds. It didn't seem to be raining, but it looked as though it might dump buckets at any minute. I strolled over to stand before the window. I could feel the damp air penetrating the glass. I breathed on it, leaving a misty field about the size of my hand. I wiped it away angrily.

Where the hell were those guys?

"Ron Smees?"

I spun around. I was being addressed by a man of about twenty-five, clean shaven, with dark hair, dark eyes: south of France, maybe—North Africa, probably. He was dressed casually but neatly. I held out my hand.

"Smith, yeah. Ron Smith," I told him.

He smiled thinly, took my hand, and released it quickly. His hand was smooth and well manicured. He wore one piece of jewelry, a gold ring.

He rattled off something in French that I didn't get. My French has never been very good.

"Je ne parle pas français," I told him.

He rolled his eyes a little and shrugged.

"Viens," he said, starting away and motioning for me to follow. I picked up my bag, looking behind me as I did so. Still no sign of the Germans. My guide looked at me and motioned again with his hand, and I followed him to the automatic doors. He went through a little ahead of me. The doors slid back smoothly, a shock of chilly air pricked my face, and my bag was knocked out of my hand.

"Tut mir leid"—sorry about that—Ako said, reaching to retrieve the bag and hand it to me. Behind him, on the sidewalk outside the terminal, Andreas stood, arm upraised, hailing a cab.

"*Es ist nichts*"—it's nothing—I told him.

He smiled as I took my bag from him. He nodded to my guide, got a cold scowl in return, and continued into the terminal.

"*Putain d'allemand*"—fucking German—my guide remarked. We walked past Andreas and headed out into the parking lot, where he led me to a maroon sedan. He popped the trunk for me. I threw my bag inside and got in the backseat.

He started the car without a word to me, and moments later we were out on the highway.

We were heading south. I could tell that much. The sun was going down to the right in a blaze of orange and red where the sky was clearer, just above the western horizon. I asked him where we were going and he just shrugged the all-purpose shrug of the French, and that was the last of our conversation. He either couldn't speak English or didn't want to, and I was in no mood to trot out my schoolbook French—besides, I had other things on my mind.

I didn't know what had happened back at the airport. Ako and Andreas are professionals, I thought. They're probably somewhere behind us right now. I didn't want to look back to see if that was true, but at the same time I could barely restrain myself from craning around and taking a look.

They're back there, Yaron, I told myself, fiddling with a gold pinkie ring that I had picked up in Amsterdam, unconsciously modeling myself in a small way after Horacio Lada and adding a facet of his personality to the personality of Ron Smith.

They're back there. They're back there.

If they weren't back there, I was going this one alone, and I had no idea what to expect. I slipped the ring off my pinkie and tossed it in my hand. I'm not used to wearing jewelry, and it was starting to annoy me.

The scenery outside was monotonous. We were in the old industrial belt around Paris. Railroad yards and gray factories gave way to more railroad yards. I had no idea where we were. I had no idea where we were going, and I had no idea whether Ako and Andreas were with me or not.

Suddenly my driver began weaving in and out of traffic. The urge to look around became overwhelming as my driver continued to speed up, cutting in and out between cars and leaning on the horn. I had to take a look, a quick glance back, before the sun disappeared completely and it became dark.

"What the fuck are you doing?" I demanded loudly, even as I looked back, scanning quickly for any sign of Ako's familiar sedan.

My driver started laughing.

Ako's sedan was nowhere in sight.

∎ ∎ ∎ ∎

About forty-five minutes after nightfall we arrived at the front gate of what appeared to be a large estate. The gates were open and we proceeded up a gravel drive. There were already a number of late-model cars parked in front of the house as we pulled up and my driver turned the engine off. The house was very grand, modeled along the lines of some nineteenth-century businessman's idea of what a château should look like. There were towers on either side with steeply sloping, conical roofs and windows that jutted out, terminating at top and bottom in pointed curlicues of weathered stone. Ivy swept up the first two stories of the front of the house, giving it a slightly sinister, House of Usher look.

My guide took me inside. Fifty people, give or take a few, were sitting and standing in scattered groups watching twelve-odd televisions of all makes and models. The people held drinks in their hands, and some of them were eating from small plastic plates. I walked up and joined a group around one large color screen. On the screen was an old couple in their sixties, maybe seventies, performing various sex acts with a small boy and girl, neither of whom could've been fifteen years old, and who were probably a couple of years shy of that. The men watching the video were dressed elegantly for the most part, in well-fitting suits with very little jewelry showing. Most people were speaking French, but I heard a lot of German and English as well. It seemed to be a convention of hard-core-porn connoisseurs from all over Europe and the States. The other televisions placed around the room were showing other films: bestiality; more child porn, with even younger children; very hard-core S&M; and films that featured the eating of feces and the drinking of urine.

The women who were there were obviously professionals. They were all uniformly young and attractive, with very done hair and long glistening nails in shades of red to match their lips. They stood by the men and sipped daintily from champagne glasses, commenting from time to time on the action taking place on the screens. Some of them wore long gowns, very tight and slit up the side, in some cases almost to their hips. Others were dressed more casually, in tight pants and tops. Whatever they wore, however, their clothing left very little to the imagination. They stood or stalked around the room, the calculating looks in their eyes belying the freshness of their faces.

I wandered from screen to screen for a while, glancing at the videos that were being shown and moving on as if uninterested. I kept an eye out for Horacio Lada, but I didn't see him. Either he was not coming or he hadn't arrived yet. There didn't seem to be any real dealing going on or any organized way to conduct business. There were just the televisions and the emptiness of the rest of the house. I wandered into a couple of other rooms, which were all as bare and lifeless as the ones leading off the hallway that I had glimpsed before. The house had either been rented specifically for this event or simply been requisitioned somehow. In any case, it seemed clear that there had been no full-time occupants for quite a while.

In my wanderings around the house I made the acquaintance of Leo. Leo was from Atlantic City. He had graying hair slicked back on his head, and he was instantly identifiable as American, as much by the coarse openness of his manner as by the somewhat less elegant cut of his suit. He did not have a very high opinion of the French in general. He referred to them in an undertone as either Frenchies or frogs. He did, however, seem to admire the cleverness with which the organizers of the "conventions" went about choosing and obtaining their locations. With very little prompting, glad to speak English with someone, he explained that the conventions went on every couple of months in a different location, but it was always similar to the place we were in. He told me that the organizers would find a place that they wanted, someplace a little secluded, with a wall or a strong fence around it, that was for sale or rent. They would send somebody to the real estate office with a bunch of show-me money and wave it in the agent's face. This would be on a Friday right before closing time—in France, where they take their weekends seriously.

They would wave the show-me money in the guy's face and say they were representing someone interested in buying the place. The agent would ask them to come back on Monday, bright and early. But the prospective buyer was not going to be in town that long. The prospective buyer needed to check the place out now because he had to leave. So the representatives of the prospective buyer offered to leave a wad of money with the agent as a security deposit, and just to make the agent feel better—"The money is usually worth about as much as a fistful of toilet paper, you know?" Leo was quick to add—a little something for the agent himself, for his time and his effort on behalf of the prospective buyer. A couple of hundred dollars usually did it.

And they had the key for the weekend.

"Slick, right?" Leo asked me.

I had to admit that it was.

I shook Leo off by making a trip to the bathroom. On my way back to the main viewing room, I glanced down a short hall and saw a brightly lit kitchen.

There was food, cold cuts spread evenly over foil-covered plastic trays on a table covered with crumbs and crowded with empty glasses and bottles. And there was a man taking orders.

North African or Middle Eastern, he was dressed impeccably in a custom-tailored suit, and he was talking on a cellular phone. As he spoke into the phone, he made notes of the conversation in a ruled-paper notebook. He scribbled down numbers and a few words in Arabic in separate columns.

There were three guys standing near him, young guys, tough looking. I started toward the man on the phone. I intended to ask him if he knew Horacio Lada and introduce myself to him. The toughs nearby slid their half-closed eyes in my direction. The man on the phone glanced at his watch, ended the phone conversation abruptly, got up, and walked past me into the other room.

I followed him out, intent on making contact. He spoke quickly to one or two men in passing, pausing momentarily to purr at a beautiful young woman speaking French with a heavy German accent.

"Ron, there you are. Have you met Jean-Claude?" It was Leo. He was shaking hands with the man from the kitchen.

Leo introduced me. Jean-Claude and I spoke briefly. He asked me if I was enjoying myself. I told him that I was. I then asked him if he had seen Horacio Lada. He told me that he hadn't. He then excused himself and made his way to one of the monitors.

Two men with long blond hair and beards were performing sexual acts with animals. Then a boy who looked to be about ten years old was brought from somewhere. He was made to penetrate a sheep that was held for him by the two men.

Jean-Claude spoke quickly with a man in front of the monitor. The two of them then went back to the kitchen. I followed and saw the man hand Jean-Claude a very thick stack of deutsche marks in exchange for two videos.

"Are you interested in anything, Mr. Smith?" Jean-Claude asked me when the other man had gone back to the screening room with his new purchases.

I told him what I was interested in.

He nodded, removed a video from a carrying case being watched over by one of the young toughs I had noticed when I first wandered into the kitchen, and led me back out to the other room.

And there was Bill Webster, the petty gangster with whom I had made contact in England, wearing a worn houndstooth blazer, slacks, and a London Fog trench coat. He was just emerging from the hallway leading to the front door. I saw him before he saw me. It seemed that the world I was working in was small indeed.

As ever, the best defense is a good offense.

I went right for him—hand out, smile cutting my head in two.

"Hello, Bill!" I said.

He looked at me for a moment and then smiled. "Ron, what the hell are you doing here?" he asked, taking my hand.

"Enjoying the show, mate. What else?"

He nodded and looked over my shoulder. "Hello, Jean-Claude. How are you?" he said.

I turned as Jean-Claude was extending his hand to Bill. They shook cordially and exchanged a few words, then Jean-Claude turned to me. "Ron, come and take a look at this—I think it might be what you are looking for," he said.

Bill glanced quickly from me to Jean-Claude and back again, his jaw muscles tightening. He was reappraising me now in a new context. I didn't ask him about our deal. I didn't ask him if he had done anything to earn the money I had given him so easily. Putting a down payment on services yet to be rendered was strictly amateur hour when it came to guys like Bill. It had been a gamble and I had lost. I looked at him and grinned. He probably thought I was an idiot.

Seeing me here, however, he would probably think again.

"You want to take a look, Bill?" I offered.

"Yeah, right, let's have a look."

We walked over to a blank monitor. Jean-Claude turned it on, put the video into the VCR next to it, and hit the play button.

Three men and one woman in what looked like an abandoned school. A couple of child-sized desks in the background, one of them with a jacket draped over it—a fatigue jacket or a uniform of some kind. The woman was held down on the floor, struggling, no shirt, short skirt hiked up. One man cut her breasts with a long knife. The woman screamed a long, high-pitched shriek through the speakers of the old television set. The man with the knife then thrust the knife into the woman's chest.

Jean-Claude stopped the video and asked me if that was what I was interested in.

"If you are, let me know. You're a friend of Bill's. I could let you have it for seventy-five thousand deutsche marks," he told me blithely.

It seemed that the currency of choice at the convention was deutsche marks. Seventy-five thousand deutsche marks was worth nearly 50,000 U.S. dollars.

"I am interested, Jean-Claude, very interested," I told him. I didn't have anywhere near that amount, or anywhere to get it. I wanted to play for time; if I could find out where he had gotten the tape, I could go right to the source.

Jean-Claude smiled. "Good, good. Why don't we—" He didn't finish. One of his toughs showed up at that moment and whispered something to him. He excused himself and went back to the kitchen.

"Ron, what about our deal? I can get you that for a lot cheaper," Bill said to me in an urgent whisper.

I turned to him. "What about our deal? The tape you got me last time was crap," I told him flatly. "It wasn't what I was looking for."

He looked me up and down for a quick second, and then shrugged, grinning. "Yeah, I know. But you know how things are. It was all I could get, and it was cheap, anyway. I didn't know you then, but I do now, right?"

He seemed almost desperate. In his mind I was about to hand over 75,000 deutsche marks, and he had played me for a sucker for less than $1,000.

I was known to Jean-Claude and seemed very much at home in the sordid atmosphere of the convention. I was now a real player in Bill's eyes, and Bill wanted to play.

"You can get me one like that?" I asked him.

"Yeah, sure. If that's what you want."

"And how's Don doing?" I asked—probing, pushing.

"Don's in the hospital. Got himself stuck with a knife," he told me simply.

"Oh, that's tough—what happened?" I asked.

"Well, Don's a good bloke, you know—but sometimes he talks too much. Maybe he talked too much to the wrong person; maybe he was just at the wrong place at the wrong time, right?" Bill told me, looking into my eyes. "You know how things happen," he added with a shrug. He expected me to know how it was. Don was a minor player and always would be. Bill and I, we understood each other.

Bill smiled at me and it occurred to me that somehow, someway, the next time we met, I would not be the one to be taken.

"Sure," I told him. "I know how things happen."

22 PROBLEMS

W**hat** the fuck happened to you guys?" I demanded loudly, scowling at Ako and Andreas in turn.

They sat side by side on the bed in my hotel room. Ako started to answer, and I cut him off with a wave of my hand.

"I mean, I hired you guys for a reason, and then there I am with no cover. What happened?"

"Yaron, I told you, we had car trouble," Ako began, looking miserable.

"Yeah, car trouble—shit! You made it to the airport! What happened then?"

"We lost him, we lost you—it's that simple. We had him out of the parking lot and then he was gone," Andreas said simply.

What could I say to that? I could see that they felt like hell about it, and I might've been generous and let it go, but I didn't feel like it. I stalked around the room for another twenty minutes demanding to know where they got the nerve to call themselves professionals. They took it with heads bowed a little. They sat there until I had almost growled myself hoarse.

And then Ako stood up.

182

"I'm sorry about what happened, Yaron. There's nothing I can do to change it. I'm sorry and Andreas is sorry. We fucked up," he said simply, holding his hands out, palms up.

"You're damn right you did. You fucked up big-time," I began. But it was Ako's turn to cut me off.

"I admit it, all right, but this yelling and shit is not going to change anything. If you want to continue working together, tell me. If not, there is nothing I can do about it," he told me.

I was shocked. Ako was proffering his resignation. He wasn't going to get off that easy, however.

I didn't apologize for blowing up. I felt that they deserved it, and it made me feel better, but I did have something for them to do.

"I'm afraid you're not off the hook quite yet—you owe me."

Ako stiffened for a moment and I thought he was going to tell me to go to hell. He wasn't used to getting treated like this. He was even less used to deserving it. He let out a big sigh then, and his large frame fell into itself a little as he relaxed. Whatever was coming, he was ready to take it.

"What can we do?" he asked.

I looked at him and then at Andreas. Andreas tried to smile at me to lighten the atmosphere a little, but the look in my eyes must've been enough to tell him that I was in no mood for his playfulness. His smile crashed to the floor, and I turned back to Ako.

"Here's what you can do . . . ," I began.

Four hours later they were on their way back to Germany.

I had two phone calls to Israel to make.

One of them was to Luke. He had worked on a story once, about two years before. Some of the details had come back to me at the château, and one of them in particular had gotten me very excited. I had to talk to him and check it out.

The other call I had to make was to Mikhal.

And she was not going to be happy with what I had to say.

The phone rang three times and a small voice spoke into the phone.

"Shalom."

"Enosh! It's your dad. How are you, my boy?"

It was my son, my ten-year-old, Enosh.

"Good, Dad. When are you coming home?" He got right to the point.

"Soon, my boy, soon. Are you being good?"

"Yeah, I got an A on my math test the other day. How soon is soon?"

"What?"

"How soon is soon? How soon are you coming home?"

"I'm coming home soon, Enosh! Don't question me. Where's your mother?" I barked.

There was a shocked silence on the other end. Enosh was not accustomed to being barked at.

"She's—she's outside," he stammered.

"Well, go and get her," I ordered him.

"OK, Dad. Dad, are you—" he began.

"Go and get your mother, Enosh, now!"

I heard a crash as the receiver on the other end hit the floor, and then a door slamming. I hadn't meant to be so harsh with him, but . . . I would make it up to him when I got home, I thought.

"Yaron?"

"Hi, Mike."

"What did you say to Enosh?" Mikhal demanded quietly.

"I told him to go and get you. Why, what did he say?"

"He said you were on the phone and then he burst into tears. What did you say to him?" she demanded again. I could tell that she was talking through clenched teeth, trying to control herself in front of the kids. This was not at all what I needed. As if I didn't have enough trouble.

"I didn't say anything to him, Mikhal. That kid's got to toughen up a little."

"What are you doing, Yaron?"

"I'm talking to you. What does it sound like I'm doing?" I asked flippantly.

Mikhal's voice became muffled. I heard her say something, but I couldn't make it out, then I heard loud and clear. "Yaron, I've sent the kids out of the room. Now you tell me what the hell you're doing and when you intend to stop this bullshit and come home."

Mikhal does not swear often. When she does, it is a very bad sign and one that I usually take extremely seriously. This time, however, it just made me mad.

"Is there a problem, Mikhal?" I asked, consciously keeping my voice level down.

"Yaron, I don't know what the hell is going on with you or why you are acting like this. Maybe you don't understand Hebrew anymore, so I'll say it very slowly. Yes, Yaron, there is a big problem. There is a problem with the kids not seeing their father and not knowing where he is. Enosh wanted to know when you were coming home because he had a nightmare about you walking around with your head cut off the other night—and then you yell at him on the phone? Are you crazy? There is a problem at the bank, where the manager is now asking when you can come in personally and speak to him about the overdrafts and how soon they are going to be remedied. There is a problem with me not knowing where you are and not knowing how I'm going to pay the bills and not knowing if you are even the same person, when you call and act like this! Are those big enough problems for you?" she finished, catching her breath.

I was stunned. I wanted to apologize and make everything all right, but before I could open my mouth, another feeling began to take over.

"Mikhal, I'm sorry that you are not happy right now, but how the fuck do you think I feel—"

"Don't speak to me like that, Yaron," Mikhal warned.

"I'll speak to you any damn way I want—you do; you just did. You tell the kids I'll be home when I get home. Tell them I'm OK."

"I can't tell them that again, Yaron."

"You tell them whatever the hell you want, then. And as for that fucker at the bank, you tell him he'll get his money, because that's what I'm doing out here, isn't it? I'm earning money. I'm making the money for the house and the schools and the food and every-fucking-thing else that you and the kids eat and wear and do and play with."

"I said don't talk to me like that, Yaron, I'll hang up!" Mikhal warned.

"Don't you hang up on me! You listen to me! I'm in the shit out here, and when I call you I want a little support. Why do I have to be the one that's got to hold things together? I'm out here doing something. I am onto something very big, and if you can't see that, I don't know how to make it any clearer!"

"You could call me and let me know, let us know, where you are and when you are coming back so we don't worry!"

"I don't have time to call you every damn day, Mikhal—I don't have time for that shit. What the fuck do you think I'm doing, going to parties every night or something?" I demanded.

There was a short silence, then, "I don't know what you are doing, Yaron. But if you say 'fuck' to me one more time, I am going to hang up."

"Don't you fucking dare hang up on me! I'm trying to talk to you now—"

Click.

I sat frozen for a few seconds listening to the dial tone. Then I slammed the receiver down on its cradle so hard I thought I was going to smash the phone to pieces. What the hell was going on? I had not meant our conversation to go like that at all. I love my wife—I love my kids. What the hell was wrong with them? Mikhal, Mike, couldn't she tell that I was under pressure here and didn't need that crap!

I put on my Walkman and went for a run, trying to sweat the anger out of me. While I ran, my favorite singer, Shlomo Artzi, sang one of his latest hits, a song called "Ambitions."

I returned to my hotel room and reached for the phone to call Mikhal back and patch things up. I dialed the number and then was surprised to hear an adult male voice answer the phone.

"Who the hell is this?" I demanded angrily.

"It's Luke. Who the hell is this?" he demanded back.

"Luke?"

"Yeah, who is this?"

"Luke, it's Yaron. I dialed your number by mistake," I told him.

"Shit, Yaron, I'd hate to be the guy you were trying to call. What's wrong with you?"

"Nothing's wrong with me," I insisted. What was wrong with everybody else?

"OK, nice talking to you," he said sarcastically, about to hang up.

"Wait, Luke, I was going to call you too. I need some information."

"About what?"

I took a deep breath—and I told him.

23 PETER

Club 44 was on the Left Bank. I checked the address against the one that I had gotten from Luke's contact, and approached the featureless burnished-metal door.

I raised my hand to press the buzzer when it swung open, revealing a very well dressed young Frenchman.

"Bon soir, monsieur. Est-ce que je peux vous aider?" (Good evening, may I help you?)

"I am here to see Peter," I told him in English.

He cocked his head at me, smiled, and shut the door.

What the hell?

I buzzed, got no answer, and buzzed again.

When the door did open again, the young Frenchman was gone, having been replaced by a hulking man in a suit, who glowered down at me.

"You want to see Peter?" he asked in slightly accented English.

"Yes, that's what I'm here for. Vasilis told me to come," I informed him.

He looked me up and down and then jerked his head. "Come."

188

I entered the 44 and was taken to a booth on the far side of an empty dance floor. The club did not open for another couple of hours, but there were people adjusting lights and wiping off tables. When I arrived at the booth, a man about my own height stood, smiling from ear to ear, and held out his hand. I reached out to shake, and a blast of dance music nearly knocked me off my feet. Peter—I could only assume that the man with whom I was shaking hands was Peter—scowled and barked something in the direction of the DJ booth across the room.

"Non, non, c'est bon, c'est fini!" the DJ, a young guy with dreadlocks, answered back, giving the thumbs-up.

Then Peter turned to me. "Mr. Smith, pleased to meet you. Have a seat," he offered in English, indicating a place next to him in the booth.

I sat down and looked around. "Nice place you picked to meet," I remarked.

"But that music, it gives me a headache. As soon as they open I leave. I don't know how they can stand it," he said. "Would you like something to drink?"

"Just a glass of water—that would be good," I told him.

Peter signaled over a young woman dressed in a body-hugging cat suit and spoke to her. As he did I looked at him and tried to put this man together with what I knew about the people he was involved with. He was Georgian mob, like Nisim Simantov; Russian mob, like the boys in the Russian bathhouse back in New York and like the man whom Luke had been kind enough to get me in touch with—Peter's boss in Israel, Vasilis. The waitress said something to Peter and he laughed and smiled at her, patting her arm with paternal tenderness.

The Russians were everywhere and into everything, and they were good at what they did and arrogant as hell, secure in the knowledge that they could not be touched—not easily, in any case. They are the richest and most modernly equipped and trained crime organization in history. They keep track of their worldwide investments by phone, fax, and Internet. They have no secret oaths or ceremonies. They own their own banks in Moscow and Kiev, and million-dollar apartments in London and Paris. They have gone global with the world economy. They cover their tracks efficiently and effectively. Their reach extends across countries and continents, and they are not afraid—not of anyone or anything. That was why they talked to Luke and why they talked to me.

The waitress went to get our drinks and Peter turned to me, about to say something. Then he slapped himself lightly on the forehead and drew his hand down his face. "Wait one moment, all right? One second?" he said, holding up a finger.

I nodded and he jumped up and raced through a door at the back of the room.

I barely noticed he was gone. When he had opened his mouth, I had seen the flash of a gold cap, and that tiny brilliant point of gleaming metal sent me years into my own past.

■ ■ ■ ■

I was a rookie. Before me on a chair sat a shabbily dressed recent immigrant to Israel. It was hard for me to believe that this man, this peasant in a stained sports coat and checkered slacks that were too short for him, was the mastermind of robberies that had set all of Israel on its ear. Over seventy synagogues had been robbed of ancient and extremely valuable religious artifacts. We knew he was the man who had done it, but he wasn't talking. He was not going to get out of that chair until I found out what I wanted to know. I sent my partner out of the room and stood over the guy.

He was cuffed to the chair. I was young and I was going to save Israel—Israel, which already had enough problems without him. I told him that he would talk to me if he ever wanted to talk to anybody again. I snapped his head back and stalked across the room.

And he started laughing at me. He opened his mouth wide and showed me all of his teeth. In the front his teeth were gold and silver. They shone in the glare of the fluorescent lights.

He said to me, "You think you are tough. You think you can scare me? You? My grandparents were killed by Nazis. My wife was sent to Siberia by Stalin. I spent ten years in a fucking camp in Siberia. They have broken every bone in my body—twice! And I'm still here! You can't break me!"

I had listened to him talk, hypnotized by his words and the glint of his gold teeth.

■ ■ ■ ■

Something was set down in front of me on the table. A glass of water. I looked up. The young waitress was leaning over me. She smiled and straightened up. She said something in French.

"Je ne parle pas français," I told her, sipping the water.

She pursed her lips. *"Moi non plus, alors,"* she said—me neither, then—and she walked away.

"I'm sorry about that. Something I forgot to take care of. Now, how much money did you say you needed?" Peter asked affably, sliding back into the booth.

I hadn't said. I wondered how many times his bones had been broken.

"One hundred and fifty thousand," I said calmly.

"No problem—you know the deal?"

I knew the deal.

■ ■ ■ ■

That night I drove north to hook back up with the Germans with 150,000 counterfeit dollars in the trunk of my car.

I had rented the money from the Russian mob. I had seventy-two hours to get it back to them. The price for using the counterfeit money was 2 percent of the total, plus penalties if I was late getting it back to them.

I didn't intend that to be a problem.

■ ■ ■ ■

About two hours out from the rendezvous point, the house of one of Ako's friends, I stopped for the night at a small hotel. I called Ako and asked him if he had been able to get together the "resources" that we needed. He assured me that he had. I told him to have them ready for me at eleven the next morning.

When I arrived the next morning, the resources that I had asked Ako and Andreas to gather for me were in the living room, sitting around chatting and smoking. There were sixteen of them, men and women in their twenties and early thirties. The men all seemed fit; a few of them looked like weight lifters, with bulging biceps shown off by sleeveless shirts. At least three of the guys were off-duty policemen. I didn't know which ones they were, but I had specifically requested that, and Ako had told me it would be no problem. The women were pretty, not like models or professionals, but pretty in an honest, open way.

Ako got their attention and told them to settle down, introducing me at the same time. They all sat there now looking at me, waiting to hear what I wanted from them. I felt like I had, years ago, when preparing to go on raids into Syria or Lebanon. I felt like I had when I was with the police—poised, ready for action, ready to give orders and see that they were carried out.

As I stood there, looking at the faces turned toward me, preparing the first words I would say to them, I realized that the gangsters that I had been dealing with must feel the same thing. They must get the same rush of power and control.

I had become the enemy.

"Ako, hast kein Bier mehr?"—no more beer?—a bearded apparition asked from the doorway to the kitchen.

With a couple of differences.

Ako said he didn't and told the guy to come in and sit down. The guy shrugged and sat cross-legged on the floor next to an attractive dark-haired woman. He whispered something to her. She looked at him, laughed, and elbowed him in the ribs.

A couple of very big differences.

I wasn't the godfather, and these people weren't gangsters, as far as I knew anyway. They were friends and acquaintances of Ako and Andreas. They had been promised free drinks and maybe a couple of bucks for participating in this wild thing that their crazy friend was planning.

It was a sobering thought.

"OK, everybody, hello. I'm Ron Smith, and I'm sure you all want to know what's going on—so let's get started, all right?"

They all nodded and relaxed, and I told them my plan. When the first hand went up with a question, I told them to save them. Unbelievably enough, the whole crowd of them were relatively attentive for the duration, listening quietly and taking in what I was saying.

When we broke, two hours later, for lunch, I was approached by one of the young women.

"Herr Smith?"

"Ja?" She was pretty. I found myself staring at her chest.

"Herr Svoray, was soll ich dann tragen?"—What should I wear?

I looked at her and smiled, wondering if anybody ever asked the godfather that.

24 BILL

Bill didn't come alone.

I pushed Andreas back into a corner. The Brit stood just inside the automatic doors of the arrivals terminal of the Frankfurt airport with a briefcase in one hand and two goons—one to the left, one to the right.

"OK, Andreas, you know what to do, right?"

He nodded, smiling. "I think I remember. I just did it last week," he said, his smile widening.

I wanted to scowl at him but I found myself grinning instead, which made me want to scowl even more. "All right—just don't fuck this one up," I ordered.

The smile left his face, and I strode forward to meet Bill Webster. I came at him arms wide, ready to embrace him in a huge hug. He wanted none of it. He stepped back, putting just enough distance between us, and held out his hand.

"Hello, Ron, how are you?" he asked.

"Couldn't be better—couldn't be better," I gushed, shaking the Brit's hand warmly.

There was nothing elegant about these guys; they were bruis-

194

ers, pure and simple—and they were there for one reason only, to make sure nothing happened to their boy.

"So listen, Bill, why don't your guys drive with Andy here, and you and I can go in my car so we can talk?" I suggested to Bill, taking him by the arm and leading him out of the terminal and into the parking lot.

He hesitated, glanced once again at his bodyguards and then back at me. "All right, then, if you say so," he agreed. He was nervous and he didn't agree willingly. But he was there to make $150,000 and to be introduced to the man, Ron Smith's man —their perverted German—who, of course, didn't exist. At that moment I held the cards, and he was ready to play what he was dealt.

I turned to Andreas. "Andy, you take care of Bill's guys, all right? We'll see you at the restaurant."

Andreas looked Bill's boys up and down, sniffed contemptuously, and spoke to me in German, assuring me that he would indeed take care of them.

"English, Andy, goddamnit," I told him.

"Whatever you say," Andreas said, looking at me like I had gone crazy.

"Good, all right, let's get going." I took Bill over to the sedan I had rented and watched his eyes pop out when a uniformed driver got out and opened the door for us. He looked at me and then the driver and then back at Andreas's car. I motioned for him to get in and he turned to me. "What the fuck is all this, then, mate?" he asked. I could tell he wasn't sure what to make of "all this" but he was impressed.

"This is business—just business," I told him, sliding into the backseat beside him. The driver closed the door behind me, got into the front seat, and started the engine.

We drove out of the parking lot and I glanced behind us. Andreas was right there, one car back.

Well, he had to make it look good, I thought.

My driver was supposed to take the scenic route until Andreas made his move. Then he was to head straight for the restaurant.

"Where are we going?" Bill asked finally as we looped a roundabout for the second time.

"We're going to a meeting and we don't want any uninvited guests, you know what I mean?" I told him, winking.

"Right," he said, sinking back into his seat, not wholly reassured.

Meanwhile I told Bill what to expect from our perverted German, glancing through the rear window from time to time to see if Andreas was still there.

He was. Dammit.

I told Bill anecdotes about our German's sick and twisted sexual tastes—little girls, little boys, dead, alive, dismembered. I told him things that made me sick to say, and all the while he nodded, eyes wide, laughing when I laughed, and glancing at his watch.

Finally I looked once again through the rear window and breathed a sigh of relief.

Andreas had finally lost us. What the hell had taken him so long?

Bill turned and looked through the window with me. "Where's the other car?" he asked, more than a little concerned.

"Bill, they're doing what we're doing, making sure that there are no tagalongs, OK? So, relax, we're almost there."

"Good, all right, as long as we're almost there—I'm gettin' fuckin' sick of sittin' in 'is car, right," he announced.

"*Sind wir fast dort?*" I asked the driver, leaning forward. Are we almost there?

"*Ja, ja—ein viertel, nicht mehr.*"

I turned to Bill. "Relax, we'll be there in fifteen minutes," I told him.

■ ■ ■ ■

Fifteen minutes turned into thirty-five, and we arrived at the restaurant one hour and eleven minutes after leaving the airport. Not bad for a drive that usually took no more than forty-five. Bill was really starting to sweat, and that was exactly what I wanted. By the time we reached our destination I wanted him eager to get the business over with and be on his way, glad to be going.

Not that there was any real business to be done that day anyway.

The driver pulled our car off the road and we bounced down a gravel driveway that wound lazily through the pines. The day was spectacular, sunny and unseasonably mild. The scent of the trees reached into the car even with the windows closed, and the sun flashed off and on like Morse code as we drove into shadow and back out again.

After about a quarter mile, the driveway opened onto a parking area that fronted the restaurant, a typically German affair of split beams and sharply slanted roofs, overlooking a valley spread out like a postcard scene in the distance.

There were three cars in the parking area. Andreas's sedan was not one of them. Bill asked me what was going on with his guys and I told him not to worry. Andy was good—he would be there.

■ ■ ■ ■

One of our guys stood by the door, massive arms folded across an equally massive chest. He was our designated bouncer, charged with the task of keeping any prying eyes away from the place until we had conducted our business.

Things looked right, and I felt good as I got out of the car on my side and felt my heel grind into the gravel as I placed it on solid ground. We had the restaurant for three hours—more than enough time. It was filled with my people, all of whom knew their parts and were ready to play them. More of my people waited offstage, so to speak, tensed and ready for the denoument, which would see me with a snuff film and the Russian money and Bill on his way back to England never knowing what had hit him. This was my show, and everything that would happen from there on in had been orchestrated by me.

That's when the first limousine arrived, followed by a second and then a third.

We were just about to walk through the front door. Bill spun on his heel as the long black cars threw dust and gravel into the air before grinding to a halt at three different ends of the parking area. These were not my limousines, and they were definitely not part of the plan. Bill looked at me and I looked at the bouncer. At that point, the owner of the restaurant came out, and without a word to me, headed, with a huge smile on his face, for the nearest limo. I signaled the bouncer. He stepped forward, hauling the owner of the restaurant around to face me.

"*Ahhh, Herr Smith—alles ist vorbereitet*"—everything is ready—he began, ducking his head and glancing at the limo door as it opened, revealing a white-shoed and stockinged leg.

I nodded at Bill and took the owner aside. "We had an arrangement," I said as calmly as I could in my best German. "Three hours—nobody else. You were paid very well. What are these limos doing here?" I demanded, my voice flat. Bill didn't speak German, and he kept looking at me and then at the limos, shifting his briefcase from hand to hand nervously.

"But, Herr Smith, you paid for the inside—and it is yours, for three hours. This party is here for the outside. A wedding. I don't see a problem. Go in and enjoy yourself. I am at your disposal." He straightened his jacket and walked purposefully to the first limo, where a plumpish young woman with very red cheeks was standing—wobbling might've been a better word; she seemed extremely drunk—in a voluminous wedding gown, surrounded by more plumpish, red-cheeked people, all in formal dress.

"What the hell is going on?" Bill asked me.

"It's a wedding," I told him, rubbing my hands together. "Isn't love beautiful?"

Bill cocked his head at me. I smiled and gestured for him to go in before me. He glanced back at the wedding party assembling for a photograph, and walked into the restaurant.

I glanced back once too. But I had eyes only for the owner of the restaurant as he bobbed and wove obsequiously among the wedding guests, shaking hands and indicating that the garden behind the restaurant was at their disposal.

Double-crossing son of a bitch.

■ ■ ■ ■

We went in and ordered something to drink: a mineral water and a beer. Bill's eyes never rested in one place but were continually shooting around the room as he drank his thick, sour beer almost compulsively, wiping his lips with a napkin after each swig.

Then Ako arrived with a briefcase. He strode into the room, towering over almost everyone there, his face hard and unreadable. He had on a business suit that fit him perfectly and only made him seem more impressive.

Bill recognized him instantly from our encounter in London and jerked his head in Ako's direction as he came on.

He arrived at our table. Without intoductions of any kind, Ako told me that the German was not coming.

"Was meinst Du—er kommt nicht?"—what do you mean, he is not coming?—I demanded, half rising from my chair.

"He could not be here and he wishes me to convey his apologies. However, I am empowered to do business in his name. I, however—"

"What the fuck—what is going on here, Ron? What's he saying?" Bill demanded.

"The German's not coming," I told Bill simply.

Bill did not react. He was not happy about it, but I am sure that this was not the first time something like this had happened to him. He scratched his chin and looked at Ako, his blue eyes cold and calculating.

"Is that it?" he asked.

"No. Ako is here to deal for him, but I don't like it; this is not how we do business. I say we get out of here and come back when the German is ready to deal himself." I stood up and rattled off some nonsense to Ako about doing things the right way. Bill did not stand but stayed in his seat with his briefcase in his lap, looking from me to Ako, his jaw muscles tightening and relaxing and his Adam's apple bobbing in his throat.

"Wait, Ron. What's the difference if it's this bloke or his boss, right? We can do business. I mean, fu—" Bill stopped himself in midoath, glancing at Ako.

"You can say whatever you want in front of him. Sometimes I wonder if he is even human," I informed Bill.

Bill smiled, more for show than anything else. It was not very convincing. "All right, let's do business, then. I didn't come all this way to go home empty handed."

"All right, if you say so, Bill. But to me it's a matter of respect. When I go to have a meeting with someone, I expect them to be there," I said. Then I turned to Ako and told him the same thing. Ako stiffened, rumbled something about that being all right with him, and turned to walk away.

Bill became frantic when he saw that whatever I had said to Ako was pushing him out the door. "What the fuck are you doing, Ron? Get him back here." He leaned closer to me and whispered. "That's $150,000 we're talking about. Don't bollix this up, right?"

"OK, I'll see what I can do—but I'm doing this for you. To me this is bullshit," I told him.

"Right, do it for me—I'll return the favor sometime," he assured me, wiping his lips and looking after Ako's back.

I got up and intercepted Ako before he reached the door. I told him that things were going perfectly. He made a show of not wanting to return to the table. I waved my hands and nodded in a great show for Bill, and finally Ako nodded once, curtly, and turned to look at Bill.

At that moment, a commotion erupted from a doorway leading to the deck where the wedding party was, and three florid, drunken men in rented tuxedoes barged in. One of them had just had an argument with some unnamed person outside. He threatened and complained while the other two held him steady and tried to calm him down.

As we stood there the owner emerged from the same door and tried to hustle them back out, which he finally did, giving me an apologetic shrug right before he disappeared back out the door. The other patrons of the restaurant—our people— looked at one another and chuckled before going back to their meals and conversations. I led Ako back over to our table and got him a chair.

He sat down and glared at Bill, who smiled back. "You speak English?" the Brit asked affably.

Ako nodded silently.

"So, give him the film, Bill, and let's get out of here," I said to the Brit.

Bill looked at me inquisitively. "Something wrong?" he asked.

"No, nothing really. I just don't like doing business like this. Just make the trade and let's get out of here."

Bill nodded and slid back the catches on his briefcase. It

clicked open; he reached inside and drew out a videocassette in a black cardboard box.

Ako reached out for it and Bill drew it back, shaking his head. "No, no, let's see the money first," he said.

Ako glared at Bill a moment longer and then reached under the table and brought up his own briefcase and laid it on the table.

Bill looked at it and then back at Ako. "All right, looks good to me." He slid the video across the table.

Loud female voices speaking German. It was the bride this time, crying in the arms of an older woman just inside the door.

Ako slid the briefcase toward Bill.

"Now we can go," he said to me. "Nice doing business with you," he added to Ako.

Ako grunted.

Suddenly, the door was kicked in.

"*Stehenbleiben!*"—everyone freeze!

One of our guys, with more behind him, leveled his gun at the room and crouched low.

And all hell broke loose.

Tables and chairs went flying in every direction. Tires squealed outside as more of our guys poured into the restaurant, dressed in borrowed police uniforms. I was grabbed from behind and thrown roughly to the ground with a gun pointed at my head. Out of the corner of my eye I could see that Bill was getting the same treatment. Ako, on the other hand, was fighting like an animal. He yelled and lashed out with his foot, but one of our "police" caught him from behind with a kick to the small of his back—and he went down.

I tried to get up and got cracked in the side of the head with a gun butt for my trouble. I was screaming for whoever it was to get off me—that I was not German. I got slapped again and my hands were cuffed tightly behind my back.

The whole time there had been one sound rising above all the crashes and yelling. The bride and her friend were screaming at the top of their lungs.

Ain't love grand?

One of our guys finally approached the terrified women, told them that this was police business, and hustled them outside.

At the same time another one of our guys was standing over Ako and Bill and myself screaming at us that we were drug dealers and that we were under arrest. He then pulled out an official-looking document and waved it in our faces.

This whole time Bill had been silent. I managed to get a look at him out of the corner of my eye. His face was tight lipped and frozen, his eyes half closed as they swiveled in their sockets. He definitely knew his business. Only TV robbers react when the cops finally close in. The real thing just goes cold and silent and waits it out.

"Ako, what is this?" I cried at the German as he was hauled onto his feet by two uniforms.

"Don't worry, these assholes—" he began. Then a fist landed in his stomach and another in his kidneys, and he doubled over.

"Who are you?" I screamed at the top of my lungs as I was hauled on to my feet in turn.

"*Polizei, Arschloch!*"—police, asshole! he screamed back at me, smacking me again for good measure.

"Ron, what's this?" Bill demanded.

The "cops" turned me to face Bill for one second, and I glared at him. "I don't know—do you?" I spit at him.

"Shit, no, Ron," he gasped out, struggling in the grip of two policemen of his own.

"Better not!" I yelled over my shoulder as I was dragged outside.

Ako and Bill and I were then thrown unceremoniously into three separate cars and driven off to our separate fates.

■ ■ ■ ■

All right, get these cuffs off of me!" I wailed miserably. I was beginning to lose all sensation in my hands as they swelled around the metal and my circulation was cut off.

We were parked on the side of the road about ten minutes from the restaurant.

My driver, a young off-duty police officer, shrugged and looked at me sympathetically. "I don't have the keys. They're back at the restaurant," he told me.

I couldn't believe it. My hands felt like they were going to fall off. My driver, whose name was Zack, smoked cigarettes and tried to talk to me about how everything had gone. I couldn't concentrate. The pain in my hands was excruciating. I tried to think about how well everything had gone and take my mind off the pain, but it was no use. All I could think about was my hands swelling into enormous hand-shaped purple balloons and popping.

That was all I could think about until I heard the sirens.

Zack and I heard them at the same time. I was standing a little ways off from the car, pacing back and forth in the tall weeds at the side of the road. We looked up and our eyes met. The sirens grew louder. They were definitely headed our way. Zack shot behind the wheel, and the engine of our black Mercedes roared to life. I yelled at him to calm down, but it was no use. His being a policeman, and the idea that he might get caught playing around at cops and robbers in his off time, made him reckless. He gunned the engine again and waved, yelling for me to get in the car. I didn't want to get left on the side of the road in Germany with handcuffed hands looking like grapefruits trailing along behind me, so I jumped into the passenger seat and we took off just as the cops came flying down the road in the opposite direction—obviously headed toward the restaurant.

Not the best way to make an exit.

Luckily, Zack had been raised in the neighborhood and knew every nook and cranny for miles around. He was a fantastic driver as well, and only once, when we were nearly creamed by a tractor trailer as we ran a red light, did I worry.

We seemed to drive in every direction at once, speeding forward, looping back, cutting across fields, and jumping intersections, until finally we ended up on a service road under a bridge. Zack pulled the car in, jumped out, and stood by the door, scanning the area for any sign of pursuit, pulling nervously on a black tobacco cigarette.

I stayed in the car. My hands were throbbing horribly, shooting fire up my arms. Two images kept recurring and flashing across the inside of my eyelids as I sat there. One was of my tortured hands and the other was of the plump bride's face when our guys had knocked in the door, guns drawn. I laughed weakly at the memory of her huge, cowlike eyes and red cheeks.

Something to tell the grandkids, at least, I thought.

Then I yelled at the top of my lungs.

"Get these fucking cuffs off my hands!!!"

25 STUNG

I thought those guys were going to kill me—or try, anyway. I almost drove them all the way to Berlin," Andreas said with just a touch of pride.

The core team was gathered back at Ako's friend's house. My hands were still an angry purplish red and swollen around a crease where the cuffs had been until the key had finally been located and they had been removed, almost an hour and a half after they had been put on.

I sat in a large leather recliner listening to how the rest of the operation had panned out while I had been under the bridge with Zack, watching my hands inflate.

Andreas had driven Bill's boys around for nearly an hour and forty-five minutes, responding to their increasingly threatening inquiries about where they were going and how long it was going to take to get there by telling them that he thought they were being followed and he had to be careful.

That worked for about an hour. After that they had begun discussing what they would do to Andreas if he did not reunite them with their boss as soon as possible. Andreas argued with

206

them, stalled a little more, and then took them to the restaurant.

In the meantime, the police cars that had burned by Zack and me had arrived at the restaurant, responding to the desperate pleas of a Bavarian wedding party that had been interrupted by guns being drawn in the main dining room of the restaurant they had rented for their reception.

By the time Andreas arrived at the restaurant with Bill's muscle in the backseat, the place was overrun with German national police and extremely angry wedding guests.

Needless to say, as far as Bill's gangsters were concerned, Andreas's feigned caution was instantly legitimized. And by the time he dropped the three men off at the train station in town, they were thankful.

"They actually thanked me and told me to visit them in London—gave me their home numbers, everything," Andreas concluded that portion of his report. He had come back in for a very important role a little later on, but that would have to wait.

Next I wanted to hear from Udo, our "chief of police." The strapping blond man smiled and told me how, according to plan, they had thrown Bill in the back of the car and started away from the restaurant. The whole time, Bill had been repeating that he was a British citizen. Udo and his partner stopped the car a kilometer from the restaurant, had a short conference in German, and then demanded to see Bill's papers.

They looked at his passport, rifled through his wallet, looked at each other, and shook their heads.

Fifteen minutes later, right on schedule, Bill was walking down the road, having just been tossed out of a German unmarked police car. He was not whom they were after, and they wouldn't waste their time on him, they said, unless he ever showed his face in that part of Germany or anywhere in Germany ever again. They gave him his wallet back but kept his passport until they were about fifty meters down the road, when they flung it contemptuously into the dirt at the edge of the blacktop.

And that's where Andreas had found Bill as he returned from dropping Bill's men off at the train station. He pulled over and motioned a very shaken Bill into the car just as a couple of cruisers came up the road, heading away from the restaurant.

Andreas offered the Brit a ride to the airport, telling him that he had just dropped his men off at the train station and was on his way back to find out what had happened.

"I didn't say anything else to him until we got to the airport," Andreas added. "Then I let him have it!"

Andreas told Bill that he hoped I wasn't too mad at him but that the cops showing up at the restaurant could cause big trouble for a lot of people. Bill protested that he had had nothing to do with that, but Andreas just shrugged and told him that as far as he knew, nobody had had any trouble before Bill came along—and it didn't look good. He told him, in effect, what I had told him as I was being dragged out of the restaurant —that he would hear from me. Then Andreas wished Bill a pleasant trip back to England and left him waiting for his plane. As he walked away he glanced back once to see the Englishman drop into a chair and put his head in his hands.

I nodded appreciatively. Everything had gone according to plan, except, of course, for the wedding party and the cops showing up. Neither of those two unplanned events had had any real effect on the end result, however. I had the money and I had the video. Bill was back in England by then, wondering what in the hell had happened and whether I might really be able to do anything about it.

There was only one thing left to do.

We had to look at the film.

I gave Udo some extra deutsche marks for a job well done and sent him on his way. I was broke, completely tapped out. But it had been worth it.

That left three of us, myself, Ako, and Andreas.

Andreas poured out small glasses of amber liquor for Ako and himself as Ako took the tape and inserted it into the VCR. They toasted and drank. They were celebrating the success of the operation. It was hard for me to join in their mutual congratulations and backslapping. I was extremely pleased that the operation had come off so well. If what I thought was on that video was really there, however . . .

It wasn't. The video showed more hard-core S&M, but this time it didn't even come close. That fucker Bill had gotten me again. I sat stock still in my chair.

"Ako, do me a favor and turn that shit off," I said in a low voice.

He looked at me and reached out obligingly, tapping the stop button on the VCR.

"Yaron, how could you know?" Andreas asked.

I didn't answer him. I sat motionless, silently processing the fact that all of my planning had come to nothing because a two-bit gangster had outsmarted me again. There was one bright spot. I hadn't paid for the piece of crap. Bill and I had scammed each other. I began to relax. I had steeled myself to relive the horror of the film I had seen in Germany, and I realized that the disappointment that I felt at not having gotten what I wanted was tempered with more than a little relief that I would not watch the murder of an innocent that night.

And I had given one asshole a real run for his money.

"Fuck him," I said out loud, smiling at the Germans, who had sat quietly, who knew me, who were my friends, and who had given me the time I needed to sort things out.

"Fuck him," I said again. Ako and Andreas smiled back at me and clinked glasses.

"Fuck 'em all."

■ ■ ■ ■

It was six hours from Cologne to Paris. I stopped three times to fill the car with gas, once to go to the bathroom when I began squirming so much that I thought I might drive off the road, and once to make a phone call.

"Mikhali, it's me, Yaron!" I said when she answered the phone.

"I know, I recognized your voice," she responded in a monotone.

"Mikhal, I—I'm sorry for being such a shit the other night on the phone. I don't know what happened, I'm just—I'm sorry," I concluded lamely.

"Don't 'sorry' me, Yaron. We have to talk about this. This cannot continue."

"I know, I know, but I can't talk right now," I told her, watching the cars speed along the autobahn and smelling the exhaust-filled air.

"Why not?" she asked.

"Truthfully, Mikhali, I'm at a gas station just off the autobahn, right before the French border—and I don't think I have enough change."

Silence.

"Where are you going now?" she asked.

"I'm going to Paris," I told her simply.

She didn't ask why I was going there; she asked only if I knew where I was going to stay.

"No—I mean, yeah, the Métropole, the one we stayed in last time we were there," I told her. "Why?"

"Because I need to know what to tell the cabdriver," she said.

"What?" I asked.

"I'm coming to Paris, Yaron. I'm coming to talk to you. If you like being married to me, you give me a room number as soon as you get one."

"But, Mikhal, the sting went over like clockwork. I'm coming home," I told her.

"Did you get one?"

"No, I got taken again."

"So, what are you so happy about?"

"Because I took him back. He tried to screw me, and I screwed him right back. It was beautiful; you should've been there, Mikhali. Now I know what I can do. I can do it again!" I told her excitedly.

"So, what does that mean to me, exactly?" she asked skeptically.

"It means that you don't have to come here, I'm coming home! I have about five minutes' worth of business to do in Paris, and then I'm on my way. I need to plan my next move. I need to think a little. I need to see you and the kids!"

"Don't sound so happy about coming home. We have a lot to talk about, you and me," she told me.

I gazed out at the autobahn again. A Trabi, one of the ridiculous-looking cars East Germany had produced for the decades before the Berlin Wall came down, was smoking and chuffing its way along the wide, crowded highway. The Trabi changed lanes suddenly, and a silver Mercedes, doing at least 160 clicks an hour, had to swerve around it dangerously in a squeal of rubber on blacktop to avoid rolling over the top of the ugly, unstoppable little car. The Trabi never seemed to notice.

"Yaron, did you hear me?"

"Yes, Mikhal, good—I can't wait to see you," I told her.

"Maybe, maybe not. Wait till you hear what I have to say. I'll talk to you soon. Good-bye," she said. She hung up.

∎ ∎ ∎ ∎

I met Peter again at the 44 and gave him back his money plus the rental fee. He asked me if my business had gone well and I told him that it had gone very well.

He smiled. He was glad when people he worked with did good business, he told me.

I shook hands with him and was about to leave when he asked me about red clay. Could I move some? He reminded me that I had spoken to an associate of his in Tel Aviv and I had told him that I could.

I wracked my brain. Red clay. An associate of his in Tel Aviv. Red clay.

Nisim Simantov—red clay . . .

Shit.

"Yes, yes, of course, no problem," I told him. All I had to do was get out of there.

"That's very good, very good," he told me.

He asked me when we could speak about it, and I told him that I would be leaving Paris but that I would put some people in touch with him.

"But I don't want to deal with 'people,' Ron, I want to deal with *you*."

I told him that was OK. I would take another flight. I told him that I would contact him the next day—day after, at the latest. No problem.

We shook hands and I left.

I had no intention of ever speaking to Peter again.

∎ ∎ ∎ ∎

I checked into the Métropole and took a shower. I stayed under the scalding water for at least an hour. I felt better afterward.

I called the airlines and made a reservation on a flight back to Israel.

When I got home, it didn't take me long to realize that whatever my next move was going to be, it wasn't going to be soon. I took some speaking engagements to pay the bills that were all long overdue, and enjoyed putting my children to bed and sitting up late at night with my wife, talking about nothing at all. I didn't forget about the investigation, and sometimes I would take time out from the comfortable domesticity that I had fallen into to map out plans for a new sting. More often than not, however, I would get interrupted by one of the kids and I would put my half-thought-out plans away for another time while I soothed away a bad dream.

My dreams of the little girl did not return immediately. I was glad of that. I had a real sense that I had done what I could up to that point. I took a little time to breathe.

In the meantime, a movie of my first book was being made. We got calls from time to time. None of it seemed real except the money that I received. Then, suddenly, it was done, and we got a call inviting us to the premiere.

That's where I met Robert De Niro.

26 ROBERT DE NIRO

De Niro told me that he had been working on a script that had something to do with snuff films but that he was having trouble making it work. He wanted to know if I could show him some films.

Then he told me that he might be interested in my story.

As I spoke to him, two thoughts were uppermost in my mind: one, if I could show this very public figure that what he was talking about so casually was real, it might blow the lid off the investigation; two, if I could really get him interested, maybe I could sell my story to him.

My family had to eat, right?

He asked me again if I could show him something.

I told him that I could indeed show him some films, but that the films he was talking about, real "slice and dice," were things that once seen could not be unseen. I didn't bother to add that I knew because I had been trying for years.

He assured me that he had seen more than his share of tragic human evil in his long career as an actor. He told me about preparing for roles by submerging himself in the attitudes and contexts of the characters he was taking on. He then reminded me of some of the roles he had played.

It's called method acting.

I told him that it would cost money. We didn't have to buy the film, but even setting up a viewing would cost money.

He told me that I would be reimbursed.

We agreed to meet in Paris.

Mikhal was not happy.

"But, Mikhali, it's Robert De Niro—the movie star!" I told her.

"But you said you were finished for a while."

"Yeah, I know, but—Robert De Niro," I said, invoking his name like some mystical chant.

"So what do you expect him to do?"

"Mikhal, can you imagine what might happen if Robert De Niro came out and said he had seen a snuff film, that they existed? Who would argue with him? Nobody, that's who. If I could get him behind this thing, there's no telling where it could go."

"Is that really why you're so excited, because you think he could help you?" she asked. I wasn't sure what she was getting at. I had an answer for her, however.

"There's that, and there's also the fact that he's looking for material for a script he's writing. If he picked my story up—we could be set, Mikhal, set!"

"Is he really interested?"

"He wants to see the films, doesn't he?"

"What about this other thing he's working on?"

"I don't know. It's some script. But it's fiction; it's got to be bullshit. This is the real thing. I'm real, the story's real. How could it compare?"

"I don't know," she told me. "But I guess you have to check it out."

"You're right, I do. This'll be good, real good. I'll let you know what's going on as soon as I do," I told her.

■ ■ ■ ■

The plan was simple. First I would get Ako and Andreas and some of their best guys down to Paris for a two-tier cover job involving Ako, Robert, and myself as an inner circle, with Andreas coordinating the movements of a loose outer circle, the rest of the team. Once I had that set up, I would go back to Peter for some more counterfeit bills to use as show-me money for the viewing. I was a little uncomfortable about going back to Peter after promising to get back to him about the red clay business. It would be only a couple of days later by that time, however, so I felt that I was still within the limit of bullshit-hustler timing.

As for the viewing itself, I would contact Jean-Claude, the Algerian who had organized the convention of hard-core that I had attended a couple of weeks earlier. The last time I had seen him was when I left the convention. I had told him that the next time we met, I would be ready to deal. I had dealt with Bill instead. As with Peter, I felt that I had to be careful dealing with Jean-Claude. He would not enjoy being disappointed a second time. This time it would not be me, however, who was disappointing him. It would be my client, Robert. He would say he did not like the film and did not want it. I would placate Jean-Claude with a little of Robert's money. Game over.

So far, so good. All I would have to do then was return the money to Peter, book a flight to Israel, wait for Robert to call, and watch the world go crazy when he broke the story.

Simple. I would be home in two or three days, tops.

This is how it worked out . . .

It took Robert a week to get to Paris. Ako could not get his best guys; they were all working and were not available. I told him to do the best he could. I could not get hold of Jean-Claude; he was out of the country. After a series of phone calls back and forth, I tried to convince one of his subordinates to show me a film. He sounded nervous, and I began to get a bad feeling.

Peter was not available, either. I went back to the 44 and ended up speaking to someone who told me he was Peter's partner. I told him what I needed and he told me that that was not possible without Peter's OK.

Things were not going well.

Robert's assistant called and told me Robert would be coming in soon, but she wasn't sure when, exactly.

Nothing was working out the way it should have, and my bad feeling kept getting worse.

What with conversations with Peter's so-called partner and with Jean-Claude's second, phone calls to Ako trying to pin him down, and wondering when Robert thought he might be coming in, I began to seriously rethink the whole thing.

The time was not right. I was not right. I began to question my motives. Was I doing this as a valid part of the investigation, or because I was starstruck? I told myself that Robert De Niro could, if he so chose, bring much more attention to bear on the subject of the investigation than I ever could. His name alone could transform it from a thirty-second bite into a worldwide sensation.

But something was definitely wrong.

I admitted to myself that I was starstruck. But, I told myself, who would not be? Besides, it was absolutely true that Robert De Niro could push the investigation into overdrive. But . . .

I wrestled with little voices in the back of my head even as I continued to try to put something together.

During one conversation with Robert's assistant, I blew up. Did Robert have any idea what was going on? Did he realize what I was going through trying to arrange this thing, and he couldn't even pin down an arrival date! The assistant apologized and said they were working on it.

Afterward, I was on the verge of calling the whole thing off. Unfortunately for me, that's exactly when everything started to come together.

Ako had found some guys. They weren't the best, they were inexperienced and young, but they were eager. He could be down as soon as I needed him. I got a call from Jean-Claude's guy and he told me he could show me something. I asked him if he had spoken to Jean-Claude and he told me not to worry about it. Peter's partner called. I could have the money, $85,000 for 2 percent for three hours—beginning from the moment I left the 44 with it.

Then Robert's assistant called to inform me that Robert would be there the next day.

I still had time to call the whole thing off.

■ ■ ■ ■

We're going to meet their guy in the Tuileries. He's got a white hat, I've got a white hat. He's going to take us to the hotel. The tape is in a safety deposit box there. We take the tape up. We watch it. We go back down. You tell him you didn't like it—and we're out of there."

Robert De Niro, one of the princes of Hollywood, nodded slowly, his eyes half closed.

Ako and I sat with Robert and a friend of his I will call Paul in Robert's suite. Robert sat back in an overstuffed, finely upholstered chair, his hands clasped in front of his face, his legs crossed casually, two inches of white, black-haired skin showing between the cuff of his pants and the top of his black sock.

Paul wore loafers with no socks.

It was hard not to think of the movies Robert had been in. It was almost eerie to sit there with a face that was so well known to me and yet utterly strange. I didn't know Robert De Niro, and yet I did—birthmark; piercing, dark eyes; longish, mobile face—at least as well as millions of other people.

It is unsettling, the power of celebrity.

Robert De Niro had a maid assigned to his suite, a palatial and overwhelming cluster of rooms at the top of one of the best hotels in Paris. The rooms gleamed with gold fixtures. They were padded with plush carpet and lit by delicate lamps that cast warm pools of light over the subtle, calming patterns of the wallpaper. There was a balcony that looked out over the city, which belonged as much to Robert De Niro as Los Angeles or New York or Oslo.

Hollywood does not recognize international boundaries.

Robert turned and asked Paul what he thought. If being face-to-face with Robert De Niro was unsettling, Paul made me feel more at home.

I knew Paul's type intimately.

Paul laughed when Robert laughed. He nodded when Robert nodded, and looked serious when Robert raised some point that he considered important. He didn't seem to have any opinions beyond those voiced by Robert.

Robert asked me if he was going to meet Jean-Claude. I told him that he might come and he might not.

He nodded again and then said something to Paul that I didn't catch. Robert and his friend had the disturbing habit of throwing bits and pieces of information back and forth in some half-whispered slang of their own, regardless of the presence of others. At times they reminded me of nothing more than teenage girls, self-consciously and coyly secretive before strangers.

Robert asked me if Paul could come.

I wanted to say no. I don't know why I didn't. That had not been part of our deal—we were not going to the Louvre, and

Jean-Claude's guy, whomever I was dealing with, would not appreciate being treated as a tourist attraction.

On the other hand, I got the distinct feeling that if his friend was not allowed to come, Robert might think twice about coming himself.

I told Paul that if he thought he could take it, he was welcome.

Robert laughed, the same sound I had heard at the movies dozens of times, his eyes gleaming. He stood and announced to everyone present that Paul could take it. Paul stood then, laughed, and got himself a drink.

"I think I can take it, Yaron," he assured me somewhat smugly.

I was already dealing with a handful of unknowns. How much difference could one more make?

Ako and I left.

When we got outside, Ako asked me what was bothering me.

"Nothing, nothing for you to worry about—you just take care of your end, all right?"

He looked at me and nodded, not quite satisfied.

I had never kept him in the dark. He knew I was holding something back.

"Everything went all right with Jean-Claude?" he asked me.

"Yeah, everything's fine. Go back to your hotel and make sure your guys get a good night's sleep," I told him.

I went to my hotel and tried to do the same.

■ ■ ■ ■

It was pouring rain. I had three hours to get Peter's money back to him, and Peter's partner had told me that, as added protection, he had detailed some of his men to keep an eye on me.

Everyone else had their eyes on Robert. Men and women

passing through the Tuileries turned and stared when they caught sight of him, wondering whether it was really him or not. He had affected a slight disguise, dark glasses and a wide-brimmed hat. It was unmistakably Robert De Niro, however.

After about twenty minutes I spotted a guy with a white cap: early twenties, dark hair, black eyes.

It was quite a relief. Not only did I want to get this whole thing over with; I felt that if we stayed there much longer, we would have to call out crowd control. People had begun to stop. They stood in the rain, singly or in small groups, trying to look nonchalant about staring at Robert De Niro.

Nothing like going undercover with one of the world's most beloved stars of the silver screen.

I approached the guy with the hat, motioning for the others to come up behind me. Our contact did not introduce himself. He simply looked us over, hesitating for a moment at Robert, and then led us to a car.

I was sure that the guy had recognized Robert. I was sure also that, at least outwardly, he couldn't have cared less. Neither Jean-Claude nor the guys who worked for him would ever allow themselves to be starstruck. They would never admit to themselves that there was anyone on the planet more important than themselves.

We were driven to the Novotel in Les Halles. Once inside the lobby, our contact told me to go look on the message board, pointed at his watch, and informed me that we had no more than twenty minutes.

That suited me fine.

I went to the message board, saw an envelope with the name Ron Smith on it, opened it, and found a key. I gave it to the concierge and told him to bring me back the box.

He did. When I opened it, I found a video cassette inside.

Our contact then led us into the elevator.

■ ■ ■ ■

The first thing Ako did upon entering the hotel room was to cock and load a pistol that he had pulled from the small of his back once the door was locked.

The small *click* of a bullet falling into the chamber of a gun is a sound that gets attention. Ako was telling all present that if there was any action, he was ready.

Our contact seemed unfazed. Robert and Paul sent questioning looks at each other. I glanced at my watch.

The video started. Ako, Robert, and Paul stared at the monitor as a woman was dismembered alive.

At the end of the first clip, I asked Robert what he thought. He said that it was shit. I said, "OK, then. Yeah, this is shit. Let's get out of here," expecting Robert to take my lead. To my surprise he shook his head. He told me to settle down; maybe there was something coming up that we would like.

I could only look at him. He told me to settle down again. Paul glanced at me. With a blithe wave of his manicured hand, he too told me to settle down.

Settle down?

I looked at my watch.

I had to get out of there. The longer we stayed, the more likely was it that whomever I was dealing with, whoever was going behind Jean-Claude's back, would think that they had a sale.

And I had to get the money back.

I left the room and I don't think anyone noticed except our contact. He eyed me frankly as I backed to the door and signaled that I was going out.

I went down to the lobby. I hoped to accomplish two things. I wanted to get some air in my lungs and calm myself before we refused the video completely and had to deal with whatever came next. I also wanted to see if I could spot whoever it was that our contact was working for.

I went out onto the sidewalk and looked around. I didn't see anybody who looked likely. Nor did I see any sign of Andreas and the other team members, which was good. I looked around a little longer to see if I could spot whoever it was Peter's partner had sent after me. It was futile. I could've been looking right at them and I'm sure I wouldn't have known it. Peter's partner had told me as much.

I turned to go back into the lobby when two guys sat down on a bench about ten meters away. A dark-haired man in his late twenties or early thirties looked my way and then scanned the front of the hotel. The other guy was big, muscular—a troublemaker.

I recognized the first guy. He had been at the convention, one of Jean-Claude's watchdogs. He was the one who had pulled Jean-Claude away for a phone call after Jean-Claude had shown Bill and me the snuff film.

That was my man. I did not like the look of his partner.

I went back upstairs. The door was locked. I pounded on the door and Ako answered it, gun held up close to his chest. Very impressive.

"All right, you like it or you don't like it?" I demanded, glaring at Robert and Paul in turn.

On the screen, a long-haired, bearded man was dragging a woman in a housecoat across a wooden floor. He grabbed her hair and screamed at her, forcing her to look up at another woman, who hung by her neck from the ceiling. The woman screamed.

Robert and Paul tore their eyes away from the screen and blinked at me. After a long minute, they got themselves together and started playing—*it's shit, it's no good, we've seen this crap before. . . .*

"All right," I told our contact, "they don't want it."

The scene on the television changed. Men with guns and patchwork uniforms. I recognized the insignia on their sleeves; I had seen it before—the tape we had gotten from Jürgen Dauer's.

"You don't want it, right?" I urged Robert and his friend. Once again their eyes were glued to the monitor. Robert looked at me and then back at the screen.

"Right, this is shit?" I urged him.

It occurred to me at that moment that I had become, in reality, the character that I had been playing and developing since early on in the investigation. I was Ron Smith—middleman. I was a purveyor of snuff films for a very wealthy and highly privileged client. I had brought Robert there, at his request, to see a snuff film. It made no difference that we had no intention of buying it. It made no difference why Robert had wanted to see it. The thought did not sit well with me.

"Right? Right? What do you think?"

Robert eyed me curiously. He didn't know about my time limits. He was there to research a role, to fill out a script. Finally he stood, his eyes never leaving the screen.

"I don't want this," he said slowly and dramatically, gesturing contemptuously at the screen and turning his back on it.

I turned to our contact and demanded what he thought he was doing getting us up here to watch crap we had seen a hundred times before. I was almost yelling by the end. I slammed my hand into the wall. Paul rose to stand beside his friend, glancing nervously from Robert to our contact to me to Ako. Finally he straightened and whispered something to Robert. Robert nodded. Paul said: "I don't like it."

Our contact shrugged and switched the video off.

We went downstairs, and as soon as we got outside, we were approached by the two I had noticed before.

I met them halfway.

Jean-Claude's guy eyed me questioningly. "So?"

I looked back at Robert and Paul standing with Ako.

"They don't want it—seen it before," I told him.

"What the fuck, 'seen it before'? You watch the whole thing. No, no good," he told me. He glanced at the big guy and then back at me.

"Well, they don't want it—what do you want me to do?"

He barked something in Arabic and our contact came over and stood next to and a little behind me.

Ako arrived a second later to stand next to me on the other side, and we faced off. My two-tier security organization was standing on its head. I had a momentary vision of the four of us surrounded by Ako's men, who were in turn surrounded by Peter's partner's men, who were ringed in by gawking, badly dressed tourists and blasé Parisians all whispering about Robert De Niro.

A pretty funny picture, I had to admit.

"I don't want any trouble. They wanted to buy, but that was shit," I told him.

He touched the big guy, who stepped forward. Ako moved to plant himself between us, and I reached into my pocket.

"Look, take this," I said, shoving a wad of francs at Jean-Claude's guy. It was all the money that the Robert De Niro organization had given me to pay expenses.

He looked at me and took the money.

"All right? Good. OK, let's go." I put my hand on Ako's shoulder, and we turned back toward Robert and Paul, who were standing and talking, not looking at us.

"Get a cab and go back to your hotel," I told Robert.

He and Paul looked at me and started to ask questions.

"Just go back to your hotel. I'll talk to you in a little bit," I ordered them.

They peeled off. I told Ako to go with them.

"Where are you going?" Ako asked me.

"I have to take the money back," I told him.

"Let's take these two back and then I'll go with you," he offered.

"Ako, I don't have time to argue. Just go, all right?" I was already starting away at a half run. "Just go, Ako!" I called over my shoulder.

▮ ▮ ▮ ▮

Ron, sit down, sit down!" Peter said, bursting through a door on the other side of his office and motioning me into the chair. I slid my backpack off and set it on the floor.

"Peter, how are you?" I asked, matching his officious, businesslike tone. I had expected to come back, drop the money off, and be out of there. I had not expected to see Peter.

He put his palms together in front of his face as though in prayer and regarded me silently, looking me up and down with cold eyes.

I sat there being examined for at least a minute. Peter said nothing. He sat stock still; only his eyes were animated, gray-blue with flecks of green in them.

I didn't know what he was waiting for, but I suddenly felt very vulnerable in that office. I reached down slowly, brought my backpack up on to my lap, and opened my mouth to speak.

Peter's hands came down on the desk hard, palms open, fingers splayed. I jumped. I couldn't help it.

"What are you doing?" I demanded, every nerve in my body tight, my heart pumping. "Here's your money." I laid the rental fee, $1,700, on the desk. "It's all there. Can we get this over with? I have a plane to catch," I told him.

He looked at me with eyebrows raised then, and smiled. "Oh, really, what time is your flight?" he asked.

"Soon," I told him.

"What time exactly?" he persisted.

"Soon. At—at ten-thirty."

"What airport."

"Or—Orly."

"What's your flight number?"

"I don't—I'm not sure," I began, fumbling for an answer that wasn't there.

"How will you get there? What airline are you flying? Where in the whole world do you think you can go?" he shot at me, rapidfire, moving around from behind the desk until he stood in front of me, his hands clasped behind his back, face neutral.

I stood up slowly, mustering every last ounce of bravado I could, and looked him in the face. "Are you done playing bull-shit games now?"

He came around the desk at me quickly and before I knew what was happening, he pushed his forehead into mine, head-butting me lightly and pushing me back at the chair. It caught me behind the knees and I sat down heavily.

"Are *you*, Mr. . . . Smith?" he asked, looking down at me. No gun or knife could've been more threatening than that light tap on the forehead, his eyes inches from mine.

"Peter, c'mon," I said, trying to keep my voice level. "I brought the money back." I glanced at my watch. "Hell, I'm early. We're businessmen; let's do business."

"First I must tell you two things that I want understood," he said, punctuating his introduction with light taps on my temple with his forefinger. "First, you don't lie to me, and second, you don't do business wearing little boy's pants. I feel that you don't respect me when you come to do business dressed like that."

I glanced down at my shorts and my thick legs.

"Peter, I came as fast as I could. I would've changed, but I— I apologize," I said, inclining my head a little.

"You understand? If you come to do business, you must look like someone I should want to do business with," he told me, the deadly cold edge in his voice fading.

"Give me your bag," he said.

"It's all there, count it," I told him.

He took my bag, opened it, and spilled the counterfeit notes onto his desk. He looked at the bills for a moment and then back at me. "I don't need to count it. I'm sure it is all there. No, I want to speak to you about something else. I want to talk about what you can do for me, Ya-ron."

What had he said? "What did you say?" I asked.

"I am asking you about red clay again, and when you could move some for us," he said casually. "It wasn't so long ago that we spoke. So what do you think, Mr. Svoray? Can we still deal?"

It took me a second to realize what he had said. I raised my head and looked into his eyes. "What did you call me?" I asked in a low voice. It's hard to talk with your heart in your mouth.

"May I call you Yaron?" he asked, smiling.

"No—I mean, yes. I, I don't know what you are talking about," I ground out—teeth clenched, jaw tight. How did he know? Why did he know? I shook my head. All games had been played.

"How did you—?"

"You have told people twice that we could do business together. The last time we met you told me that we would speak in two days—'at the latest,' were your very words, I think. Then I don't see you or hear from you; and then you come to take more money. What are you thinking, Yaron? Don't lie. It's a bad habit, and it can get you into trouble," he told me, shaking his finger at me. "You don't know anyone who wants red clay, do you, Mr. Svoray?"

I shook my head.

"A shame to lie like that. I know people who would kill whole families for a hundred dollars. Did you know that that was possible?"

I nodded. I had been a cop. I had arrested guys like this. I had fought the men who worked for men like him.

"Good. Then you know that I am not playing games."

I believed every word he said.

"What are you going to do?" I asked him.

"Me? Nothing," he told me, smiling humorlessly.

That was something, anyway.

■ ■ ■ ■

Outside, there were very few people on the street. The Pompi-dou Center loomed not far away, like some great alien machine.

"Où vas-tu, mon vieux?"—Where are you going, pal?—a voice behind me wanted to know.

I spun around to be confronted by two big guys.

One of them grabbed me and pushed me up against the wall. The other one clamped his hands on my ears.

I knew immediately what was coming.

He started shaking my head back and forth very quickly, whipping my skull forward and back.

He continued for thirty seconds, maybe a minute. Then he let me go.

I staggered forward, momentarily blinded, my eyes sparking, my head pounding.

It's a very good way to get someone's attention—and it leaves no visible marks. I vomited, reeling forward, and collapsed on the sidewalk. I felt like someone was squeezing my head in a vise.

When I could finally see clearly again, the two guys were gone.

■ ■ ■ ■

Ako had escorted Robert and Paul to their hotel room and then gone back to hook up with Andreas and the others.

I walked into Robert's hotel suite just as Robert and Paul were debating whether what they had seen was real or not.

Robert was of the opinion that what they had seen could not have been faked. Paul agreed with him.

In this instance, I couldn't fault the yes-man in him. What he had seen was undeniably real.

Robert and Paul asked questions and drank vodka from a crystal decanter provided with the fully stocked bar. They asked questions but not the right ones. They didn't ask how what they had seen could've been allowed to happen, or what they could do about it. They asked about me and Ako. They asked what we had been thinking and how we felt about what had happened.

I answered them as best as I could. I still had a blinding headache from the shaking I had been given. And it didn't help to realize that, as far as I could tell, although I knew Robert and his friend had been affected by what they had seen, they were still Hollywood. They were interested in motivation. They were interested in the psychology of what we had done. They did not seem interested in the fact that they had just witnessed murder—not acting, not theater, not drama, but murder: real, premeditated, vicious, and senseless.

Finally, I couldn't take it anymore. I asked Robert what he thought. Did he realize what he had seen?

He told me that he did. He considered his glass full of clear liquor for a moment and said something to Paul, who nodded.

Robert told me that he was still unsure if my story was the story he was looking for.

I knew before I left his suite that Robert was not going to take the story and run with it. He was not going to make sure that the world knew that these movies existed, that they were real.

As real as Ron Smith. I had done my job and I was now being dismissed. I had done what my wealthy and privileged employer had asked of me, and my usefulness was at an end.

And he wasn't going to play me in the movie.

Just as I was leaving, he asked me if I had any other films to show—it might help him make up his mind. I looked at him, the prince of Hollywood. He sat in his chair as in a throne. He accepted the luxuriousness of his surroundings without a second's thought. It was a little unfair of me, I knew. Robert De Niro had struggled once.

I didn't have any other films.

He was on a plane back to New York the next day.

■ ■ ■ ■

I had one thing left to do before I could crawl into bed and curse myself to sleep.

"Ako, I'm going to have to send you the money. I just don't have it right now, I'm broke," I told him in the hallway outside his room. Inside his room, Andreas was baby-sitting the others.

"You don't have anything?"

"A little."

"Do you have enough to pay my guys?"

"Maybe—I don't know." I took out my wallet. The money Robert had given me was gone. I had some cash left, and one credit card that was not totally maxed out.

"If you do, pay them. We can work things out between us later. But I have to give them something. I promised them, Yaron."

I put all the cash I had left in his hand. His fingers closed around the bills slowly, his eyes never leaving my face.

"Yaron, what happened out there? You weren't telling me everything. Why?" he asked, stuffing the money into his pocket without counting it.

"Ako, believe me, you don't need to know everything about this one."

"Why? You don't trust me all of a sudden?"

"There are just things going on that are strictly on a need-to-know basis."

"Like with your friends in the Mossad?" Ako asked.

"How many times do I have to tell you I am not in the Mossad?" No matter how many times I did tell him, Ako had gotten the idea somewhere that I was a member of the Mossad, and he clung to it.

"I am not a secret agent," I added, smiling.

"I don't know what you are anymore. What was all this Hollywood bullshit about, anyway? I mean, it was fun meeting Robert De Niro and everything, but what was it all about?"

What could I tell him? That I thought Robert De Niro would help? That I thought I would become a celebrity? I had kept so much from him up to that point. I hadn't told him about Peter's partner's men or that I was almost positive that Jean-Claude's man was double-crossing his boss. I hadn't told him so much. I saw no reason to start then.

I told him nothing.

Ako wasn't used to being kept in the dark. He felt that for some reason I had not trusted him, and it offended his sense of professionalism and honor.

We parted that night neither friends nor enemies, but estranged. When Ako said good night I heard a tone in his voice that he had never used with me, but that I had heard him use countless times with business associates and friends of friends.

There was no warmth in it, only stiff, formal courtesy.

The Germans went home that night.

27 MIKHAL

The next morning I woke up and all I wanted to do was go back to sleep for the rest of my life.

My ego had gotten me off track. Because of that I had blown it with Robert De Niro, if I had ever stood a chance in the first place. I had blown it with Ako, and I had blown it with Peter.

That last part worried me.

I couldn't help but wonder why I had gotten off so easily. Unsummoned visions of a recent double murder in Israel flashed through my mind. A young boy and an old woman, two generations of a family that had recently immigrated to Israel from the Ukraine. They had both had their throats cut almost to the point of decapitation. Luke had covered that story. It was due to the connections that he had made nosing around that he had been able to get me in touch with Nisim Simantov and with Peter.

At that moment the doorknob turned and Mikhal marched into the room.

"Are you finally awake?" she asked me.

233

"Mikhal, when did you get here?"

"This morning," she informed me.

I glanced at my travel alarm. It was three o'clock in the afternoon.

She looked at me, reaching out her hand and laying it on my shoulder. "Are you sick?" she asked.

"No."

"Yaron, what's been going on?"

I told her.

■ ■ ■ ■

It felt good to have Mikhal there. Her presence and warmth worked on me the way it always did, and once we had our family business taken care of, I began to feel better. Her mind was like a bright spark illuminating the dark pit I had fallen into, and slowly I began to climb out.

We made love a lot. Thank God for room service.

Our daylight hours not spent in bed were spent walking around the city. We took in the sights, strolling hand in hand along the river. It soon became apparent, however, that we were looking at two different cities. I had to concentrate to appreciate the obvious beauty of the Luxembourg Gardens or the Pont Alexandre at sunset. It was much easier for me to see the darkness around the edges—and the people who inhabited it.

At Saint-Michel, Mikhal sighed at the beauty of the ancient fountain.

I pointed out the punks, hustlers, and Eurohippies breaking bottles and scaring tourists headed for Notre-Dame.

Mikhal went into little shops and bought souvenirs for the kids. I sat by the Fountain of the Innocents and sniffed the air for the scent of the decaying bodies moved out of the cemetery in the last century. The fountain was part of a church. The church had had a cemetery that was so full the bodies had had to be moved out of the city because the stench was poisoning the air.

We held hands and walked through Les Halles, once the largest open-air market in Paris, *le ventre de Paris*—now, and for a long time past, a tourist attraction, yuppie hangout, and flash point for young runaways, street kids, and the people who preyed on them.

Everywhere I looked I saw junkies and pickpockets and secret deals going down in shadowy corners.

Near Les Halles was Saint-Denis. Whatever else used to be sold in the covered stalls of the old market, this was where the meat market had ended up. Women of every size, shape, and color plied their age-old trade along the stretch of Saint-Denis beginning a little north of Les Halles and terminating, a handful of blocks farther on, at a grand triumphal arch turned public urinal.

"Will you stop it!" Mikhal said finally.

"Stop what?"

"Stop not enjoying yourself. Or start enjoying yourself, or something. This is the first time we've had together without the kids in years. Can't you just forget about all that other crap for a minute?"

I told her I would.

One night we walked past the 44 on our way back to the hotel. I didn't say anything at all.

■ ■ ■ ■

After a week in Paris, Mikhal told me that it was time to go home.

I told her that I had to do something first.

"Oh, what now?" she demanded.

"I have to see Ako. I have to talk to him. I have to make it right with him."

"Can't you just call him?" she asked. She knew that I couldn't, but I didn't blame her for trying.

I just looked at her. I was about to answer when she answered for me.

"No, you can't—I know, I know," she said dramatically.

"I can't," I agreed.

"Well, I have to get back. I can't wait for you."

"I know, go ahead. I'll go up and work it out with Ako and get a flight from Germany. A couple of days."

"Where've I heard that before?" Mikhal mused.

"I know, but I mean it this time. A couple of days, and there's something else."

"Oh, anything, Yaron," she said sarcastically.

"Do you have any money?"

"What?"

"I owe Ako and I'm flat," I told her, bracing myself.

"You want more money—you're asking me for money?" she asked me, shaking her head.

"I have to give it to him. I can't go without it."

"Money? From me?"

We made love three times that night.

28 RANKO

I went through Saarbrücken again and laughed to myself as I crossed the border, remembering the anxiety with which I had awaited the arrival of Ako and Andreas the last time I was there.

Then, I had been worried about encountering the worst that Germany had to offer, in the form of skinhead neo-Nazis hungry for vengeance against the man who had exposed them. This time, I was worried about coming face-to-face with the best—Ako Reinhardt.

Once in Germany, I felt a huge weight lift from my shoulders. The inadvertent offense that I had given Ako and the bad blood the last time we had seen each other had really gotten me down. Now, for better or worse, I was going to fix that. It was the only loose end that remained to be tied, and I intended, if possible, to tie it up like a Christmas ribbon.

The only thing that bothered me was the "if possible" part. I had never known Ako to hold a grudge. Of course, he had never been mad at me before.

237

I would fix it, I told myself. I would tell him everything—and pay him.

I would fix it.

■ ▮ ■ ▮

Hello, Yaron. It's good to see you," he told me stiffly, opening the door of his small, neatly kept flat on the outskirts of Cologne.

I put an envelope with the Hotel Métropole letterhead on it in his hand.

"What's this?"

"It's what I owe you," I told him simply.

"Thank you," he said without the slightest trace of surprise.

"May I come in, Ako?"

He stepped back from the door. "Yes, of course. Please come in."

■ ▮ ■ ▮

That's the story, Ako; that's all of it," I said. We sat at his kitchen table. Ako had a beer and I had a glass of mineral water. I had told him everything.

"So, why didn't you let me in on it?" he asked.

"I don't know. I couldn't. The whole thing with Peter's guy and Jean-Claude—I just thought that what you didn't know couldn't hurt you."

He considered that for a moment, and then he smiled. It was the first time he smiled since I had arrived.

"It sounds like it could've killed me," he said finally.

"Not you, my friend," I told him, slapping him on the shoulder.

"And they just shook your head, that's all?"

"Oh, Ako, you don't know. That was one of Savak's favorite

methods. It feels like your brain actually moves. Come here, let me show you."

"No, that's OK." He laughed, waving his hands at me.

"I won't do it, no. But they grab your ears"—I clamped my hands on the sides of his large head—"and they shake for a minute or so."

Ako stood up. He is much taller than I, and his head just rose out of my hands.

"Thanks, I get it. I don't need a lesson in the shah of Iran's secret-police torture tactics. You want some more water?"

"No, thanks."

Ako went to the refrigerator and got himself another beer.

"And you know—I don't know, I got off track, Ako. The worst thing is that I realized I had become the people I had been trying to get to."

"What do you mean?" he asked me, sitting back down.

"I just, I felt like—I had become a guy who gets snuff films for rich, privileged people. Who does that sound like to you?"

"Ron Smith," he said.

"Yeah."

"But that's not you. You know that," he said.

"I know, it was just a shock. The whole thing with Robert, it was a mistake."

"Die machen wir alle," he said—we all make them.

"Thanks," I said. "I just wanted to make sure we were good. Now it's over—if you're good."

"I'm good," he said, grinning.

"Then it's over," I said, laying my hands on the table.

Ako looked at his watch. "You know, I'm supposed to meet a friend of mine for dinner. You want to come?"

"No, you go ahead. I'll get a hotel in town. I'm heading out in the morning."

"Quatsch." Nonsense. "You stay with me tonight. And I think

you should come to dinner. This guy—remember when we saw that first film from Dauer's?"

"Yeah." How could I forget?

"Remember I told you I knew someone who could tell us who those soldiers were? This is the guy. His name is Ranko. He just got back from Bosnia."

I considered for a moment. It couldn't hurt, and besides, it would kind of close the circle.

"Why not? Sure."

■ ■ ■ ■

Dinner was typically heavy. Ako and his friend, introduced to me only as Ranko, ate slowly and drank large glasses of beer without any visible effects. Ako had told me that they were not old friends but had met fairly recently. They had found themselves fighting side by side in a street battle with skinheads not long before. After the fight they had gone to a bar and discovered that they had many mutual interests: weapons, hand-to-hand combat, military history, that kind of thing. I felt totally relaxed, in the company of friends.

At some point, as a pretty waitress delivered yet another round of sour beer, Ako reminded Ranko who I was and asked him to tell me what he had been doing.

That's when things got interesting.

Ranko had been born in Germany to Croatian parents who had fled their country when Germany lost the Second World War.

He had recently returned to his parents' lost homeland as a volunteer, fighting the Serbs and the Bosnians and whomever else they told him to fight.

He had been a member in good standing of a unit that went by the initials HOS.

In my travels, someone else had mentioned those initials to me.

A terror unit, I had heard.

Then it hit me. All the way back to Jürgen Dauer's, events falling over like a line of dominoes revealed something that I couldn't believe I hadn't seen before.

Jürgen Dauer. Horacio Lada telling me he could talk to Arkan. The film I had seen at Jean-Claude's, with a uniform draped over a child's desk.

I told Ranko to continue.

He talked for three hours, smoking two packs of cigarettes in the process. He told me about a country being torn apart from within and without. He told me about taking villages of civilians and then moving on, leaving the villages with half the population they had had before his unit came. He told me about cities turned into playgrounds for criminal warlords and charismatic militia leaders. He told me about a nation ravaged by war while a small group of people on all sides of the conflict got rich as hell.

And he denied over and over again that he had taken part in any of the massacres or rapes that the HOS unit was known for.

I didn't dispute it.

Then he told me about the cameramen. One had been with his unit. They made propaganda films for the generals and politicians. They made videos of men going into war so that when, like Ranko, they got home again, they could prove that they were heroes. And the cameraman with the HOS unit, in particular, shot film of the soldiers ravaging towns that had been taken.

I asked him what that meant, and he shrugged, blowing out a cloud of blue-gray smoke.

"What do soldiers do when they take a town?" he asked me.

He told me about rape and he told me about murder.

I asked him if he had ever seen a film of soldiers raping and killing women.

He told me that they never saw those films.

I asked him what happened to them, and he told me that the cameraman with his unit had told him once that he made good money with them.

He sold them.

Did he know to whom the cameraman sold the films, where he sold them? Did he know anything about them?

Ako glanced at me, his eyes glazed. A small voice in the back of my head told me it didn't matter. . . .

"No," Ranko said flatly.

I closed my eyes, my head lowering a little. I didn't realize how tense I had gotten until I relaxed and felt like I was going to melt out of my chair.

It was a dead end. It didn't matter anyway. It was over.

■ ■ ■ ■

When we got back to Ako's that night, he asked me what was wrong.

"I just don't know why I didn't see it before," I told him.

"See what before?"

"See all the signs. The films I've seen—they all—oh, fuck it, it doesn't matter." I threw myself into the battered easy chair in Ako's cramped living room.

"What signs? What are you talking about?" he asked.

"Yugoslavia, Bosnia—you heard what your friend said. It seems so obvious now. Shit."

Ako switched on his stereo, put a CD on—nothing I recognized. He turned to me.

"You going to check it out?"

I shook my head. "I can't—Mikhal would kill me, and I'm broke. I have nothing left. No, I'm not going to check it out," I said positively.

"But you want to." It was a statement.

"It doesn't matter, I can't. It's over."

Ako nodded slowly. He walked out of the room and came back a moment later with something in his hand.

"Here."

It was the envelope from the Hotel Métropole.

"What do you want me to do with this?" I asked him.

Ako shrugged. "I don't know, take a trip somewhere. Someplace inexpensive. It's not much—my boss is kind of cheap."

I looked at the envelope and back up at Ako.

Mikhal would kill me. On the other hand, I had told her that I would be a few days. How far was it to Pale, anyway?

"Just do me a favor," Ako said, grinning.

"What?"

"Don't tell Mikhal it was me, all right? No sense in making it a double funeral."

29 TARA

The man at the desk of the Hotel Inter-Continental in Belgrade looked at my passport and then peered closely at me.

"Is there a problem?" I asked.

I had entered the capital of the former Yugoslavia legally, with a visa issued through the Israeli consulate in Paris.

"No sir, no," he told me, shaking his head slowly, laying my passport down on the desk and copying down the number into his registration book.

I looked around as I was checked in. There were small knots of people chatting in low voices scattered around the lobby. Journalists from a dozen countries, easily identifiable by their vests and expensive adventure clothing, sat and stood around the carpeted room smiling and laughing as if they hadn't a care in the world.

Outside, a city and a nation were dying.

"Sir?"

I turned around and took my passport and a key from the deskman. "Thank you." Taking out my wallet, I gave him a $20 bill. "Thanks for everything."

244

He looked at the money and tried to give it back, but I assured him it was all right. I wanted him to have it.

He positively beamed at me as he finally slid the bill into his pants pocket. "You need anything, you tell me, I get it," he said, repeating himself three or four times. I smiled and assured him I would. The $20 bill I had given him was equivalent to at least a week's wages. I had just bought a good friend.

I started away from the front desk toward the elevator, and then turned around, moving back toward my new friend. "You know what, there is something you might be able to do for me right away," I told him.

"What is it, Mr. Svoray? Anything," he said happily.

"First of all, while I'm here, my name is Mr. Smith, all right —you get it?"

He nodded quickly. "Yes sir, Mr. Smith," he said.

"Secondly, I need a guide, someone to show me the city, a translator—you know what I mean?"

He seemed to consider for a moment while a sly smile crossed his lips. "Yes sir, I know what mean. I see what I do, OK?"

"OK," I told him and I went up to my room.

■ ■ ■ ■

A half hour later there was a commotion outside my door. I was trying to get some sleep after trying to call home to tell Mikhal that I had arrived safely. I had been unable to do either. My mind was racing with half-thought-out plans, and the phone did not work. I was lying on the bed staring up at the ceiling when I heard voices in the hallway outside and the sound of hard-soled shoes running on thick carpet. A moment later I heard a male voice say something quickly in what sounded like English, and then a female voice, much louder, speaking Serbo-Croatian.

I walked to the door and opened it, to be confronted by two men looking every inch U.S. Secret Service, with gray suits and earphones in their ears. Between them they held a very attractive young woman in a short, black leather miniskirt, high, scuffed white heels, and a formfitting sweater, who struggled more for show than anything else and rattled off what were probably very bad words in her own language.

"What's going on?" I asked the dark-suited men.

Their heads jerked in my direction. They had probably not been expecting to be questioned in English.

"Go back inside, sir," one of them told me in an official monotone as another suit emerged from the room next door to mine and joined them. The new suit spoke quickly to the young woman, got an answer, and all four heads turned to look at me.

It was an unsettling experience.

"You Mr. Smith?" one of the suits asked. It was hard to tell them apart.

"Yeah, yes I am," I told him. "What's the problem?"

"This woman, sir, she says she's here to see you."

"Well, I don't—I don't know her. Who is she?" I asked.

The translator suit addressed the woman again, got his answer, and turned back to me. "She says she's your translator. The front desk told her what room you were in," he said skeptically.

The front desk.

My translator.

"It's OK, fellas," I told the suits. I led the woman toward my door, ushered her inside. "You just wait inside for a minute, I'll be right in," I told her. I then closed the door and turned back toward the suits. "What are you guys doing here? I mean, thanks—you're Americans, aren't you?" I asked, smiling.

They nodded. "Nothing to worry about, sir, we're just sweeping this floor and the two above and below. We ran into your— translator," he said, eyebrows raised, "and we didn't have a translator handy. We're sorry for any inconvenience."

"Oh, no inconvenience at all. You don't know how happy I am to have you guys around. Couldn't be better as far as I'm concerned—but what's going on?" I asked.

"Special envoy Holbrooke has just checked into the hotel, sir."

"Richard Holbrooke?"

"Yes sir," the more officious, older-looking one of the original two answered me. He then put his finger to his ear, listened for a moment, told the other one to continue the sweep, and took off at a quick walk down the hall, taking the translator suit with him.

I looked closely at the remaining suit. He looked young, new to the game, and was probably pretty excited with the role he was playing.

"So, what's happening? Is the war over or something?" I asked.

The guy smiled and really showed his age, mid-twenties, tops. "Will be, soon as those bombs start coming down," he told me conspiratorially.

"Bombs?" I asked, feigning shock.

"Yes sir, the U.N. OK'd it this morning," he began; then he put his finger to his ear, nodded, listening, and walked away down the hall in the other direction, with a nod at me.

Bombs. Great.

∎ ∎ ∎ ∎

I went back into my room and found the woman sitting on the edge of the bed. As I pushed the door closed behind me she stared at me silently. She was very pretty, with large dark eyes and a finely drawn mouth.

She didn't look like a translator. She had refused to speak English with the Secret Service guys. I remembered the front desk guy's smile.

"You want something to drink?" I asked.

No response.

"Do you speak English?" I asked. I thought that would be a good place to start. It was definitely my minimum requirement for a translator.

She said something inaudible. Her mouth moved.

"What was that?"

She looked at me; her large eyes opened and closed slowly. "Dirty motherfucker CIA sons of bitches," she said.

She could speak English. We were getting somewhere.

I held out my hand. "Hi, my name is Ron Smith—and you are . . . ?" I asked.

"My name is Tara," the young woman said, shaking hands.

That was how I met Tara.

■ ■ ■ ■

I am here to talk about peace, not war," Richard Holbrooke was saying.

He was at the center of a mob of reporters thrusting their cameras and microphones at him. Flashbulbs exploded, popping white light everywhere as journalists from all over the world recorded this historic occasion. Tara and I had talked for a while in my room and then decided that we could both use something to eat. We had taken the elevator down to the lobby and emerged into a true media feeding frenzy as Richard Holbrooke, U.N. special envoy, began to read a prepared statement to the electronic representatives of the world gathered there in the lobby of the Hotel Inter-Continental, in downtown Belgrade.

"Mr. Holbrooke, Mr. Holbrooke, is it true that NATO planes are going to start bombing Serb positons around Sarajevo?" a frantic voice rose above the throng.

"The use of discriminate force will begin if the demands being put forth by the U.N. Security council are not met within the allotted time," Holbrooke answered.

"When is it scheduled to begin, Mr. Holbrooke? Mr. Holbrooke—!"

"What if the Serbs don't pull back, Mr. Holbrooke?" another frenzied voice demanded.

"Then the use of discriminate force will continue until there is proven compliance by the Bosnian Serb forces. That's it, ladies and gentlemen; we'll have another statement for you tomorrow," Holbrooke said. Immediately he was surrounded by dark suits and whisked away into an elevator.

The crowd of journalists stayed knotted together for a moment as if they could not untangle themselves, and then, in ones and twos, they started peeling away, laughing and complaining about the brevity of the statement as they rushed to file their stories.

"They make me sick," Tara said. Her command of English was remarkable. She had almost no accent when she spoke. Whatever else her qualifications, her linguistic abilities were excellent.

"Why? They're just doing their jobs," I commented as we emerged out of the hotel into a bright, cloudless day. Not far away the Danube River shone in the sunlight, a bright line of sparkling light in the otherwise drab city.

Belgrade was mostly destroyed in World War II and then rebuilt by the Soviets after they had taken control of the region. The renovation job had been typically postwar-Soviet shoddy. There remained very little of the Old World charm found in Prague or Budapest or other capitals of the region. The city was, apart from a few short streets and small areas of preserved Austro-Hungarian splendor, gray and bland and shabby looking.

The hotel was situated near the Danube in a large, new-looking, flashy complex of hotels and shops and open spaces that would have been filled with people had it been anywhere else. In Belgrade, however, it was lifeless. The energy was slowly being wrung out of Belgrade by sanctions and world opinion, and the colorless city seemed to reflect that.

"Exactly. They're just doing their jobs, no more, no less," Tara said. "They don't care about what is going on here or about what is really happening to the people out there," she said, pointing across the river. "All they care about is getting their stupid story, no matter how full of propaganda it is or who is telling it to them—and then sending it back and having a drink and finding some poor girl to fuck for the price of a dinner," she finished.

"But at least they're trying to tell a story, letting the world know," I countered, drawing her out. Up in my room she had said little more than what her price would be per day and what she would do for that: translating, driving, office work. She had asked me what I was doing in Belgrade and I had simply told her that I was looking into some interesting business opportunities that I had heard about. She had looked at me then as if she were going to comment on the ridiculousness of doing business in Belgrade, but she didn't. She didn't ask me what kind of business I was in. I had tried to ask her about her background after that, and she had become evasive. That's when I suggested we go out and get something to eat.

"But whose story are they telling?" Tara said. "Whose story *could* they be telling? They hardly ever come out of their hotel, most of them. Bosnia is a country—Serbia is a country too. And they don't understand what is going on; they don't even care. They just write down what they are told to write down, and that's it for them; it's over."

We were walking past a small park area in the midst of the complex. Two or three teenagers were roller-skating to rap music from five years ago.

"What real story do you want them to tell?" I asked. "As far as the world is concerned, Serbia is where the problem started, they are the aggressors! Do you want them to dig into that?

You're Serbian. Do you want them to prove that the government here is funneling arms and men to Bosnia so that they can wipe out entire villages of men, women, and children?" I demanded.

I half expected her to walk away from me at that point. I did not expect her to turn to me and say what she did.

"I'm Yugoslavian. I don't give a fuck about Serb or Bosnian. I'm a lawyer who has to rent herself out because she can't practice," she began.

Then she stopped herself and looked closely at me. "What business did you say you were in?" she asked.

"I didn't say, but if you want to know—"

"I think I should if we're going to work together."

"I'm in the movie business," I told her.

She laughed. "What kind of movies?"

"Pornography," I told her flatly. For a second time I expected her to walk away from me. Instead she shrugged and smiled. Her teeth were even and white.

We walked silently into the monitored parking lot and arrived at a very beat-up Audi.

"It's a big world, I guess," she said then. "Here's my car. I know a great place, it's where all the bosses eat. We'll go there."

She took me to a restaurant in downtown Belgrade. The place was glitzy and bright, chromed and mirrored, with thick carpets and silent, efficient servers. This was where the real power in Belgrade dined. This was where the people patiently suffering through the embargo, scraping together what they could for a meal, hoped one day to go.

This was where the gangsters ate.

They were unmistakable. There were the fashionable suits and the gold chains and the conspicuous displays of wealth in an otherwise economically dead city. They were loud and demanding and seemed to be arguing incessantly, pointing at one another with forks loaded down with meat and chicken before stuffing them into their mouths. Tara pointed people out to me casually, reading off a list of names that I had never heard and giving me their pedigrees. When she got to Malatesta, I stopped her.

"Which one is he?" I asked.

She motioned at a slim man with black hair, dressed elegantly in a suit and sitting quietly, eating by himself with only two well-groomed young men in shirtsleeves for company.

"He works with Arkan, right? I've read about him in the papers," I told her. I also remembered what Horacio Lada had told me about getting films from Arkan. He had told me that he would have to go through Malatesta.

"He's Italian. As far as anyone knows, he had to leave Italy. He got in trouble with some people over there. He's Arkan's connection to the outside world. Everyone knows that without him, Arkan would just be another nothing, getting what he can out of a war nobody cares about," Tara confirmed for me.

"I want to meet him," I said. I started to get up, when Tara grabbed my arm and pulled me back into my seat.

"You can't just go over and meet him like that. He wouldn't talk to you. You have to go through channels. Don't be an idiot."

An idiot?

"Listen, my friend," I said, glaring at her. "I've been doing all right up to now, meeting who I wanted when I wanted on my own terms, all right? When I want advice from you, I'll ask for it."

"Doing what? Where have you been? You haven't been in Belgrade, that much is certain," she told me.

I looked at Malatesta and then back at Tara. He was right there, right across the room. But she was right. I could blow everything if I just started barging around now.

"All right, then. I want to meet him. How can I do it?" I asked her. "Can you make the introductions?"

She seemed to consider for a moment. "You plan on doing business in Belgrade. You would have to meet him eventually, anyway, if you're thinking about making more than fifteen cents in his city," she mused.

"Can you get me to him?" I persisted.

"I might be able to. I'll see what I can do. When do you want to see him?" she said—"Him," with a capital *H,* as if she were arranging an audience with the pope.

"As soon as possible," I told her.

That night we drove back to my hotel and I said good night to Tara in the parking lot. The night was as clear as the day had been. The large parking lot was well lit and practically empty. Along the river, Belgrade spread out, dotted with lights and restless with an occasional car horn or blast of music—the inarticulate cries of a fevered body asleep.

As I got out of the car Tara told me that she would make some calls for me and try to arrange a meeting for the next day. I thanked her and told her that that would be good.

I paid her what I owed her for the day. She took the bills and nodded, shoving them into a small purse she carried.

She asked me then if I was really a pornographer.

I told her that I was, among other things. She looked at me, tilting her head to the side a little. I felt an inexplicable urge to tell her everything.

"I'm into a lot of things. Maybe I'll tell you about it sometime," I said. It wasn't time.

"You tell me whatever you want. You're the boss."

"So, you call me in the morning."

"Right, good night, Mr. Smith."

"Good night, Tara." I didn't know her last name.

I closed the door and began walking away across the parking lot. I heard her start her car, gassing the cranky engine into coughing, sputtering life. Then she was rolling along slowly beside me. I stopped and she smiled at me.

"Smith is a very common English name, isn't it?" she asked, leaning out of the window.

"Yeah, I suppose it is," I told her, looking at her suspiciously.

"That's what I thought. It's very, very common," she persisted.

"What is that supposed to mean?" I asked her.

"Nothing, it's just something I remembered from my English lessons at school—Mr. Smith does this and Mr. Smith does that. It was always Mr. Smith—when I was a kid I thought everybody in America was named Mr. Smith," she said, laughing.

"Well, I'm not from America," I told her.

She looked at me and shook her head. "That's funny, I thought you were. So, good night."

She hit the gas before I could respond. I stood where I was and watched her drive up to the security station. The green-and-white-striped gate rose, the guard nodded to her, and she was gone.

30 THE *DIJALOG*

The next day, about mid-morning, Tara picked me up in her car and we drove through Belgrade to a small park along the Danube River. She had arranged a meeting for me that she said was the first step on the way to Malatesta. These guys would check me out, and if things went smoothly, they would pass me along.

We got out of the car and walked along the river. It was another cloudless day, the weather seeming to mock the hopelessness that hovered in the air over the city. Tara told me that before the war, the area we were in had been a popular spot for picnics in the daytime and young lovers at night. She told me that she herself used to come there often with friends on hot summer nights and drink wine in one of the nearby cafés or just lie in the grass under the trees, watching the river flow by, talking about what they were going to do when they got out of school.

I looked at the overgrown and untended parkland. In some areas the grass was a wilted yellow, dying from lack of water. In other areas it was wild and overgrown; it looked more like a

255

meadow in the mountains that ringed the city—long, slender wands of green-and-yellow waving in the small breezes that swept occasionally over the Danube.

"No one talks about what they are going to do anymore. The war is killing everybody, but despair—" She stopped and turned to me. " 'Despair,' that means deep sadness, right?" she asked.

"Hopelessness, without hope," I told her.

"Yes, exactly. Despair is killing everyone even more. A friend of mine is a businessman, import-export. He needed a fax machine for his business. He waited three years to get it—three years. Finally he got it, and you know what happened then?"

"No, what?"

"They told him he only has to wait six more years for the paper." She laughed.

There were no lovers in the park that day, nor were there any picnics. The only people I saw were sullen groups of men standing and sitting around in knots, speaking in low voices and sending the smoke of a thousand cigarettes into the air.

It seemed that no one in Belgrade could be seen outside without a cigarette smoldering between his or her fingers, including Tara.

We were headed for one of the riverboats moored not too far from the bridge linking the old and new sections of the city. The riverboats were floating restaurants where the well-to-do in prewar Belgrade society used to take lunch alongside tourists and native splurgers. Now they were mostly empty and in various states of disrepair—peeling paint and smudged, foggy windows.

"There it is," Tara said. She pointed at a boat about thirty meters ahead. Unlike a lot of the others I had seen, this one shone in the sun in a faceted sparkle of polished brass, gleaming windows, and bright, fresh-looking paint.

"Tara, I have something to tell you," I said suddenly. I stopped and grabbed her arm, glancing at the boat. I could make out the name on the stern. It was called the *Dijalog*.

"What is it, Mr. Smith?" She called me only Mr. Smith.

"I, I—" I was torn. On the one hand I wanted to tell her what I was doing there and why I wanted to meet these people. I wanted to tell her that I wasn't a pornographer and that I wasn't a criminal. She was an honest and intelligent woman. I felt very strongly that she could be of more use to me if she knew what the stakes were. I felt I could trust her. On the other hand, I knew it was too late now. If we went into this meeting cold, without any preparation, she might blow it if she knew who I was and what I wanted. I couldn't put her in that position.

Somehow, in the face of this strong young woman, my cover felt like a lying cheat rather than a means to an end.

But I couldn't put her in that position.

"I hate those damn cigarettes," I said lamely. "They make me sick."

She grinned devilishly and took a cigarette out of her pack.

"These you hate?" she asked innocently.

"Yeah," I told her.

She lit up, never taking her eyes off my face. Blowing out a lungful of blue-gray smoke, she shook her head and tapped the ash off onto the sidewalk. "You better get used to it, Mr. Smith," she told me.

■ ■ ■ ■

We stepped aboard the *Dijalog:* very clean, pleasant looking; white tables and chairs spaced evenly around the deck. Tara immediately went for a table occupied by three men. One man in jeans and a Hard Rock Cafe T-shirt was speaking into a cellular telephone, an extremely expensive and showy way to get around the communications crunch in Belgrade. He was flanked on either side by two men in full Adidas running suits, one gold, one green, who rose as we approached the table.

The man on the phone motioned with one hand for us to sit

down. There were only four chairs, so I made Tara sit and dragged a fifth seat over from a neighboring table.

As soon as we were seated a waiter came over and asked us what we wanted. We ordered some mineral water and a glass of white wine. Mr. Cell Phone continued speaking for a moment. The running suits spoke in a friendly, leering manner to Tara, who returned their comments graciously with a quick glance at me.

Mr. Cell Phone stopped talking, flipped his phone shut with a large, flamboyant gesture of his right hand, and smiled at me.

Tara leaned forward and spoke to him quickly in Serbo-Croatian, glancing at me from time to time. He looked at her appraisingly, nodded once or twice, and settled back in his chair.

"She only translator you? You don't need with me. I'm speak English good, yeah. If only translator you, you waste money," Mr. Cell Phone told me, laughing.

"Tara is working for me as a translator and consultant," I told him.

He reached out and stroked Tara's cheek. She let him touch her briefly and then pulled back, smiling.

"She very pretty, Tara, but too smart, too smart," he said, looking at her. Then he turned to me. "So, what you want?"

"I'm looking for films, very special and hard-to-get films that I was told I could get here in Belgrade," I told him.

He sat forward and waved his hand. "Porno, so little—bull-shit. You don't do anything else?" he asked.

"No, not right now. Right now I have customers waiting for these movies, as many as I can get." I told him what I was looking for.

I glanced over at Tara but she wouldn't look at me; she was looking out at the river.

"Bad movies, very nasty—films, women get fucked, killed, very nasty," he told me.

"Yes, very nasty—and very expensive. With a few of those I could make enough money to set myself and my partners back home up real nice here," I said, looking around and taking a deep breath.

"How many money is one?" Mr. Cell Phone asked me casually.

"Oh, about $250,000," I told him, grinning.

He didn't even blink. "You know we are fight a war here, Mr. Smith?" he asked.

"Wars cost money," I told him.

"You know who is Arkan?" he asked me in an obvious effort to impress.

"I've certainly heard of him, my friend. I'd like to meet him," I said brightly.

Mr. Cell Phone grinned at me and then translated for the running suits, as they apparently did not speak English.

They all had a friendly laugh over that one.

"Arkan not meet you, Mr. Smith. Arkan is patriot. He is fight Serbia!"

"I've heard he has a great soccer team, too. But I thought I had to meet Malatesta. That's what I'm here for, isn't it, to get checked out for him?" I decided to stop bullshitting and get down to business.

"Yes, is why you are here. Maybe you meet, maybe you not," Mr. Cell Phone said after a moment's pause, smiling. "I will speak some friend. Tonight maybe. Call me at afternoon," he told me.

"I'll try, but the phone system doesn't seem to be working very well in Belgrade right now," I told him.

"You call, Tara has number. I am easy to call," he said, leaning forward with a big smile on his face. "I am a patriot also."

■ ■ ■ ■

We left the *Dijalog* in silence, Tara walking a little ahead of me. When we got to her car she opened her door and then looked at me over the roof of the car.

"Mr. Smith, are you really looking for films of women being raped and killed?" she asked me point-blank.

I wasn't sure what to say. If I went halfway, I would have to go all the way.

"Yes, I am," I told her evenly. "There are people who want them; they are worth a lot to some people I know."

She rubbed her eyes and then glared at me. How could she know that I was talking about people who wanted to stop this horror?

"I can't work with you, Mr. Smith. I can't be involved in that," she told me, mouthing the words precisely and evenly in a cold monotone. I was more amazed than anything else. Of course she couldn't be involved in it, of course she wanted no part of it. But no horror showed on her face, only a dignified, steely calm.

"I will drive you back to the hotel and you can pay me what you owe me," she told me, sliding into the car.

"Tara, wait. There's more to it. I, I can't tell you what right now, but you have to believe me; it's not what it seems," I said quickly, yanking open the passenger door and falling into the seat.

"Why, why should I believe you?" she asked, jamming the key at the ignition, her hand unsteady. A simple question.

"No reason, except I'm asking you to."

"You want me to trust you? For no reason at all? In the middle of a war?" She looked at me. For a moment I could not tell whether she was going to attack me or start crying. If I had had to, I would've bet on the former.

I nodded.

She looked out through the windshield. "Better a pornographer than a journalist," she said finally, turning the key in the ignition.

We sat idling for a few moments, the small car vibrating underneath us, her key chain, suspended from the ignition, jingling against the worn plastic around the empty space meant for a car stereo.

"We have some time," she said after a few moments, looking at me, her face softer, almost puzzled. "Would you like to see a little of the country?" She said it in a conversational tone, but I knew it was some kind of challenge, and if I didn't take her up on it, I would lose big points. I would lose her.

"Yes, sure," I said, nodding.

■ ■ ■ ■

There are four major roads leading out of Belgrade. Traffic was not a problem, because there was no gasoline available, or very little, anyway. The gasoline that was being sold was strictly black market. You pulled over to the side of the road and got in a line that sometimes stretched twenty or twenty-five cars long, and inched forward until you arrived at the "pump," usually a couple of guys with containers of all kinds filled with stolen gasoline. They sold you gas in a milk bottle or a thermos or a five-gallon jug; you emptied it into your tank with the help of a plastic funnel, and off you went, having paid ten times what the same amount of gas would've cost you before the war.

According to Tara, black market gasoline was one of Arkan's most thriving businesses.

And there, in the midst of so many potential Molotov cocktails, everyone was smoking. It seemed to me to be just more evidence of the despair that Tara had spoken of.

The buses were running. Soviet-made behemoths from the

sixties and seventies, belching massive clouds of black diesel smoke, stopped at seemingly random spots along the roadside, wherever enough people had gathered to designate the point a bus stop. The people boarded the bus, pushing and shoving into the overcrowded vehicle until the last person got on, and then the bus lurched forward, another angry thunderhead of exhaust temporarily marking the location like an animal marking its territory.

I tried once or twice to engage Tara in a conversation regarding the meeting on the boat, but she wanted none of it. I asked what she thought would happen and if they actually would set up a meeting for me, but she only shrugged.

I dropped it after that and decided to enjoy the ride.

There was just one thing.

"Will you stop smoking those godawful cigarettes!" I shouted at her as she stuck yet another paper tube of black tobacco in her mouth.

She looked at me like I had to be kidding. I made it very clear to her that I was not, and we came to the decision that it would perhaps be best if, when she wanted a cigarette, she stopped the car and smoked on the side of the road.

We stopped about every ten minutes after that.

We stopped in a village where old men and women sat in ancient squares before ancient churches, vaguely possessive of small squares of cloth, displaying a few old, rusty forks or a small pile of straight pins. These were for sale, these pins and forks. They were all that the old people had gathered, and they sat there with their pathetic wares, Tara told me, not because they thought anyone would buy them, but because they had nothing else to do. And maybe there *was* someone who needed an old fork or a straight pin.

One old woman looked somewhat better off than others I saw. She squatted, toothless and proud, behind a high pile of shoes. When I approached to examine her merchandise, however, I saw that none of the shoes had soles on them, and in many cases there was only one of a pair—one shoe, worn and ragged as though an entire litter of puppies had broken their teeth on it.

I picked one up and looked at it. Fishing in my pocket I proffered a handful of coins for it. The woman shook her ancient head and held up the correct amount on stringy, knobby fingers.

■ ■ ■ ■

Apart from the shoe woman's, two other images are etched in my mind from that trip through the countryside around Belgrade.

One was that of a human figure, too old and bent and covered with mud-stained and ragged clothing to be identifiable as either man or woman, trudging along the side of the road pushing a wheelbarrow piled with what looked like all of his or her earthly possessions.

I made Tara stop the car and I got out. I was drawn to the figure by its machinelike movements as one foot after the other seemed to reach out, brush the ground with the tread of a ghost, touching the dirt and gravel lightly, and then retreat as the other foot moved forward, pushing the wheelbarrow ahead.

I approached the figure slowly and saw that it was an old woman. There were no houses nearby, nothing but fields of sick-looking corn and the road, which went from nowhere to nowhere, with a dying little village at each end and nothing in between but a light sun shower that had begun to fall from a suddenly overcast sky.

I told the woman in English that we could give her a ride. I asked her if she wanted some help with her load, and only after I had spoken and the woman had not so much as turned her head did I realize that I was speaking to her in a language she probably did not know.

I motioned Tara out of the car and she came over. I told her to tell the old woman what I had said. The old woman stopped, shook her head, and said she was not interested. I took some bills out of my pocket and put them in the old woman's hand. She looked at me then and smiled weakly. Through Tara she said thank you and then told me she did not want us to take her anywhere because she wanted God to take her. She had lost her daughter and grandson the week before, and she was ready to die.

She thanked me again, placed one ghost foot forward on the ground, and put the wheelbarrow in motion. I stood for long minutes watching the old woman diminish slowly as she moved away, while Tara blew smoke into the wet air. Finally, it started to rain harder, and Tara convinced me to get back in the car. She wanted to get back to Belgrade.

On our way back to the city we passed through a village of neat, well-kept homes that seemed somehow untouched by the desperation and poverty that I had seen so far. Tara told me that the inhabitants of the village played no part in the war that was raging only a handful of miles away.

"What? Are they Quakers or something?" I asked her jokingly.

"No, they are Muslims," she responded.

I was surprised. I told her that I would've thought that a village of Muslims would've been the first to be cleared away at the beginning of the war.

She told me that there were enclaves of Muslims in various parts of Serbia. The villages were unmixed, and the inhabitants did not wish to secede from what was once Yugoslavia, and therefore they posed no threat to the integrity of the state.

"In any case, the war is not being fought here. It is Bosnia that is at war," she reminded me. I couldn't tell whether she was being sarcastic or not.

"And there is no mixing of blood in the villages?" I asked.

"No."

"Is that the villagers' choice, or are they forced to remain pure?"

"It is everyone's choice," she told me simply.

"It sounds suspiciously like a ghetto," I told her.

"It does, doesn't it?" she agreed.

"But no one calls it that?"

" 'Ghetto' is an English word. I suppose the people who live here just call it home," she said, stopping the car at an intersection in the center of the town.

A man and a boy, father and son, crossed the intersection in front of us diagonally, splashing through the rain, the father holding an umbrella over their heads with one hand, the other hand wrapped around the boy's shoulder, hugging him to his side.

Tara moved the car forward through the intersection as they went together into a store, the father folding the umbrella, the boy looking up at him.

"Stop," I said quickly, laying my hand on Tara's leg.

Tara hit the brakes and the car stopped ten feet into the intersection.

"What? what is it?" she asked, peering at me and then out into the rain.

The man and boy disappeared into the store.

"What is the matter?" Tara asked again.

"The man and the boy, did you see them?" I asked.

"Crossing the street? Of course I saw them. I stopped so I wouldn't hit them," she responded.

It was the opposite of the old women, hopeless and abandoned. There was love between the boy and the man, and trust. The war raging all around them seemed very far away, from the look of absolute confidence that the boy had given the father as the man lowered the umbrella and gently guided the boy out of the rain.

"There was so much—I can't explain, that guy and his kid—"

Tara looked at me and shook her head, understanding without having to be told. "Mr. Smith, there are fathers and sons all over Bosnia and Serbia and Croatia—everywhere," she told me.

■ ■ ■ ■

As we got closer to Belgrade we started seeing military vehicles barreling up and down the road in both directions, and checkpoints, manned by militiamen from Belgrade, stopping trucks going toward the city.

Tara told me that the checkpoints were to identify and turn back Bosnian Serb soldiers and militiamen who were not citizens of Serbia proper. Those caught trying to enter Belgrade without the proper papers were hauled out of their vehicles and loaded on trucks. When the trucks were full they were driven back to the border, wherever the border was at the time.

By all accounts, what Serbia wanted most was a Greater Serbia, a linking of Serbian-populated regions within the breakaway republics of Bosnia and Croatia. It did not seem that they wanted to fight for it, however, and those fighting for a Greater Serbia got no welcome in Belgrade. They were turned back, refugees from their own fledgling nation and refugees from a nation that had once been theirs.

On the road from Banja Luka we were stopped at one of these checkpoints by a portly militiaman about thirty-five years old who waved us down with a yellow sign that read "Stop" in Cyrillic.

Tara stopped the car and rolled down her window. The militiaman bent down and asked for our papers, a sour smell of old sweat and beer and tobacco wafting through the open window as he smiled, showing yellow teeth.

At the edge of the trees that lined the road, a tarp was set up, dripping with rain. Seven militiamen in makeshift uniforms stood under it desultorily, with cigarettes either hanging out of their mouths or knuckled between first and second fingers. Two of the men were manning a mounted machine gun, while the others were armed with automatic rifles and handguns.

Tara handed the militiaman her resident's papers and my hotel pass.

Because a foreign passport was too great a temptation for people desperate to get out of the former Yugoslavia to bear, the passports of all extranationals were kept at their hotels, locked safely away, and they were issued what was called a hotel pass, which gave anyone who needed to know all the information they needed.

The militiaman made a great show of examining the papers, eyeing them close up and then holding them at arm's length from his face as he squinted at them, one at a time. He folded back the corners and waggled them in the air, testing their tensile strength, no doubt, and then asked Tara to get out of the car.

He spoke to her in Serbo-Croatian. Barking questions at her, which she answered in a soft, submissive voice, he looked her up and down, an obscene smile stretching his leathery face.

Behind us, drivers began standing on the horns, and even the other soldiers, under the tarp, began shifting nervously, eyeing the line of cars that was building up behind us.

Tara was getting soaked as she patiently and politely answered the man's questions. I had the urge to get out and see if I couldn't speed things along a little by throwing around my status as a foreigner, but I held the urge in check. Better to let her handle it; she knows what she is doing, I thought.

The militiaman then slipped his hand around Tara's waist and put it on her ass.

I gave in to temptation.

"What is going on here?" I demanded loudly, exiting the car and slamming the door.

The militiaman and Tara both looked at me at the same time, the militiaman's eyes showing faint surprise, Tara's eyes showing nothing at all.

The man said something to Tara and she translated. "Get back in the car, Mr. Smith!" she told me.

"The hell I will," I said, coming around the car and facing the militiaman. The men under the tarp looked on, interested, their stances shifting a little with buried tension. I was banking on the fact that a foreigner's bullet-riddled body was not the kind of press that the already beleaguered Serbia wanted.

It was a hunch.

"You translate word for word what I am about to say, Tara," I told her, looking at the militiaman. He had backed off a little, a faint, contemptuous smile playing over his thick lips.

Through Tara, the conversation went like this:

"What's the deal?"

"No deal, get back in the car."

"Why are you stopping us? Why are you harassing us? I am a foreign national, and I'm here on business. This is my assistant. I want to know why you are holding us up."

"Get back in the car."

"I'll get back in the car when my assistant is allowed to get back in the car and you let us move on!"

"Get back in the car or I will take you to the station and keep you there!"

"Fuck you!"

Tara looked at me. "I don't know how to say that," she told me as the man's eyes flashed from me to her and back again.

"Yes you do, Tara, tell him."

"I don't, there's no word for it," she insisted.

"Well there must be something close—tell him what I said!"

Tara nodded slowly, turned to the man, and spoke one word. The man's eyes went wide. His jaw muscles tightened under his skin. He repeated the word and Tara nodded. The man's hands balled into fists and he took a step toward me, repeating the word to himself.

I braced myself for the worst. I thought I could take this guy, or at least put on a good show. The other seven—probably not.

"What is problem here?" asked a voice in heavily accented

English. It was one of the seven from under the tarp. He was taller than I, with a thick moustache and darting, intelligent eyes.

His uniform was as pieced together as the others were. An officer?

"There is no problem except that this guy is holding us up and harassing my assistant," I told him. "It's upsetting me."

"Why problem? We check roads, everyone check," he told me. He spoke slowly and deliberately, as if he were concentrating on every word.

"I am obviously not a refugee. My assistant has the right papers. Why is he holding us up?"

The officer spoke to the militiaman. He produced our papers, and the officer examined them. Then he handed them back to me and, without a word, waved us on.

A few kilometers down the road I asked Tara what she had said to the militiaman.

She shrugged. "I said, 'Fuck you,' " she told me.

" 'Fuck you'? I thought there wasn't a word for that."

" 'Fuck you,' basically," she told me.

"Basically?"

"Yes, basically the same."

It was good enough for me.

31 PALE

We got back to the hotel and Tara put in a call to Mr. Cell Phone. Their conversation did not last long. She nodded her head and scribbled something on a piece of stationery. When she was done, she hung up the phone and frowned at me.

"Malatesta is busy. Maybe next week, maybe the week after he can see you."

"I don't have a week," I said, more to myself than to Tara.

Tara started to say something, glanced at what she had written down, and started to put the paper in her purse.

"What is that?" I asked her.

"It's him, acting like a big man," she told me.

"What does that mean?"

"It's nothing."

"What is it, Tara?" I demanded.

"It's nothing, a name and address. Some man in Pale. He said if you had the balls, you could go there and talk to him."

"Who is he?"

270

"He makes pornography."

"In Pale?"

"Yeah, yes—but you can't go there," she told me flatly.

"Did he say this guy had what I wanted?"

Tara hesitated. "Yes," she said finally.

"If I wanted to go to Pale, could you arrange it for me? Can you do that?"

She stood up and walked across the room. When she got to the windows she turned and glared at me. "Yes, of course I can. I can arrange anything. That is what I do—but you can't go there. Bombs are falling there," she told me.

"Not yet, they're not," I corrected her. And it was true. NATO had yet to make good on its promise to push the Serbians back from Sarajevo by force. I had no doubt that they would. The great alliance could not afford to look any more ridiculous than it already did with regard to the situation in the Balkans—a situation that was already five years old with a hundred thousand bodies down the drain. Besides that, the United States was beginning to show some impatience and starting to move. NATO had been waiting for them, and it looked like the wait would soon be over. Bombs would fall soon on the Bosnian Serbs who had had a stranglehold on Sarajevo since early on in the war. Whether it would put a stop to the madness was anyone's guess.

Whether it would stop me from going to Pale was another thing altogether.

"You can't go there. You have to talk to Arkan first," she insisted.

"Fuck Arkan. If I can get what I want, I have to go there. End of story."

She sagged a little, letting out a long breath. "You really are looking for movies of women being raped and murdered?"

"Yes . . . I am."

"I don't believe you, Mr. Smith," she said flatly.

"Why the hell are you always calling me Mr. Smith? It's annoying as hell!"

"That's your name, isn't it?" She tilted her head up a little, looking at me suspiciously.

I drew a long breath and looked at her. "No, it's not," I said finally. "My name is Yaron Svoray . . . and I'm not a pornographer."

She smiled victoriously and fell back on the bed. "I knew it. I knew you weren't a fuck pornographer. So what are you? Are you U.S.? Are you CIA? What are you?"

"How did you know I wasn't what I said?"

"Oh, c'mon. The old ladies and the father and the kid. You were almost crying . . ." Her voice trailed off. "So, what are you? Are you CIA?" she asked brightly.

"No, I'm not American, I'm Israeli."

"So, what are you?"

"I'm a journalist," I told her.

Her eyes went wide and she made a face as if she were spitting out a piece of rotten food. "Fuck—fuck! A journalist, what the hell!" She stood up and started pacing the room, cursing and swearing half in English and half in Serbo-Croatian. Finally she turned and glared at me, her eyes rimmed with red and bulging. "Better if you were a pornographer! A fucking journalist—shit!"

When she had been told that I was looking for snuff films, her only reaction had been to stiffly tender her resignation. I wasn't quite sure what to make of this.

"Tara, calm down, let me explain."

"No, what do you need to explain? What do you need to explain? You want to tell the story of poor Tara and the poor crazy Serbian people? Tara and the poor evil Serbs? You don't give a shit—you get your story and fuck you!" she screamed at me.

I walked over to her and shook her by the shoulders, hard.

"What is the matter with you? Calm down a minute and I'll tell you what I'm doing here. I'll tell you everything, but you have to calm down first! All right?"

She nodded, biting the inside of her lip.

"Now sit down." I led her back to the bed and she sat.

"Do you want a glass of water?"

She shook her head, eyes down.

"Well, I sure as hell do," I told her. I went over to the sink and filled a plastic cup with tepid water. She lifted her head and watched me drain the glass, refill it, and drain it again.

"You don't even drink," she said ruefully.

"What does that have to do with anything?"

"You don't drink or smoke, or anything else. How could I know you were a journalist?"

She had me there.

I told her everything. Finally, I repeated that if I could get snuff films in Pale, I had to go there.

"Where the bombs are dropping, and you want to do it behind Arkan's back?" she said quietly.

"I want to go there and check this out. I want to finish this thing and get what I came for. If you could help arrange that for me, I could wrap it up and be gone in a couple of days. You understand now?"

"It's crazy," she said.

"What's crazy?"

"The whole thing is crazy. Stupid."

I looked at her uncomprehendingly. "What's stupid?"

She put her hand on the back of my neck and looked at me sadly. It was the first time she had touched me like that, gently, because she wanted to. Her hand felt soft and cool.

"Never mind. What will you do when you get the film?"

"I'll go home," I told her. I was immediately sorry.

She drew her hand away, but the sad smile never left her face. I would go home. I would leave this mess of a country behind me and go on to other things. For Tara, this was home.

She tilted her head and pushed a few stray strands of brown hair behind her ear.

"Tara, I—" I began.

I didn't get to finish, however. Tara suddenly looked at her watch and gave my knee a resounding slap with the flat of her hand.

"Oh my God, the restaurant!"

"What restaurant?"

"We have to eat, don't we? I made reservations. I almost forgot—we have to go!" she exclaimed, jumping up and rushing for her coat.

"Tara, I don't want to rush," I complained. More than anything, I wanted to stay where I was. I wasn't sure what I wanted, but I wanted Tara to stay there with me.

"You better rush," she told me, wagging her finger at me. "They'll give our table away—and you owe me dinner."

Even in Belgrade, reservations were reservations.

∎ ∎ ∎ ∎

Tara was a lovely dinner companion. The scene in my hotel room earlier was completely forgotten as she told me stories of her school days and her friends and family. She told me about her childhood, first in a village a hundred kilometers away, and then high school and university in the big city, after her mother had died and her father had brought the family back to Belgrade, where he had been born. She told me that she had liked me right away because I reminded her of someone.

"Who?"

"An old boyfriend."

"Where is he now?"

"He died in the first week of the war."

Something had changed between us. I had known soon after meeting her that she was an extraordinary young woman, and she only rose in my opinion as she explained to me her very well thought out views on the war and the situation in her own country, as well as the reaction abroad.

And she no longer called me Mr. Smith.

■ ■ ■ ■

Tara drove me back to the hotel and came upstairs with me. She had left her change of clothes in my room. She gathered her things slowly, looking at me out of the corner of her eye as she stuffed the jeans and blouse she had had on earlier into a worn, bright pink duffel bag.

"You will need a lot of money to go to Pale. Do you have it?"

"You tell me how much I'll need and I'll tell you if I have it," I told her.

She told me. I had enough, barely.

"When can you arrange it?"

She didn't answer. Instead she picked up the phone and made three or four calls. When she finally hung up, she looked at me and said wearily, "Tomorrow morning at eight, in front of the hotel."

"You're good," I said, smiling.

"I know." She ran her fingers through her hair. "You can't leave the country from Pale. You will have to come back to Belgrade," she said, sitting down on the edge of the bed, her bag between her feet.

"I'm leaving tomorrow morning; I'll be back tomorrow night."

"No, you won't."

"Why not? It's only—what? A hundred fifty kilometers from here, three hundred round trip. How long could it take?"

"You're not going on a picnic." She shook her head and rolled her eyes. "And you're not a bird. There are checkpoints every couple of kilometers. Don't you get it? There's a war go-ing on!"

I nodded. "Yeah, I get it. I know that, but I'm just going to get in and get out—talk to this guy and get back here. With a good driver . . . I don't see a problem."

I opened my wallet and counted out her day's fee. She took the money, stood up, and hefted her bag onto her shoulder. "I'm going to go now."

"All right, go get some sleep, and thanks for everything. Listen, meet me here in the lobby tomorrow night at ten," I told her.

She regarded me silently, went to the door, laid her hand on the knob, and then stopped. "I knew you weren't a pornogra-pher," she said, turning around to face me.

"I know you did. I guess I wasn't very convincing."

"No, you weren't. But I don't think you're a journalist, either. I don't know what you are."

"But I am, it says so on my passport," I said playfully.

She didn't smile. She wiped her hand across her eyes and squared her shoulders. "If you were really a journalist, it would've been understood," she said, a slight quaver slipping into her voice. "Shit," she added a second later, digging her nails into her thigh and grinding her teeth together.

I was at a loss. I walked toward her. "What? What would've been understood?" I asked.

She swallowed hard and looked at me. "Me, Yaron," she said. It was the first time she used my real name. "I am included in the price for my services—you didn't even know." She laughed sadly and reached out, laying her slender hand on my chest. "I don't know what you are, but you are not a journalist." She tapped me with her forefinger.

I could only stare at her.

"Good night," she said, pulling the door open and stepping into the hall.

"Wait, Tara. You'll be here? Tomorrow night, right?"

She turned and looked over her shoulder at me as she went for the elevators. Her smile was back, but it was forced. She waved.

"You won't be here," she called.

"The day after, then, at ten—in the lobby."

"Yes, all right. Good luck," she called. The elevator came and she stepped in. She did not look at me again.

■ ■ ■ ■

My ride to Pale arrived right on time, at a quarter to ten the next morning—exactly an hour and forty-five minutes late—in the form of a very beat-up diesel-burning Mercedes-Benz blasting American heavy metal music. My drivers—there were two of them—were a thin, tall guy in his late thirties with deep-set blue eyes and a younger guy.

I yanked the door open as they pulled up to the curb in front of the hotel, and began coughing as a huge cloud of cigarette smoke billowed into the air.

"What took you guys so long?" I demanded.

"Pardon?" the younger one yelled over the music.

"I said what the hell took you guys so long? Turn that shit down!"

He smiled and nodded, reaching for a battered ghetto blaster on the seat next to him.

"Sorry, we have problem, but no problem now, right?" he said after he had turned the music down. Both of them were clad in ripped and faded Levi's and T-shirts.

"So, get in."

The other guy hadn't said anything yet. He was checking me out from the backseat. He leaned forward as I got in the car and said something to the younger guy.

"You got enough money?" the younger one asked when the other had finished speaking.

"Yeah, I got enough money—don't worry about it." Tara had

seen right through me; I wasn't going to give these guys the chance. "Just get me there in one piece," I told him. "I'll take care of the rest."

He shrugged. I had barely got the door closed when he hit the gas and we flew away from the curb, tires squealing, trailing a large cloud of black diesel fumes.

The younger guy's name was Dusan. The other guy's name was Dragan. Dragan did not speak English.

We drove for about half an hour, arriving eventually at a garage behind a post office in a small town twenty or twenty-five miles northeast of Belgrade.

As we pulled to a stop in front of the garage, Dragan jumped out of the backseat, undid a lock on the large, sliding wooden doors that fronted the building, shoved the doors open, and waved us in.

I wasn't sure what to make of this. I had trusted Tara to hook me up with people I didn't have to worry about, but as we pulled into the dark garage and Dragan slid the doors shut behind us, I began to feel a little uneasy.

"What the fuck is this?" I demanded.

"No problem, take it easy," Dusan soothed me.

It was pitch black. There was a shout from Dragan. Dusan answered him, and then there was another shout as something crashed to the floor somewhere in the dark.

Dusan laughed and turned on his headlights. In the glare of the double lamps, Dragan stood, sharply illuminated, hopping up and down on one leg with his hands wrapped around his other knee. Beside him was a metal table, about knee high, piled with rusty tools.

Dusan chuckled. "Dark, yeah?"

"Yeah. What are we doing here?"

"Supplies," he told me, jumping out of the car.

An hour later we were back on the road. Dragan was driving, Dusan sat next to him, and I sat next to the window. The three of us sat in the front seat because the trunk and the backseat were loaded down with our supplies for smoothing the road to Pale.

There were boxes and boxes of cans of meat and vegetables. There were, it seemed to me, an inordinate number of sardine tins, and there were definitely, as far as I was concerned, way too many cartons of cigarettes. They topped off the pile of goods: Marlboros from the States, Gauloises from France, and many other brands, which I didn't recognize. There were also about ten or twelve bottles of the local brandy, slivovitz, a great favorite with the soldiers.

The trip itself was relatively uneventful. I was geared up and tense for some great adventure, life threatening and daring, but by the time we had cleared the third or fourth checkpoint, the whole thing had become almost routine. At each checkpoint, Dragan would get out of the car and chat with the soldiers or militiamen, who were standing smoking and looking bored. He would distribute some of the trade goods we had brought along, and twenty minutes or half an hour later we would be back on the road, our load of cans and cigarettes and liquor lightened by a couple of cartons or a bottle, or a half dozen cans of peas.

Dragan and Dusan shared the driving. They listened to their music and spoke with each other, occasionally addressing a comment to me. Dusan was like a kid; he acted younger than he looked, and seemed to think the whole trip was nothing more than an extended drive in the country. Dragan, on the other hand, was more sober and less chatty, and at some points along the way he would stare pensively up the road without speaking, his face tense, as the Mercedes chugged with a boat-like rocking motion, negotiating roads that in some places were badly in need of repair and in others looked exactly like two-lane highways anywhere else in the world.

At one point, as we made our way over a badly degraded stretch of highway between two provincial towns, a pair of jets streaked overhead through an otherwise empty sky. Dragan was driving then, and he slowed the car even further as he peered up through the windshield at the con trails left by the aircraft, white streaks in blue light.

They had to be NATO jets. There had never been much of an air war over the former Yugoslavia.

At eight o'clock in the evening we rolled into Pale. It had taken us almost ten hours to traverse a little over 170 kilometers.

Tara had been right again.

There were no bombs falling. There were no firefights. There were people going about their everyday lives in an everyday provincial town that just happened to be the seat of government and center of operations for the army of the Bosnian Serbs.

There were also journalists, dozens of them, prowling the streets in marked vehicles, snapping pictures, and trying to speak to people who, for the most part, seemed to be trying to ignore their existence entirely.

At an intersection, Dragan said something to Dusan, opened his door, and jumped out of the car. I asked Dusan where he was going, and he told me that Dragan had friends in Pale he wanted to see. We would hook up with him later. I accepted this without comment.

I then produced the piece of paper that Ranko had given me, and showed it to Dusan. I asked him if he could find the address for me. He shrugged and told me that Pale wasn't a very big town.

32 STEPHAN

Stephan Tomasovitch was short and beefy, with the overdeveloped physique of a dedicated weight lifter. He answered the door of his small, one-room apartment with a big grin on his face, his eyes shifting quickly between Dusan and myself. He asked me what I wanted and who I was, in that order.

"My name is Ron Smith," I told him, Dusan interpreting.

I introduced Dusan as my assistant and I told Stephan that I was there to do business. I told him Mr. Cell Phone had sent me.

Stephan looked us over again, wheels turning, and showed us inside.

In the living room, a battered couch was occupied by a man and a woman, both of whom seemed drugged or drunk or both. The bedroom had a mattress on the floor and stank of old cigarette smoke and brandy. The kitchen was littered with crusted-over plates and dishes. Food was rotting on the counter, with flies buzzing everywhere. Very homey.

Stephan offered us a seat on the couch. When the woman

281

and the man already occupying it didn't move fast enough, he yelled at them and threatened, with gestures and words, to throw them out physically. They reluctantly got up. The woman made some kind of protest regarding money, because after a brief exchange Stephan produced a couple of dinars, slapped them into the woman's hand, and then pushed her out the door along with her comrade.

With Dusan translating, we got down to business.

Stephan had started out as an actor in porn films himself. He had enjoyed it immensely, judging from the gusto with which he recounted some of the scenes he had participated in.

"But it was never a big business in Yugoslavia, and one day I realized that I should be making the movies and not acting in them. I decided that I was going to become the king of Yugoslavian porn. I worked in Belgrade for a while, and then I moved everything out here," he told me.

"Why?"

"When the war started, there was a whole new talent pool out here. So many refugee women were hungry and scared, they would do anything for some money or a place to stay. The best one was this beautiful woman, not young—a mother. She had with her two pretty little girls, and she offered herself and them to me for almost nothing. One of the little girls screamed so much she must have been a virgin. That film did really well. I made it with the girls and three soldiers that I knew," he informed me proudly.

"Soldiers?"

He explained to me that that was where he got the men to act in his films—from the front lines. They got to enjoy themselves and make a little money.

I told him that that was the kind of thing I was looking for. Raw stuff—fresh. Stephan jumped out of his seat suddenly, went into the other room, and came back out with a bulky, ten-year-old video recorder. He punched some buttons, put his eye to the viewfinder, nodded, and told me to take a look.

It was the woman whom Stephan had thrown out of his house upon our arrival. In the video, two men were having sex with her on the bed in the other room. They had finished shooting it half an hour before I showed up.

"Yes, yeah, exactly. That's exactly the kind of shit I'm looking for," I told him. I loved everything he showed me, and he got more and more excited as he brought out stacks of magazines filled with badly reproduced photographs of men and women engaged in various sex acts. Proudly he drew my attention to his name at the top of the masthead.

He told me that he was one of the biggest suppliers of girls to Europe. When I asked him what he meant, he produced a number of "seventeen" magazines.

"I discovered most of the girls in those ones. I take their pictures and give them a little money. Then I get them fake passports and ship them off to brothels all over Europe," he said, poking himself in the chest for emphasis. "Not bad business."

As Dusan and I looked over the magazines, Stephan went into the kitchen to make some coffee. According to a brief disclaimer, all the girls in the magazine were over the age of seventeen. In proof of this, all the girls sported the headbands I had seen before, wide red ribbons holding their hair back, emblazoned with the number seventeen. None of them looked seventeen, however, and most of them looked quite a bit younger, some without developed breasts or pubic hair. I had seen the magazines a number of times over the course of the investigation. I was finally getting an idea just how big their operation was.

"You're not afraid of the NATO air raids?" Stephan asked me from the kitchen.

I told him that I was not—it was business as usual. In point of fact, I had almost completely forgotten about them. Stephan told me that no one else was worried about them either.

"NATO does not bomb civilians," he told me with great conviction. And as far as he was concerned, the fighters on the hills surrounding Sarajevo, just a few miles away, could take care of themselves.

He brought a cup of coffee in for himself and Dusan, and a glass of bottled water for me. He sat back down and asked me if I was working with anyone else in the country. I told him I was not.

"You have any deals with Arkan?" he asked me.

I told him that I had not spoken with Arkan and that we didn't have any kind of an arrangement whatsoever.

I heard thunder. We all heard it, a low rumbling that sounded like thunder but seemed to come from inside the earth rather than from the sky. Stephan got up and walked to the door. Dusan and I looked at each other. Then we heard the scream of low-flying aircraft.

The bombing had begun.

There was more thunder at regular intervals as we continued to talk about the growing porn industry in Yugoslavia. Dusan did not look terribly pleased to be sitting there, but Stephan was unfazed. His only comment directly related to the barrage was that they were definitely bombs that we were hearing. Tomahawk missiles had a different sound as they came in. I asked him to describe the difference but he said he couldn't, it was subtle. I would know it when I heard it, however.

Dusan was fidgeting and glancing at the window every couple of seconds. I barked at him to pay attention. I wanted him to be very careful in translating what I was about to say. He licked his lips nervously and nodded.

I told Stephan what I wanted to do. I wanted to go into partnership with someone in Yugoslavia, someone like himself, who was already set up and knew where to get the talent. He seemed immensely pleased at this. I told him I needed some very unique films first.

"What kind of films?" he asked.

I told him I wanted snuff movies. I told him I needed movies of women being raped and then killed; that I knew people in the States and in Europe who would pay a very high price for them. I told him that with the money we could make off one film, we could turn Belgrade or Pale or anyplace else on the map into the porn capital of Europe.

Stephan listened to what I said, his face set and businesslike. He ran his fingers through his greasy hair, looked toward the other room and then back at me, scrutinizing my face, looking for something.

How many times had I seen this hesitation over the course of my hunt for these things? Everywhere I had gone so far, when it had come down to it, what I was looking for was always available, but hard to get. Somewhere else, someone else had them or could get them, but not now, not this minute. Give me a week, ten days—I'll take care of you, but be patient.

My patience was at an end.

I looked Stephan in the face, leaning forward, locking his eyes.

With Dusan translating, I said, "I know you have films like that. I want them, as many as you can get me."

"You said you don't have any deals with Arkan, right?" Stephan asked me for the second time, glancing away from me.

I told him again that I positively did not.

Stephan shrugged, got up, and went into the other room, mumbling something.

Dusan didn't translate immediately. At that moment the sound of jets overhead made him look up. I saw his body tense for the rumbling that he expected. None came.

"Dusan, what did he say?"

Dusan slowly lowered his head and looked at me. "He said, he said, no problem. He want know if any deals, is all."

I was about to ask Dusan to clarify that for me when Stephan's voice called from the other room. I looked at Dusan.

"He said go in—come in. Look."

I stood and started for the other room. Dusan stood with me but I shook my head. I told him I wouldn't need him. He went to the window and pulled back a tattered curtain, peering out into the dark.

Stephan was shuffling through a stack of videocassettes. He picked one up, examined the label, handwritten in Cyrillic, discarded it, and found another. This one he considered for a moment longer than the first, finally setting it aside. Then, hooking a battered television set to a VCR, he looked up at me and then glanced behind me, looking for Dusan.

"I don't need Dusan for this," I said in English, shaking my head, wondering grimly what was on the tapes he handled so carelessly. There had to be fifteen or twenty of them, with more scattered here and there around the room.

Stephan raised his eyebrows and then shrugged. He secured the cable between the monitor and the tape player and switched the television on. It took a moment to warm up, a small dot appearing in the middle of the screen. The dot grew larger as I looked at it, and then suddenly the screen flared into life, slashing out in wavy lines of green and blue fire before it settled into a color bar accompanied by a loud, high-pitched whistle.

Stephan reached out, turned the sound down, and hit the play button on the VCR.

Death.

Clips of death strung together in a reel. A snuff sampler.

Rape and massacre. It was all there in thirty-second bites. Women running, tied up. Blood on young faces, torn clothing. A knife, a gun, bullets tearing flesh. Men in uniforms laughing, drinking. Girls' bodies left lying on concrete floors, legs bloody, hair matted and plastered against wet faces.

I heard a screaming sound from somewhere else—inside my head? No, outside. I looked over at Stephan, his face bathed in shifting patterns of blue light. He said something. I didn't quite catch it, and he went into the other room as I turned back to the television screen.

Men blindfolded, executed, shot from behind, shot in the face, cigarettes dangling from swollen lips. Soldiers with machine guns firing on crowds of men, young and old, rapid-fire bursts echoing soundless laughter. Girls tied up together, young, young, two at a time pushed into bare rooms, naked, struggling, screaming, faces like frightened animals, sense gone, humanity gone—raped, murdered, burned, stabbed. Throats slit like cattle, taken by men with guns at their heads. A handful of hair, yank head back, scream, show teeth—slap, kick, shoot, cut, and always blood, more and more blood and more . . .

I reached out and turned the television off. The screen went white and then shrunk back into a tiny spot that slowly disappeared. I stood and walked out into the other room. A low rumble ran up through the floor and into my feet.

They're bombing the Serbs, I thought. I remembered the bombing. The good guys were bombing the Serbs, who were the bad guys . . .

The living room was empty. I heard voices and stepped out onto the porch. A low whistle that grew into a scream assaulted my ears.

Stephan turned to me and pointed at his ear. "Tomahawk, yes—yes?"

About half a mile away, a hillside, a dark outline in the moonlight, exploded in a flash of white incandescense. They must've got an ammo dump, I thought.

I had what I was looking for.

Stupid.

I heard Tara's voice saying that it was stupid and my voice asking her what was stupid.

No answer.

NATO was bombing the Serbs, who had been killing the Bosnians, and I had swum into an ocean looking for a glass of salt water.

Stephan was saying something to me. I turned to look at him.

Dusan translated. "He said he has another like that, sample short. He let you have—free gift."

Another explosion, farther off this time, beyond the hills. The sky flashed, and long low thunder rolled out underneath us.

I looked at Stephan. "Tell him thank you," I said tonelessly.

Tell him thank you very much.

33 GAME OVER

It took us only seven hours for the homeward trip. By the time we got to the outskirts of Belgrade, most of our supplies were gone, Dusan was asleep, I was driving. Dragan had elected to stay in Pale.

It was over. It was finally over, and I had done what I had set out to do—and I felt like hell about it.

I had been searching for snuff porn. I realized now that the videos were only a minute piece of something. They were evidence, yes. But they were evidence of something so much larger and more horrible that it made the few minutes of violence caught on the videotapes in my backpack pale in comparison.

It was over for me, but it wasn't over for Tara or Dusan or the people of what had once been Yugoslavia, or the countless women and men and children that the huge, formless, thoughtless monster I had been tracking for a year and a half caused to suffer and die in silence, alone.

It wasn't over for Horacio Lada or Malatesta or William McCall either, for that matter. They would go on, eating lives like so much ripe fruit.

And what could I do about it?

Nothing.

That was where all lines converged. I couldn't fight the power of the Russian mob, or Arkan, or even the ridiculous posturing and small-time havoc of a Bill Webster or a Don Swinborne, despite the fate that had awaited him in particular.

As I drove into the hotel parking lot, I realized that the videos in the backseat would cause a havoc all their own. It was true that they were only tiny lights compared to the huge darkness that surrounded them. But they were lights nonetheless; they were proof.

I honked the horn as I pulled up before the swinging arm that barred my way into the parking lot. The security booth, manned twenty-four hours a day by three different men, seemed empty.

Dusan stirred and woke up, opening his eyes and rubbing the sleep out of them like a child. He asked me what was going on, and I told him to stay put. I got out of the car and stepped over to the booth.

No one.

At the same time a car with its headlights out pulled up behind the Mercedes. Dusan got out and stood next to the open passenger door. I looked at him and then at the car that had just pulled up. As I stood at the door to the security booth, four men got out of the car. One of the newcomers peeled off and approached Dusan, while the others came straight for me.

"You guys know what's going on?" I asked them in English. "The security guy's not here."

They answered in Serbo-Croatian and flashed badges of some kind at me.

I called to Dusan. "Ask these guys what they want."

Before Dusan could speak, I got my answer. Two of the guys grabbed me roughly by the arms and pushed me back against the Mercedes, slamming me down on the hood.

"You arrest," Dusan called to me.

"Why? What for? By whose authority?" I demanded.

They frisked me and found nothing. They pulled me back to a standing position and barked at Dusan.

"You arrest," he told me again. "You go with them. Get in car and follow the—you, no, is my car!" Dusan turned and began a heated exchange with a police officer or militiaman or whoever he was standing next to him, during which I thought I heard Arkan's name mentioned several times.

The exchange ended when Dusan hit the ground, silenced by a fist in his mouth.

My two guys pushed me roughly into the Mercedes, smashing my head against the roof in the process.

"Go, yes?" the one who seemed to be in charge told me roughly, sticking his head through the driver's side window and glaring at me.

The keys were in the ignition. I started the engine.

The men got back in their car and pulled out onto the two-lane service road that accessed the parking lot. I backed out after them, catching a glimpse of Dusan, still prone, as the headlights slashed over him.

Another car appeared behind me and I had no choice. I drove.

■ ■ ■ ■

We drove for about twenty minutes and arrived finally at what looked like some kind of official building—a police commissariat or an administrative complex. I was directed to park the car, which I did. I then got out of the car slowly, leaving the keys dangling from the ignition, and was taken inside.

My escort and I marched through an archway large enough to allow vehicles to pass, guarded by a tired-looking sentry who waved, sucking absently on a hand-rolled cigarette. We

292 GODS OF DEATH

traversed a courtyard littered with the skeletons of cannibalized cars and trucks and boxes of garbage, climbed a short flight of stone steps, and entered the main building.

The men who had brought me there relaxed visibly as we entered the building. They lit cigarettes and spoke among themselves, smiling and nodding as we stopped at a desk manned by another guard, who with words and gestures demanded my papers and shoved a sheet of paper at me and motioned for me to sign something, an affidavit of some kind written in Cyrillic.

I tried to find out what it was they wanted me to sign and got nothing but shrugs and sighs for my trouble. The one who had told me plainly to "go" back at the parking lot now refused to talk, and the four of them stood by murmuring impatiently as I finally scribbled "Yaron Svoray" on the line indicated.

My hotel pass was returned to me. Three of my guards then left me for parts unknown, mouthing gloating good-byes at their comrade. I was taken by the remaining guard up two flights of stairs, deposited in a decrepit room—fallen plaster, paint hanging down from the ceiling in ribbons, a few wooden chairs scattered around haphazardly—and left there.

That was it. I hadn't been searched. I hadn't been told what was happening or why I was being held. Apart from the initial violence of the encounter, I had not been mistreated. As far as I knew the videos were still in my backpack in Dusan's Mercedes, and the keys were still in the ignition.

I looked at the cracks in the walls and the ceilings. There was a window, nailed shut and made opaque by who knew how many years of grime and dust. There was a poster on one wall, curled at the edges and yellow with age. It showed a policeman in what I assumed was the uniform of the former-Yugoslavian police force with his hand on a child's head. The child, a little girl, was smiling up at the policeman, who was looking out into some unknown distance where a safe future for the little girl, and all humanity, for that matter, lay shining on the horizon.

So I was in what was, or had been, a police station. The men who had brought me there did not look like the starched and fine-lined officer in the poster. Their uniforms had been mismatched patchworks of trousers and tunics of all shades of blue and green, the only official marking being the flag of Serbia sewn on their sleeves.

As I examined the room, I realized slowly that I was not afraid; but there was no good reason for this. I did not delude myself. No one knew where I was, and I had no way to tell anyone what had happened to me. Dusan had probably gotten word to Tara, who may or may not have been trying to find out what was going on. If my hunch was correct, however, she would not get very far.

Whom could she go to for answers? I didn't know if I was in the hands of the regular police or not. If I was not, then I was in the hands of some militia.

Tara could go to her friend Mr. Cell Phone. His interests, however, lie in one direction.

Arkan.

It was only a hunch. There were a couple of arrows pointing in that direction, however. Stephan had been very careful to ask me, more than once, if I had made any deals with Arkan before my trip to Pale. Tara had also warned me about going to Pale without meeting with Arkan first. . . .

It was all conjecture. I was sure of only one thing. Whether Arkan was the cause of my sudden arrest or not, all roads in Belgrade led eventually to him and his partner Malatesta.

In the meantime, I was being detained. I stood and walked to the door. The man who had brought me to my de facto cell had ushered me inside, motioned for me to sit, and disappeared, closing the door behind him.

I had my hotel pass. I also had about 200 deutsche marks as well as about the same amount in dinars.

But I was not afraid, and that was good. Again, it was not that I had any delusions that somebody would come to help me. There would be no one. I was not important enough. My lack of fear was due more to a sudden clarity of vision regarding my situation. I could not stay where I was. I had to find out what was going on, who had ordered my arrest and why, how long I was to be held, and what my ultimate destination, if indeed I had one beyond that long-neglected room, would be.

I rapped on the door. Thinking like a police officer, I assumed that my guard was standing watch on the other side. I got no answer and rapped again, harder this time, slamming my fist into the chipped layers of paint.

The door shivered and opened a crack. It was not locked. I stood still, unsure of what to do. I grasped the handle, pulled the door open, and stepped quickly back into the room, expecting to see my guard's face appear.

Nothing happened. I approached the door and looked out into the hall, in both directions. It was empty.

Was I a guest, or a detainee? I stepped out into the hall. I could hear voices coming from one end. There was a chair, like the ones in the room, set next to my door, unoccupied.

The hall was lined with doors identical to mine and stretched fifty meters in each direction. Fluorescent lights ran along the center of the ceiling, every third or fourth one blinking and buzzing as it slowly died.

I stepped across the corridor and opened the door opposite mine. It was empty. I closed the door and stood in the middle of the hall.

At the far end of the passage I could see the doors I had been led through on my way up. Behind those doors and down two flights was the man at the desk who had examined my papers; beyond him was the courtyard, and beyond that was my life. Not Ron Smith—my life, the life of Yaron Svoray.

I decided to stop playing. I knew somehow that if I stayed there in that room, I would be dead sooner or later. Whoever had ordered my arrest would come for me eventually; they would find out that I was not Ron Smith; they would find out everything.

I wasn't going to wait for that. Why was there no guard at my door? I walked a few feet down the hallway and pulled another door open—again, nothing. I checked a few more doors, and every room that I looked into was uninhabited. I could still hear voices coming from the other end of the corridor. They were faint, and they were speaking a language that I did not understand. I realized then that this was what I had been doing for the last two years. I had been opening doors only to find the rooms behind them empty and dead.

Why was there no one guarding me? Why did no one come rushing at me, gun drawn, to push me back into the room that I had been left in?

I turned back and walked toward the voices, my footsteps ringing up and down the passageway. I had just reached the double doors at the end of the hall when they swung open abruptly, pushed from the other side, revealing a man in a militia uniform, who looked at me blearily. We stared at each other for about half a minute. The man finally croaked something at me in Serbo-Croatian. He was not armed, as far as I could see. He did not seem threatening. He ran his fingers through his lank dirty blond hair and spoke to me again, a few short words. I pulled my hotel pass out of my pocket and waved it at him, telling him that I was an Israeli citizen and that I demanded to see whoever was in charge. He looked at my pass, shrugged, and disappeared back the way he had come.

I waited. I waited five, ten, fifteen minutes. He never reappeared.

Fucking bureaucracy. That had to be it. The empty corridor and the empty rooms and the militiaman who couldn't be bothered with me. It was all a bureaucracy functioning in a vacuum, moving forward out of inertia because no one had ordered it stopped. No one could stop it—not Arkan, not anyone—because there was nothing to stop. There was no organization, there was no center. There were only circles within circles of drunken men, performing duties out of habit or self-interest. I had been ordered arrested and taken to the place. Had someone specifically been ordered to watch me? To keep me there?

I couldn't believe that this was happening, but it had been happening all along. The world that I had immersed myself in was very similar to the Kafkaesque castle that I now found myself in. There was a semblance of order; there was a semblance of hierarchy; but it was all a facade, a mask, hiding a much deeper and far older truth.

I started toward the other end of the corridor, smashed through the double doors, and took the stairs two at a time.

Pornography was not the problem, it was a symptom. Yes, people made movies of women being raped and killed. Yes, people made movies of small children being sodomized and being forced to fuck barnyard animals, and yes, it was a god-damned shame. It was a horrible, rotten, stinking shame that nothing was being done about it. I had been looking for the source of these outrages, and I had uncovered only that there was no source. I had gone from the suburbs of Connecticut to the middle of a war zone, and if I had learned one thing, it was that the degradation of individuals was only a small part of a much larger problem.

The obvious question, then, was, what was the problem?

Blood sells. Simple, right?

As I got to the bottom of the stairs and approached the man at the desk who had examined my papers earlier, he had his back to me. He swung his head around slowly at the sound of my footsteps.

It wasn't he. It wasn't the guy who had so carelessly looked over my hotel pass earlier. I made as if to walk past him, and he stood. This one, unlike the militiaman who had confronted me upstairs, was armed. He barked something at me and I stopped. He began to come around the battered desk at me, and I brought out my hotel pass, waving it in his face like a talisman.

I was not going to play along anymore. I told him I was leaving. He didn't understand a word I was saying. We carried on quite a conversation in two languages, neither of us understanding the other. He could've shot me at any moment. I knew this, of course. He had a pistol slung on his hip, gunfighter style. All he had to do was take it out, point it at my chest, and fire.

He wouldn't do it, though. How did I know that? I didn't. But no one was there to order him to do it. It was not his job to make decisions. It was not his job to guard me; that was someone else's job, someone else's responsibility.

It was just the chaos that goes on every day underneath our feet. The chaos to which we are oblivious, most of us, if we are lucky.

I could not remain oblivious. It is my misfortune to have been born with a need to look under the carpet. Like everyone else, when I looked for something, I expected to find it. Three years before, I had found Nazis in Germany. Over the course of this last investigation, starting with the film I had seen in Germany and my dreams of the little girl, what had I found? I had found this militiaman. I had found this guy, a little fat around the middle, with bad skin, troubled eyes, and probably a wife and kid at home. What did he want? He wanted to go home every night with the least amount of trouble. He didn't give orders; he got them, from somewhere, and carried them out.

And I didn't blame him one bit.

I told my militiaman that I was leaving and I started for the door. I could almost feel the bullet entering my back and tearing through my spine.

It never came.

I walked across the courtyard. I wasn't playing anymore, not

Arkan's game, not Peter's, not Bill's, not Don's, and not William McCall's.

I approached the booth with the sentry, expecting to be stopped at any moment. I walked past the booth. No one ordered me to halt. There was no sound of hard-soled boots ringing on pavement. I continued through the entryway and stopped.

There was the Mercedes.

I turned back toward the building. The sentry had his nose in a paper. Yellow lines of plastic snaked up into his ears from a Walkman. For reasons that I will never understand, I turned and walked toward him. When I was about five meters away, he lowered the paper a little and saw me.

I looked at him. He looked at me. It looked like the same guy who had been there when I had been brought in.

I couldn't be sure.

He scowled at me and waved me off, flapping his hand at me as if to say, We're closed, come back in the morning.

I turned slowly and walked to the Mercedes. The keys were in the ignition. The door was unlocked. I pulled the driver's door open and felt a strange sensation in my knees.

A voice called to me at the same time. I turned. The sentry seemed concerned about something. He left his booth and stood in front of it, hands on hips.

I waved at him. "It's all right," I told him. "All a big mistake!"

He started across the pavement.

I fell into the driver's seat and reached for the keys. There was something wrong with my hand. I had to concentrate. I didn't remember the ignition being that cranky. With my left hand I steadied my right and twisted the key, and the engine started. The sentry was almost to the car. He was saying something. I could see his mouth moving. He raised his hand, fingers splayed.

I put the car in reverse and smiled at the sentry. He stopped.

My leg was not working. I suddenly felt very tired. I pressed down on the accelerator, the gears caught, and the car moved.

I turned the wheel hard, made two points of a three-point turn, and left the sentry behind me. I wasn't sure where I was. I would find the Danube. The complex where the hotel was would be visible from a long way off.

I glanced once in the rearview mirror and saw the sentry still standing there. He shook his head and turned back to his booth.

That's when I reached behind me and felt for my backpack. It was gone. The images that the video contained had disappeared back into the nightmare they had come from. It didn't even occur to me to question the fact that though the backpack was gone, the Mercedes had been right where I had left it, with the keys still in the ignition. That's how far gone I was. Somehow, in the twisted world I had been inhabiting, it made perfect sense.

I came to an intersection and stopped. While I waited for the light to change I heard a slapping sound and saw that my hands were shaking, fluttering against the steering wheel like the moths that crowded around the porch light in front of my home in Caesarea.

The light changed. I pressed down on the gas and drove on, free.

EPILOGUE: ISRAEL

Fifteen days later I was home with my family.

I could hear Mikhal telling the other two kids to sit down and start eating. I stopped for a moment in the hallway and listened unseen to their childish bickering, the *clink* of silverware, and Mikhal's gentle admonitions to settle down.

Two weeks before, I had walked away from an investigation that had taken me deep into a world of pornography and death. I still didn't know what it all meant. I was piecing it together, hoping that a larger picture would emerge.

The only thing I knew for sure was that I had walked away from the chaos, and in the end it had been unable to touch me.

I had had somewhere to go.

"Yaron, what are you doing? Come and eat!" Mikhal appeared in the hall.

I smiled at her.

"Are you all right?" she asked.

"Yes, yeah, I'm fine, let's eat," I said, grabbing her around the waist just as Enosh pushed past us in a dead run for the dinner table.

We sat down. Mikhal had outdone herself, and I was hungry. I took big helpings of everything, told the kids to stop fighting, and told Mikhal how good everything was, pinching her leg under the table.

The phone rang.

"I'll get it!" Elie cried, making a dash for the phone.

"Whoever it is, tell them I'm busy. Take a message!"

"He says it's important. He has to talk to you!"

I grimaced and put my fork down. I walked out to the living room, and Elie handed me the phone.

"Yeah?" I said.

"Mr. Svoray?"

"Yes, who is this? I'm eating dinner, so make it quick," I told the unfamiliar voice.

"Mr. Svoray, I'm calling on behalf of my employer, Kiril Ivanesko. He would like very much to speak with you." Whoever it was spoke Hebrew with a slight accent. I couldn't place it.

"You must have the wrong guy," I told him. "I don't know any Kiril Ivanesko. Sorry."

"But Mr. Ivanesko knows you, and he would like to speak with you at your convenience."

"Call back tomorrow. Maybe I can arrange something—"

The voice cut me off. "He would like to speak with you at your convenience tonight, Mr. Svoray. It won't take long. We know you are a busy man."

Kiril, Kiril. It was familiar somehow. It came to me then. Kiril Ivanesko. I had heard the name before. He was reputed to be a powerhouse within the Russian mob, like Peter, like Nisim Simantov. I glanced back toward the kitchen.

"Mr. Svoray?"

"Yes, yeah, I'm here. Look, I'm eating dinner, could I—"

"Please finish your dinner. Would two hours be enough time?"

"Yeah, yeah—OK," I told him.

"Good. Mr. Ivanesko is very anxious to meet you."

He gave me the address of a café in Rhamat Gan, the Rasputin.

"In two hours, then, Mr. Svoray," the voice said.

I hung up.

■   ■   ■   ■

The Rasputin was not crowded. The directions had been precise, and I arrived an hour and fifty-five minutes after getting the phone call. As I stepped through the door of the well-lit café, I was immediately approached by a blond man, thirty-five, maybe forty, in a tailored navy blue suit. He confirmed that I was Yaron Svoray and led me to a table at the back occupied by an older man with white hair and watery blue eyes, flanked by two younger men who looked me up and down and then ignored me.

"Mr. Svoray, this is Mr. Ivanesko," Blue Suit told me, sitting down beside me.

The old man reached out a desiccated hand. It was as light as paper, and just as dry.

This frail-looking old man was Kiril Ivanesko, a reputed powerhouse within the Russian mob. This was Peter's boss.

He smiled and said something, his voice a rasping whisper. I asked him to repeat himself, and Blue Suit did it for him. "Mr. Ivanesko would like you to know that it is a great pleasure to meet you," he told me. He then leaned forward and confided in a whisper, "Mr. Ivanesko's Hebrew is not very good. I will translate for him."

The old man then wheezed something at Blue Suit in Russian. Blue Suit responded, and the old man waved his hand at him, chuckling damply.

"The tea is very good here. Mr. Ivanesko would like to know if you would like a cup."

I told him that I would, and shortly afterward, a steaming cup of tea was set on the table in front of me.

With Blue Suit translating, Kiril then told me that he had expected me to be taller. He had seen my picture. He thought I would be taller.

I apologized that I was not, and he waved his hand. Not important.

He asked me if I liked the tea. I told him that I did, at which he nodded approvingly.

Finally I turned to Blue Suit. "Please ask Mr. Ivanesko why he wanted to see me."

Blue Suit translated. Ivanesko fixed me with his watery blue eyes.

"You are famous, very smart, very good at what you do, that's all."

That's all?

"Mr. Ivanesko understands that you had an accident in Paris, Mr. Svoray. He would like to apologize for that."

Paris—Peter.

"It was not supposed to happen. It has been dealt with."

I had no idea what was going on. Kiril Ivanesko was apologizing to me for the beating I had received at the hands of Peter's henchmen. I had come fully expecting to apologize myself. I didn't know how to react to this.

"Would you like another cup of tea, Mr. Svoray?"

"No, no thank you. Please tell Mr. Ivanesko that it was a misunderstanding, that's all. It was my fault and I apologize. Please tell Mr. Ivanesko—"

Blue Suit raised his hand and laid it gently on my shoulder. He smiled, his eyes cold. "He knows, Mr. Svoray."

I turned to Kiril and he shook his finger at me, croaking in Russian.

"It's bad to lie, Mr. Svoray. Very bad."

I lowered my head and apologized again.

Another wave of the hand. Water under the bridge.

He turned and spoke to Blue Suit. Blue Suit thanked me on behalf of Mr. Ivanesko for coming.

As I rose to leave, Ivanesko began speaking. The translation went: "You are good at what you do, Mr. Svoray, but we are better at what we do. You stick to your business and we will stick to ours. Do not make promises that you cannot keep. How many times did you tell people that you would do business with them? Here and in Paris. Where else? These things can always come back to you. It's not good business."

I had told both Nisim Simantov and Peter that I could move red clay. That's what he was talking about. Promises to deal in stolen nuclear devices, promises to run guns and sell women into white slavery. All the lies came back to me then, all the bullshit and bluffing. And I had thought I was so smart. I had thought that I had gotten away.

"Now go home and enjoy your family, Mr. Svoray. Family is a good thing," Ivanesko finished.

At the mention of my family my blood froze in my veins, and I began to apologize all over again. I had to explain. He had to understand. My family wasn't involved. They were not a part of this.

Ivanesko cut me off with another wave of his hand. Leaning forward and licking his lips, he spoke to me in very old-fashioned Hebrew, his phrasing almost biblical. I didn't understand at first what he was saying. He had to repeat himself twice, searching me with his blue eyes.

When I finally understood him, I could only sit back and stare.

"*Aba shell aba shelcha. Limeo oti psanter ey az beir Cherno-vitz.*" The father of your father taught me to play piano way back in Chernovtsy.

Chernovtsy, my grandfather's hometown. Kiril looked eighty years old. He could not have been more than sixty.

"Isn't that amazing?" he asked me, smiling.

Amazing, I thought, dumbfounded. What had this coincidental connection saved me from in Paris? I sincerely hoped that I would never find out.

"I know you are only doing your job," he began again after a moment, Blue Suit translating once more. "And you are not bad for an amateur. But we are professionals. Don't make promises that you cannot keep. That is a sign of disrespect. It is saying, You are nothing to me, so my promises are empty."

I nodded. Ivanesko sipped his tea, the bottom of his cup clicking loudly against his saucer as he set it down.

"And these films you are looking for—horrible," he added after a moment. "Who would think that people could do such things? Only monsters could make those films, monsters," he said.

I sat silently, searching Ivanesko's watery blue eyes. I was safe. My family was safe. All because my grandfather had taught this man to play piano.

Ivanesko told me to go.

As I left the Rasputin, one thought screamed in my head like the Tomahawk missiles that the good guys had launched at the bad guys—bad guys who had been good guys who had been bad guys.

No one is safe.

Monsters, indeed.

ABOUT THE AUTHORS

Yaron Svoray is the author of *In Hitler's Shadow: An Israeli's Amazing Journey Inside Germany's Neo-Nazi Movement* (with Nick Taylor). He has been a paratrooper in the Israeli Defense Force and a detective in Israel's Central Police Command, and is currently an investigative journalist. He lives in Israel.

Thomas Hughes cowrote the script for the upcoming film *Breathing Room*. He lives and writes in New York.